The Agrarian Question

KARL KAUTSKY
The Agrarian Question
IN TWO VOLUMES
Translated by Pete Burgess

VOLUME 2

LONDON   WINCHESTER, MASS

First published 1899 in German by Verlag. J.H.W. Dietz Nachf., Stuttgart

This edition published 1988 by Zwan Publications
11-21 Northdown Street, London N1 9BN, and
8 Winchester Place, Winchester
MA 01890, USA

Copyright © Verlag J.H.W. Dietz Nachf. GmbH
Godesberger Allee 143, D-5300 Bonn 2

Translation Copyright © Zwan Publications 1988
Introduction Copyright © Hamza Alavi and Teodor Shanin 1988

Typesetting: Ransom Typesetting Services, Woburn Sands, Bucks

Printed and bound in the United Kingdom by
Billing & Sons Ltd, Worcester

No part of this publication may be reproduced, copied or
transmitted without written permission from the publisher

British Library Cataloguing in Publication Data

Kautsky, Karl
   The agrarian question.
   1. Agriculture—Economic aspects
   I. Title II. Die Agrarfrage. *English*
   338.1   HD1411
   ISBN 1 - 85305 - 023 - 7 v.1
   ISBN 1 - 85305 - 024 - 5 v.2

Library of Congress Cataloging-in-Publication Data
(revised for vol. 1)

Kautsky, Karl, 1854–1938
   The agrarian question.

   Translation of: Agrarfrage.
   1. Agriculture—Economic aspects—Germany.
2. Socialism—Germany. 3. Communism and
agriculture—Germany. I. Title.
HD1306.G3K315 1988   338.1   87-20593
ISBN 1 - 85305 - 023 - 7 (v. 1)
ISBN 1 - 85305 - 024 - 5 (v. 2)

      ECC/USF LEARNING RESOURCES
      8099 College Parkway, S.W.
         P.O. Box 06210
     Fort Myers, FL 33906-6210

Contents

VOLUME 1

Glossary	viii
Translator's Note	ix
Introduction to the English Edition: Peasantry and Capitalism by Hamza Alavi and Teodor Shanin	xi
Foreword by Karl Kautsky	1

Part I: The Development of Agriculture in Capitalist Society

1. Introduction	9
2. The Peasant and Industry	13
3. The Agriculture of the Feudal Period	20
The Three-field System	20
The Restriction of the Three-field System through Large-scale Farming by Feudal Lords	22
The Peasant Becomes a Starveling	27
The Three-field System Becomes an Unbearable Burden on Agriculture	31
4. Modern Agriculture	35
Meat Consumption and Meat Production	35
Crop Rotation, Division of Labour	38
The Machine in Agriculture	43
Fertilisers and Bacteria	52
Agriculture – a Science	56
5. The Capitalist Character of Modern Agriculture	59
Value	59
Surplus-value and Profit	63
Differential Rent	71
Absolute Ground-rent	77
The Price of Land	83

6.	Large and Small Farms	95
	The Technical Superiority of the Large Farm	95
	Overwork and Underconsumption on the Small Farm	110
	The Cooperative System	120
7.	The Limits of Capitalist Agriculture	133
	Statistical Data	133
	The Demise of the Small Enterprise in Industry	141
	The Limited Nature of the Soil	145
	The Larger Farm is not Necessarily the Better	147
	The Latifundium	153
	The Shortage of Labour-power	159
8.	The Proletarianisation of the Peasantry	168
	The Tendency Towards the Dismemberment of the Land	168
	The Forms of Peasant Supplementary Employment	179

VOLUME 2

9.	The Growing Difficulties of Commodity-Producing Agriculture	199
	Ground-rent	199
	The Law of Inheritance	202
	Entailment	204
	The Exploitation of the Country by the Town	212
	The Depopulation of the Countryside	217
10.	Overseas Food Competition and the Industrialisation of Agriculture	236
	The Export Industry	236
	The Railway System	239
	The Regions of Food Competition	244
	The Decline in Grain Production	253
	The Unification of Industry and Agriculture	263
	The Displacement of Agriculture by Industry	284
11.	Prospects for the Future	298
	The Mainsprings of Development	298
	The Elements of Socialist Agriculture	303

Part II: Social Democratic Agrarian Policy

12.	Does Social Democracy Need an Agrarian Programme?	311
	Off to the Land!	311
	Peasant and Proletarian	313

Class Struggle and Social Development	325
Nationalisation of the Land	329
The Nationalisation of Forests and Water	335
Village Communism	339
13. The Protection of the Rural Proletariat	345
Industrial and Agricultural Social Policy	345
Freedom of Combination, the Servants Ordinance	346
Protection of Children	349
The School	361
Women's Labour	370
Migrant Labour	372
The Normal Working Day – Sunday Rest	377
The Housing Question	383
Rent on Land	388
14. The Protection of Agriculture	390
Social Democracy – Not the Representative of the Employers' Interests	390
Feudal Privileges – the Hunt	391
Mixed Land Holdings – the *Gemenglage*	395
The Improvement of the Land	398
Control of Epidemics	401
State Insurance	403
The Cooperatives – the Agricultural Training System	407
15. The Protection of the Rural Population	410
The Transformation of the Police State into a Cultural State	410
Self-administration	412
Militarism	413
Nationalisation of Expenditures on Schools, Poor Relief and Roads	417
Free Administration of Justice	420
The Costs of the Modern Cultural State	423
Bourgeois and Proletarian Taxation Policy	426
The Neutralisation of the Peasantry	438
16. The Social Revolution and the Expropriation of the Landowners	442
Socialism and the Small Enterprise	442
The Future of the Independent Household	449
Bibliography	454
Index of Authors	458

The Agrarian Question
Volume 2

9

The Growing Difficulties of Commodity-Producing Agriculture

Ground-rent

The modern large-scale enterprise has been the vehicle by which the capitalist mode of production rescued agriculture from the depths to which it had sunk towards the close of the feudal period and elevated it to its present outstanding heights. This same mode of production also generates powerful forces which obstruct the development and expansion of the large-scale enterprise, preventing it from attaining sole dominance within agriculture in the prevailing social order. Not only do these forces hold agriculture back from the highest level which it could attain under given technical conditions: by encouraging the parcellisation of land they can even lead to technical regression.

The constraints placed on the large-scale farm are not the only means by which the capitalist mode of production impedes the development of agriculture: ground-rent is no less damaging.

The purchase price of land is, in essence, nothing more than capitalised ground-rent: this is, of course, the price of the *land*, not the *estate*. Prices of buildings, live and dead stock are determined in the same way as any other commodities, in the last instance through the socially necessary labour-time required for their production.

Even an industrial capitalist has to pay ground-rent. But its cost only represents a small part of the total amount of money advanced in production.

Matters are different in agriculture. So-called ground-capital, that is, capitalised ground-rent, represents the bulk of the sum of money which farmers have to spend if they wish to practise agriculture on land which they own.

On the middle-sized and larger farms of Central Europe, combining farming and stall-feeding, working capital only amounts to between 27 and 33 per cent of the initial capital. This can fall to 15 per cent or rise to 40 per cent, depending on the intensity of farming. The average level of working capital in the Kingdom of Saxony is 410 Marks per hectare, with an average *purchase price* of 1,930 Marks per hectare (Krämer, in Goltz, *Handbuch der gesamten Landwirtschaft*, I, pp. 277–79, and

Krafft, *Lehrbuch der Landwirtschaft*, pp. 58-60).

Buchenberger cites the example of a large peasant holder in Baden whose farm was valued at 46,233 Marks. Of this, 6,820 Marks (14.72 per cent) were stock, buildings accounted for 5,480 Marks (11.9 per cent), and the land 33,923 Marks (73.4 per cent) (Verein für Socialpolitik, *Bäuerliche Zustände*, 1883, III, p. 249).

Of the total expenditure of capital only a *quarter* is actually active in the process of production.

Only a proportion of the farmer's capital is therefore available for the actual operation of the farm. By far the bulk of it, *two-thirds* to *three-quarters*, has to be handed over to the previous landowner merely to obtain permission to undertake farming at all. The farm will, therefore, always be either smaller or less intensive than would otherwise be possible given the size of the total available capital. Theory notwithstanding, the practician nevertheless tends to prefer a larger estate, even if it is indebted, to a small unencumbered one, given an equal investment of capital within the constraints noted above. In fact, it is very rare for a farmer to pay for an estate in cash. The farmer will regard virtually all his available capital as working capital, and fix the desired size of the farm accordingly. The land is not bought outright, or only a small part of it: the farmer goes into debt for the price of the land and this is registered as a mortgage on the estate. That is, the buyer takes on the obligation to pay ground-rent to the mortgage creditor, the real owner of the land.

Every change of ownership therefore encumbers the estate with debt. Although it would be overstating the point to claim that change in ownership is the sole source of the excessive mortgage indebtedness weighing down on land-ownership and that the need to carry out improvements is negligible in comparison, it is nonetheless the major cause of the increase in mortgage debt.

Under tenant-farming, the agricultural entrepreneur can use all his capital for agriculture. Agriculture can most fully take on a capitalist character. In fact, tenant-farming is the classical manifestation of capitalist agriculture.

Apart from the full utilisation of entrepreneurial capital, the tenant-system also has the advantage of allowing the owner of the land to select the most assiduous and best-capitalised tenants from those competing for land. Under the system of owner-farming, the identity of the farmer is largely a matter of accident of inheritance.

This is not desperately important with the small enterprise. Peasant farming remains a simple and routinised affair. The peasant's children have to work on the farm from a very early age and can acquire the necessary experience. Although differences in ability may develop between individual farmers, these remain within fairly narrow limits and do not have too much effect on the running of the farm.

Matters are different when we turn to large-scale agricultural enterprises. The large farm is a complex structure whose management requires both all-round practical experience and basic scientific and commercial training. However, as capitalist development proceeds, large landowners tend to become more and more of an urban breed, a class with urban tastes and inclinations: they live in towns, and give their children an urban upbringing. The sons of large landowners can no longer be assumed to have grown up in an agrarian environment. They do not receive a solid agronomic or commercial education. And despite its urban character, land-ownership is still utterly steeped in feudal traditions. The offspring of large landowners receive their schooling at court and in the military. Accident of birth may often bequeath the role of farmer on to a young man whose 'studies' have been confined to the racetrack and grand restaurants, and whose abilities, at best, merely embrace connoisseurship of wine and a knowledge of horseflesh – not the best fitted person to demonstrate the practical superiority of the large agricultural enterprise. But ownership of land, especially with rising ground-rent, can keep his head above water for quite some time before the onset of bankruptcy.

The tenant is in a different position. Ground-rent cannot make up for any shortfall in profits. And ownership of land cannot be used as security against debts. The annual rent has to be paid on time. The ability to pick the most competent tenants has its counterpart in the rapid bankruptcy of the incompetent. Competition is felt much more severely than in the case of farmers who are also landowners.

And since the tenant does not have to spend money to buy land, or often buildings too, the entire capital can be given over for farming. The largest estate possible can be farmed at the maximum level of intensity for any given capital. Under the capitalist mode of production, the tenant system therefore yields the highest net product. Nevertheless, the tenant system also has its gloomier aspects. The tenant has the greatest interest in extracting the highest possible yield from the soil, and is also best fitted to do so: but they have little interest in the constancy of yields, an interest which diminishes in proportion to the length of the tenancy agreement. The quicker they suck the fertility out of the soil, the more profit they make. Although the contract can forbid methods of cultivation which deplete and impoverish the land, and tenancies do contain very detailed regulations on such matters, at best this causes agriculture to stagnate at a given level. The tenant system is less suited for achieving agricultural *progress*. Tenants have no interest in effecting improvements, or introducing initially expensive methods of cultivation whose beneficial consequences may either partly, or even wholly, only be felt long after the agreement is terminated, and which would probably simply provide an excuse for raising rents – increasing ground-rent rather than boosting agricultural profits. The tenant will avoid undertaking any improvements unlikely to pay back the capital cost plus interest during the duration of the tenancy agreement.

Under the tenant system, agricultural progress is favoured by long tenancies. However, rising ground-rents encourage landowners to shorten tenancies as much as possible to ensure that increased ground-rents disappear entirely into their own pockets. Just as with owner-farming, ground-rent also emerges as a powerful obstruction to rational agriculture under the tenant system.

The *law of inheritance* ranks alongside it.

The Law of Inheritance

The feudal shackles which constricted both agriculture and industry could only be broken by the introduction of full private property in land, and the lifting of privileges, not only of rank but also of *birth*. Bourgeois society not only demands the complete equality of all its citizens before the law, but also the equality of all children in the family, and hence the division of parental property into equal parts. However, these same institutions which allowed a rapid advance of agriculture soon became shackles themselves.

The division of parental property in the form of capital is also a major obstacle to the accumulation of capitals in the hands of one owner. Nevertheless, the concentration of capital is not merely a product of the centralisation but also of the accumulation of fresh capital: this latter process is so powerful that despite the continuation of divided inheritance, the concentration of capital continues to make rapid progress.

In those countries with long-established cultivation, where all land is already in private ownership, there is nothing in the sphere of land-ownership to correspond with the accumulation of fresh capital. The centralisation of ownership also encounters much greater difficulties than the centralisation of capital. The division of inheritance is a strong factor in the progressive dismemberment of land ownership. However, despite the powerful and profound influence which juridical relations have on economic life, in the last analysis it is always the latter that emerges as the decisive force. The dismemberment of land-ownership can only become a reality where economic relations allow it, relations which have been sketched out in the previous chapter. And where this is the case, the division of inheritance in fact proves to be a highly effective means for accelerating development.

In contrast, where a farm serves commodity-production rather than production for the household, that is, is subject to competition, and where the large farm is superior to the smaller and the fragmentation of ownership implies direct and obvious disadvantages – for example, where grain-growing predominates and there are no opportunities for supplementary employment for the farmer – the dismemberment of estates *in natura* on the division of inheritance is both difficult and rarely sustainable. The more common form is that one inheritor receives the estate undivided and pays the co-heirs for the shares. But since such an inheritor does not usually possess the necessary capital, the property has to be mortgaged. This is essentially an instance of buying an estate with insufficient capital. The specific difference is that inheritance is an involuntary transaction, and one that is necessarily repeated from generation to generation. The law of inheritance forces heirs to take over their inheritance encumbered from the very outset: instead of using any surpluses to accumulate capital and improve the estate, they have to pay interest on the mortgage. And even if one heir succeeds in paying off the debts, his successor will be back in the same position, and maybe even in greater debt should ground-rents have risen, or interest on capital fallen in the meantime – or possibly both factors may combine to increase the value of the estate.

Rising prices for estates are an advantage for those who cease farming, who sell their estates, but not for those who are turning to farming, who are buying an estate or inheriting one in company with others. Nothing could be more mistaken than to suppose that a steep increase in the price of estates and the artificial maintenance of such high prices is in the interests of agriculture. The short-term landowner, the mortgage bank, and the speculator all gain – but not agriculture, and least of all agriculture's future: the next generation of farmers.

Fragmentation, or the increased *encumberment* of estates – this is the alternative which bourgeois inheritance offers the farmer.

In some areas, in particular in France, the rural population attempts to sidestep this alternative by means of the two-child system. Although this undoubtedly offers a means for avoiding the disadvantages of the existing law of inheritance, like other means designed to help the peasant it does so at the ultimate expense of society as a whole. The development of capitalist society requires vigorous population growth.

Any nation with a relatively slow-growing labour force will be left behind in the international competitive struggle. And it also runs the risk of forfeiting its political power because it will no longer possess the necessary military might, based essentially on the number of people of military age it can throw on to the scales.

In France, the prominence of the two-child system is not only leading to a decline in the country's relative military strength – population only grew by 2 million, from 36 to 38 million, between 1872 and 1891 and since 1886 has scarcely grown at all, compared with Germany which grew by 9 million from 41 to 50 million over the same period – but is also forcing capitalists to import Belgians, Italians, Germans and Swiss to provide the labour-power which their own rural populations cannot supply. In 1851 France had only 380,000 foreigners within its borders, 1 per cent of the population: by 1891 this had risen to 1,130,000, 3 per cent. In contrast, in 1890 the German Empire contained only 518,510 persons born abroad, 1 per cent of the population. At best the unburdening of land-ownership through the two-child system is at the expense of military power and industrial capacity. France's politicians and economists are not especially enthusiastic about rescuing agriculture through such a device.

Entailment

In France, revolution made a very thorough job of sweeping away the feudal economy and the feudal law of inheritance. In contrast, large land-ownership in England and Germany managed to retain a significant amount of its power within bourgeois society. One expression of this is the particular form of the law of inheritance which it preserved for itself, or at least the most favoured of its members, namely the *Fideikommiss*. Under this system of entailment an estate ceases to be the free property of an individual owner and becomes bound to a family: although usufruct falls to one individual member of the family (usually the deceased's first born) they may not sell or diminish the property. Their siblings share equal title only to moveable property: they are excluded from the entailed property of the *Fideikommiss*. The number of entailed estates has grown markedly in Prussia since the onset of the agrarian crisis.

Until this century	153
1800/1850	72
1851/1860	46
1861/1870	36
1871/1880	84
1881/1886	135

Within the space of the 16 years since 1871, more property was entailed in this way than in the first 70 years of the century, and the process is still on the increase: 13 more estates in 1896, and 9 more in 1897 as this work was in preparation. It is quite evident that these foundations are not for the 'welfare of agriculture', but the well-being of a few aristocratic families.

The peasant form of entailment [*Anerbenrecht*] represents a kind of peasant sub-species of *Fideikommiss*: it does not bind property ownership so strongly and allows the owner a little more freedom of movement. Both forbid the division of the inheritance. In certain parts of Germany and Austria, where large peasant holdings predominate, this law has been maintained, if not as statute then as custom. More recently, a number of legislative provisions have given this custom a more secure basis in law – the reason being that conservative politicians and economists regard it as a powerful means for conserving the peasantry, and hence a bulwark for private property.

Entailment is undoubtedly capable of warding off those dangers to land-ownership threatened by the division of inheritance, at least where the practice is carried through with some conviction. But in effect this means nothing other than disinheriting otherwise entitled children, saving peasant *agriculture* at the expense of the majority of the peasant *population, saving private property* through the *confiscation of the rights* of entitled heirs and erecting a dam against the proletariat by multiplying the proletariat.

With entailed large-scale land-ownership the disinheritance of younger sons, as is common in England, is not a particularly serious matter: the Church, the Army, the Civil Service are all entrusted with the task of supplying a sufficient number of sinecures for the disinherited sons of the aristocracy. Peasants are not so well provided for. They have no influence with the state or the Church, and cannot use it as a welfare institution for their younger offspring. Entailment means nothing more than condemning all the peasants' children, bar one, to wage slavery.

Entailment also encourages the proletarianisation of the rural population in another way – all the more so, the more it comes to resemble the *Fideikommiss*: that is, the more it prevents the fragmentation of the land and its encumberment with debt as a result of the division of inheritance. It gives a powerful boost to those tendencies which favour centralisation rather than fragmentation of the land. It therefore encourages opportunities for extending and more rationally organising the farm, at the same time ripping a large number of small landowners from the soil which previously bound them to their homes.

Entailment applies to the smallest of holders neither as custom nor as statute. It would merely be a fetter on them: their wellbeing is based less and less on their landholding and more and more on their money earnings outside the farm. The law of entailment is intended to protect the large peasant. In Austria it only applies to estates of 'medium size', in Mecklenburg to holdings which are at least 37.5 bushels, in Bremen to estates of at least 50 hectares, in Westphalia and Brandenburg to estates with a net land tax yield of at least 75 Marks.

The large peasants' right of entailment not only proletarianises their younger siblings and children, but also tends to proletarianise their smaller neighbours. Inasmuch as this acts as a spur to the flight from the land, the ensuing depopulation of the countryside will hamper the development of rational cultivation. For example, we read in the case of 'districts with closed inheritance' in Hesse:

> For many years, complaints have been heard about shortages of labour. Emigration to the industrial districts by young people and able-bodied men who have nothing to call their own has increased very considerably: only the women, children and elderly remain and the farmers – both peasant and estate owner – have to choose their workers from amongst these individuals. (Auhagen, *Die ländliche Arbeiterverhältnisse in der Rheinprovinz*, p. 233)

The same applies, but even more so, with *Fideikommiss*, one of the most potent means for establishing and extending latifundia. However, claims that the tendency towards decentralisation is the sole tendency in agriculture, and that this can only be combatted by artificial barriers are utterly false. Wherever commodity-production predominates in agriculture, both tendencies will coexist. According to Conrad, there were 2,498 private landowners with over 1,000 hectares each, with a total land-ownership of 4,684,254 hectares in the eastern provinces of Prussia in the late 1880s. Of these 308 were subject to *Fideikommiss*, and owned 1,295,613 hectares, around a quarter of the land area comprising holdings over 1,000 hectares. In France this system does not exist. Despite this, the large farm is growing there even more so than in Germany, as the table on p. 135 clearly showed. In 1895 in Germany, farms over 50 hectares accounted for 32.65 per cent of land in agricultural use: in 1892 in France farms with more than 40 hectares accounted for 43.05 per cent. Unfortunately, the French statistics only show the number and not the area of farms of 40 hectares and above. However, the largest farms have grown considerably.

Difficulties of Commodity-Producing 207

	1882	1892	+/-
Farms over 40 hectares	142,000	139,000	-3,000
of which 40-100 hectares	113,000	106,000	-7,000
" " over 100 hectares	29,000	33,000	+4,000

Admittedly, these are only farm statistics and not ownership statistics: nevertheless, they illustrate the general trend. Land-ownership statistics would show more, certainly not less, centralisation.

Although the protection offered by fee-tail is not the sole reason for large-scale land-ownership, the protection it does provide is certainly highly favourable to its emergence and growth; and in doing so, it creates the preconditions for the highest stage of agriculture attainable within the capitalist mode of production.

The great size of the latifundia enables the individual farms on them to be arranged in accordance with their specific nature, and their land tailored accordingly. A number of farms can be merged into one planned economic organism. And entailment also facilitates the accumulation of capital which can be used to intensify the operation of the enterprise, since it shields the farm from the burdens which accompany the division of inheritance. According to the survey of indebtedness carried out in 42 Prussian administrative districts in 1883, recorded debt per Thaler of net property tax yield (without deduction for the mortgaged value of buildings) was as follows:

Estates held under *Fideikommiss* or through a foundation	Holdings with net property tax yield of:		
	Over 100 Th.	100-500Th.	30-100 Th.
20.30 Marks	84.40 Mks	54.10 Mks	56.20 Mks

The security of ownership unique to entailment encourages extensive improvements, and also encourages the development of tenant-farming which flourishes the most where tenants feel sure that their rights will not be curtailed by change of ownership or insolvency on the part of the owner.

It is therefore no coincidence that the latifundia system, protected by entailment, has produced the two highest forms of capitalist agriculture: the capitalist tenant system in England, and the giant conglomerate enterprise in Austria.

Nevertheless, although the latifundium form of ownership, more than any other, makes capitalist farming in the fullest sense *possible*, the protection provided by entailment releases it from regarding rational agriculture as *necessary*.

First and foremost, the owners do not have to defend their holdings in the competitive struggle. Although we do not share the view that the competitive struggle on the market is one with the struggle for existence, a nature-given necessity, a certain degree of rivalry between the members of society and the selection of the fittest does seem to be an indispensable prerequisite both for social progress in society and for maintaining the level already attained. There is no reason to suppose that the essentials of a socialist society would be irreconcilable with such rivalry and selection. The elimination of class differences, the equalisation of living standards between classes in no way implies the elimination of every other social difference, some of which can serve to stimulate individuals. Consider contemporary trade unions: their members are not divided by class differences or differences in standard of life, but there certainly are differences of opinion, power, individual behaviour and, as a consequence, both rivalry and a process of selection in determining those called on to represent and administer the whole. A complex structure such as a modern socialist society would inevitably display even greater diversity and difference. Far from equality in living standards suppressing rivalry, and making it impossible to choose the fittest for the most responsible, important and difficult posts, such equality would constitute its foundation. A race between horses who begin at different starting points along the racetrack is a nonsense: the same is true of rivalry between people who are unequal to begin with. The selection of the fittest can only take place amongst equals.

Such rivalry and selection are not competition as understood by bourgeois economics: they already exist *within* the capitalist enterprise, not under the sway of competition as conceived by the economists, but where planning and cooperation prevail. Competition begins to rule and regulate economic life at the point at which planned cooperation ends. The relationship between individual, independent establishments engaged in commodity-production is determined by competition. Within the individual firm or enterprise, production is regulated in a planned and maximally economic fashion. Production within society is unplanned: this situation is only rescued from degeneration into utter chaos by the fact that those products produced to excess are devalued, and those which use too little labour time, and which therefore do not meet the demand for them, are paid above their

Difficulties of Commodity-Producing 209

value – a more wasteful or inconvenient procedure is barely imaginable.

The lack of planning within commodity-production corresponds with the methods used to select who shall own and manage enterprises. Under the rule of private property in the means of production, *accident of birth* is the main route. Competition only comes into play *after* this selection process is over: and then it operates less by elevating the virtuous than by eliminating the unfit, not by dismissing them – as in the case of a poor manager – but by ruining the entire establishment, a method which in terms of cruelty and waste is indeed comparable with the struggle for the existence of the individual organism, although it has little else in common with it.

As brutal and wasteful as this method may be, it is the only possible way to bring about maximum economy and rationality in the arrangement of production in the individual establishment under the system of commodity-production and private property in the means of production.

These dictates have been abolished as far as entailed property is concerned – the very private property in the means of production which makes such dictates so essential. The owner of such an estate can manage it appallingly, their earnings may fall, but their title to the land will never be put in jeopardy.

It would be absurd to try and protect industrial or commercial capital by entailment. Such capital is far too mobile and changeable to tolerate such a fetter. Capital is engaged in an unceasing metabolism: one day it exists in the form of money, the next in the form of means of production, the day after that as commodities – contracting and expanding, alternating between crisis and prosperity and so on. Land, in contrast, regardless of how often it may be equated with capital, is subject to quite different laws. It does not represent a value which has been created by labour, and is not subject to a process of circulation. In material terms, it is quite different to those means of production which represent capital. These wear out – land cannot be destroyed. Means of production are constantly rendered obsolete by new discoveries – land remains the natural basis of all production. Competition between capitals grows as capital accumulates, as industry and population expand; the same processes increasingly give land the character of a monopoly.

Irrational as it would be for a family to seek to secure its capital through entailing a factory or a bank, such a step is very much in the interests of a landowning family – despite the fact that entailment is the least conducive form of land-ownership for rational cultivation. A passing owner can only damage himself by a poor standard of farming by causing a temporary reduction in ground-rent: he cannot destroy the basis of the family's income. This will survive the generations.

That *Fideikommiss* and a poor standard of farming go together is evident from the start. Modern entailment requires that the state take a strong interest in individual landowning families, since it is the state which permits and protects this system. It is the families of court nobles who enjoy this privilege – families whose occupation keeps them away from agriculture and makes them unsuitable as farmers. The fact that, despite this, latifundia held under this system of inheritance do not number amongst the poorest farmed estates – and in fact occasionally contain model farms – is due to two factors: first, the capitalist tenant system, the development of which is favoured by such estates, and second, the modern system of agricultural training, which produces more than enough competent administrators, cheaply available to the noble latifundia owners, in whose employ they find the best circumstances in which to apply their knowledge and skills.

Of course, a neglectful or incompetent landowner can still easily make serious mistakes in choosing their tenants or estate managers. At any event, the superior cultivation practised on a number of latifundia does not testify to the advantages of entailment but to the superiority of the large-scale agricultural enterprise – a superiority which still manages to show through under the most unpropitious circumstances.

Entailment also hampers rational agriculture in another way. Such property is either a latifundium from the outset or, as we saw, becomes one by overruling the tendencies towards the decentralisation of ownership, leaving free rein to the centralising ones. However, the larger the land-ownership, the greater the mass of ground-rent which it generates, and hence the greater the landowner's luxury. The most obvious such luxury is luxury in land, and in particular, land subject to entailment, on which feudal traditions remain strong. The larger the holding, and the better farmed one part of it, the larger the ground-rent, and the greater the desire to devote the rest of it to the pursuit of pleasure – mansions, ornamental gardens, parks, game enclosures – and consequently the smaller the part devoted to growing food.

Capitalist exploitation in the towns is heading in the same direction. The more this exploitation and the mass of surplus-value grows, the greater the luxury of the bourgeoisie, expressed – among other things – in the purchase and establishment of country seats, ranging from the magnificent castle of the finance baron to the simple small country house of the small merchant or manufacturer, country seats designed primarily for pleasure and in which agriculture is merely an adjunct. The more the means of communication develop, the easier the link between town and country, the more such country seats will encroach into the countryside

Difficulties of Commodity-Producing 211

and drive the peasants off their plots.

The increase in the mass of surplus-value and the easing of communication between town and country is not only expressed in the establishment of country seats, but also in the increase in *hunting*, which undergoes a transformation from feudal privilege into bourgeois pleasure. This not only leads to an expansion in forests at the expense of peasant holdings, but also encourages the excessive protection and multiplication of game stocks even where woodlands are not increased in size. And as far as the game is concerned, the fodder offered by arable fields and pasture is far preferable to what they can find in the woods.

Both the increase in woodland and the increase in game ruin peasant farming. Despite this, peasants may often welcome the extension of hunting for sport. They can rent out their cottages and huts, and where demand exceeds supply, rents have leapt up enormously. The odd hare can be very expensive for peasants; instead, it may pay them to deliberately feed their produce to hares and partridges rather than people and cattle. Some peasant localities do very well out of renting out their hunts. But the extension of hunting for sport always obstructs rational agriculture.

Even the increase in surplus-value in the towns joins with ground-rent and the laws of inheritance to damage agriculture. The problems caused by the law of inheritance are most clearly recognised by economists the more of an inkling they have of agriculture. But as representatives of the interests of *bourgeois* society they do not generally go as far as actually urging the abolition of inheritance in land and its replacement by common ownership. In theory common ownership in land is not incompatible with bourgeois society: nevertheless, bourgeois instincts are sharp enough to realise that the individual spheres of society are closely interrelated – and react upon one another. Despite the fact that common ownership of land would liberate agriculture from a number of its most oppressive burdens – burdens which are growing from generation to generation – they consequently maintain a resolute defence of private property.

Bourgeois economics prefers to attend to the symptoms – such as easing the indebtedness caused by inheritance – by dreaming up new forms of credit. Its customary position is that both the equal division of inheritances and monopolisation of the inheritance by one member of the family are equally damaging: and then concludes that both are in fact essential. Each serves as the antidote to the other. If England is the country of entailment, and France of equal inheritance, then Germany will draw praise for having both systems running parallel. Whether this will give German agriculture a lead over English or French is far from obvious.

But this is not the end of the story. The capitalist mode of production either creates or fosters a host of other processes inimical to agriculture.

The Exploitation of the Country by the Town

We saw how ground-rents and farmers' indebtedness grow. But only part of ground-rent and debt interest are retained – to be consumed or accumulated – in the country: the bulk flows into the towns, and this portion is steadily increasing.

Rural backwardness forces farmers to look for potential lenders in their immediate locality – their creditors not only include the village Jew, corn and cattle merchants, grocers and innkeepers, but also highly Christian large peasants, who are as skilled at blood-sucking as the next. In the course of development, as the incurring of debts ceases to be a matter of accident, ill luck or poor farming – an act usually performed surreptitiously as it would be seen as a sign of distress – and becomes a necessary part of the process of production, as commodity exchange develops between town and country, such primitive, furtive usury is supplanted by specific institutions for the open granting of credit as a normal act, not a desperate resort. Extortionate rates of interest are replaced by normal rates. Such institutions are either based in towns from the outset – banks, the numerous cooperatives and so on – or they borrow the required capital from urban capitalists. This transformation of the credit system is a necessary development. But although it is useful for the individual peasant, taken as a whole it represents an increase in the country's tributary obligations to the towns. An ever-growing portion of the values created on the land pour into the towns, without any compensating flow of value travelling in the opposite direction.

The same is true of ground-rents. The more that capitalist development advances, the greater the cultural differences between town and country: the more the country gets left behind, the greater the means for pleasure and amusement which the town can offer in comparison. Small wonder that owners whose estates are large enough to be cultivated by tenants or hirelings, and who enjoy high enough ground-rents, prefer to spend a good deal of time – and their rent income – in the city. Under extreme circumstances this leads to absentee landlordism – the complete decamping of the owner from their estate. This is seen, for example, in Ireland or Sicily, where centuries of mismanagement of a system of enormous latifundia have engendered a barbarism which makes even a short stay by the owner into something far short of a pleasure – and pleasure is the sole aim of such an individual's life. Irish and Sicilian agriculture illustrate the pernicious consequences of the protection provided by entailment in a context in which the large-scale agricultural enterprise has not developed to a stage where it can overcome such consequences.

Even where the extremes of absentee landlordism are not seen, the periodic absence of the large landowner in the town, accompanied by part of their ground-rent, is the rule. And while their rural luxuries – hunting, pleasure palaces – are ruining agriculture, cutting back the cultivated area and removing peasant workers, their urban enjoyments encourage industry and trade, increase employment, draw in labour-power and promote the accumulation of capital.

Money taxes also work in the same direction: these are steadily growing, and fall most heavily on the peasantry.

From its beginnings, production in the towns is predominantly commodity-production. Money taxes are a product of its development. Production in rural areas, especially in smaller establishments, is still, even now, primarily for direct consumption. Urban development imposes money taxes on the countryside. Such taxes are not the product of this form of production: in fact, they stand in contradiction to it, but nonetheless act powerfully to transform it. Money taxes are one of the driving forces behind the development from production for direct consumption to the production of commodities: however, money taxes, and the other cash needs of the peasant, usually grow much faster than rural commodity-production and the institutions of commerce and credit corresponding to it. In many instances this is still the source of the perpetual financial embarrassment of the peasant farmers and their dependence on middlemen and usurers.

The taxes which are such a burden to the peasantry are not intended to serve the development of the countryside: instead, they serve the *towns* – and in particular the large *cities*. Only a fraction of tax income is spent in rural areas: the barracks and arsenals are in the towns; the ministries and courts – and with them the lawyers whom the peasant has to pay – are in the towns; state secondary and higher schools are in the towns; museums, state-subsidised theatres and so forth are all in the towns. Both peasant and town-dweller have to pay their share of the costs of civilisation – the difference is that the peasant has precious little access to it.

Hardly surprising then that peasants show no understanding for culture and are hostile to what is – as far as they are concerned – merely a burden. This is all highly gratifying to those reactionary demagogues who, out of supposed concern for the public purse, call for the cutting of all expenditure for cultural purposes rather than the export of culture into the countryside, and the abolition of the antithesis between town and country. This will be one of the most important tasks of the society of the future.

The concentration of government in the towns is not a product of hostility to agriculture but rather economic forces much stronger than the will of politicians. In fact, present-day governments are very much the friends of agriculture, and the powerful support they give through tariffs, gifts and grants is only too familiar.

Despite the enormous movements in wealth which state policy brings about, it neither halts nor hinders the flow of unrequited commodity-values from country to town. In the final analysis, the sole beneficiaries are the *landowners*. State policy is essentially a means for *increasing ground-rents*. As we already know, these constitute a burden on agriculture, clearly visible in the tenant system, indirect and hidden in the mortgage system, but no less effective for all that. Under the tenant-system such state support enables the tenant to pay a higher rent. Where the landowner and the farmer are one and the same person, both gain so to speak; but the increase in ground-rents leads to an increase in the price of estates. This can raise the burden of debt even on the present owner, and will certainly encumber his successors by purchase or inheritance. After a while state support to agriculture simply becomes state support to the real owners of the land, the mortgage creditors.

Most of the latter live in the towns; even the larger landowners consume the bulk of their rents there. The increase in ground-rents through tariffs and subsidies does not therefore tax the town to help the countryside, does not serve to reciprocate any inflow of values. Rather, the increase in ground-rents means that along with *agriculture* the *mass of urban consumers* are also fleeced to benefit a few landowners, most of whom live in the towns, together with their urban creditors.

The outflow of so much value into the towns, uncompensated by any flow of counter-values, corresponds to a constantly mounting loss of nutrients in the form of corn, meat, milk and so forth which the farmer has to sell to pay taxes, debt-interest and rent. At the same time the increased demand for industrial products from the town and the steady demise of rural domestic industry for local consumption increase the outflow of values for which there is a counterpart. Although such a flow does not signify an exploitation of agriculture in terms of the law of value, it does nevertheless lead – as with the other factors cited – to its material exploitation, to the impoverishment of the land of its nutrients. Technical progress in agriculture, far from making up for this loss, is, in essence, a method for improving the techniques of wringing the goodness out of the soil and increasing the mass of nutritional material removed each year for despatch to the towns.

But doesn't modern agronomy emphasise the maintenance of agricultural equilibrium and the replacement of nutrients removed from the soil by the application of appropriate fertilisers? Yes, but this does not contradict our claim in the slightest. That the soil is becoming exhausted is beyond dispute. Without supplementary fertilisers, and given the current relationship between town and country, and current techniques of cultivation, this would soon lead to the complete collapse of agriculture. Such fertilisers allow the reduction in soil fertility to be avoided, but the necessity of using them in larger and larger amounts simply adds a further burden to agriculture – not one unavoidably imposed by nature, but a direct result of current social organisation.

By overcoming the antithesis between town and country, or at least between the densely populated cities and the desolated open country, the materials removed from the soil would be able to flow back in full. Supplementary fertilisers would then, at most, have the task of enriching the soil, not staving off its impoverishment. Advances in cultivation would signify an increase in the amount of soluble nutrients in the soil without the need to add artificial fertilisers.

Significantly, despite all the advances in agronomy, wheat yields fell in England between the 1860s and the 1880s after a period of uninterrupted advance. Average annual yield per acre was:

1857–62	28.4 bushels
1863–68	30.8 bushels
1869–74	27.2 bushels
1875–80	22.6 bushels

This fall came to a halt after the 1880s. This is not attributable to any increase in soil fertility, however; merely that land less suitable for wheat-growing has been turned over to pasturage as a result of foreign competition, leaving only the most fertile in cultivation. Since the 1860s the area under wheat has fallen from 3,800,000 acres to 1,900,000 – virtually half.

The advance of capitalist methods of cultivation has also been accompanied by an increase in the various animal and plant diseases afflicting agriculture.

Some of these pests have assumed such dimensions over the last few decades that they threaten to devastate the agriculture of entire countries. One only has to reflect on the ravages of vine-pest and colorado beetle, foot-and-mouth disease, red murrain and swine fever.

The damages from phylloxera in France, on which a tax abatement was allowed, have been estimated at 125.9 million francs in 1884, 165.6 million francs in 1885, 175.3 in 1886, 185.1 in 1887 and 61.5 in 1888 ... According to most recent reports, the devastation caused by phylloxera continues. Since its first appearance (1880) this dangerous insect has already spread through 63 *Départements* (1890) and laid waste hundreds of thousands of hectares of vine-growing land. (Juraschek, *Übersichten der Weltwirtschaft*, p. 328)

Foot-and-mouth disease affected the following numbers of farms and animals in Germany.

Year	Farmsteads	Animals
1887	1,242	31,868
1888	3,185	82,834
1889	23,219	555,178
1890	39,693	816,911
1891	44,519	821,130
1892	105,929	4,153,519

The disease abated somewhat after 1892, but in 1896 afflicted a further 68,874 farms with 1,584,429 animals.

These are horrifying numbers.

The main cause of the rapid increase in the danger of pests and diseases lies in the supplanting of natural breeds by 'refined' breeds, by the products of artificial selection. Natural selection leads to the selection and reproduction of those individuals most fitted to maintain the species. Artificial selection in capitalist society ignores this aspect, and is simply concerned with breeding individuals which offer the greatest profit, incur the least cost, mature early and in which the exploitable parts are as large as possible, and the non-useful organs as atrophied as possible. Such 'refined' strains yield a much higher profit than natural breeds, but their stamina and resistance is abnormally low.

Nevertheless, whilst their resistance may be declining, their numbers are on the increase. Thanks to the efforts to keep the small farmer going, and improvements made in their methods of cultivation, 'refined' plants and animals requiring great care and knowledge have now entered the small farmer's orbit. At the same time the character of farming is changing, a fact particularly evident in stock-rearing. Summer pasturing, which refreshed and strengthened animals, is being abandoned: but the peasant's lack of money means their stabling has not improved. The peasant stall which once provided confined and unhygienic winter shelter for the tough cattle of the Middle Ages now becomes a prison for the delicate modern breeds. Even in England, which maintains a high level of stock-rearing, the stalls are no longer adequate.

Mr Wilson Fox states, in his Lancashire report, that unhealthy and ill-constructed cattle-sheds and byres, with want of space and air, have contributed to the spread of tuberculosis. Instead of 600 cubic feet of air, in some cases a cow gets only 260 cubic feet, and there are no means of isolating diseased animals. One witness stated that if the Dairy and Cow Sheds Act was put into force in the Chorley district, seven-tenths of the buildings would have to come down. (Royal Commission on Agriculture, 1897, p. 363)

One of the factors favouring the devastation caused by pests is the disappearance of insect-eating birds, a result not only of hunting them out but also of the reduction in nesting opportunities prompted by the extension of cultivation. In forestry, the destruction of forests by pests is encouraged by modern large-scale operations, the replacement of a planting by a felling system, and the elimination of slow growing deciduous trees by rapid-growing, and more rapidly exploitable, conifers.

Whilst modern breeding reduces the resistance of plants and animals to the tiny organisms which threaten them, modern transport facilitates the rapid spread of these pests and allows them to devastate ever larger areas. As the land deteriorates, its products need more and more mollycoddling. The costs of fertilisers are joined by those of pesticides – and anyone who tries to save on these expenses is rewarded with crop failures: and then blights and pests arrive to complete the ruin of the farmer.

The Depopulation of the Countryside

The growth of towns and the expansion of industry, which increasingly exhausts the soil and imposes new burdens on agriculture in the form of the fertilisers needed to combat this exhaustion, does not rest content with this achievement. It also robs agriculture of its *labour-power*.

Chapter 7 noted how the growth of large-scale agricultural enterprises pushed out the peasantry, and with them the reservoir of agricultural labour.

On the other hand, the previous chapter revealed the periodic migrations which arise from the peasant's need for supplementary employment. This also depletes the labour which agriculture needs for its rational operation. But workers also bring new capital into agriculture from industry, from the town, and this helps the rational organisation of farming.

However, the flight from the land generated by the attractions of the cities and industrial areas has quite a different effect.

Towns offer wage-labourers quite different opportunities for employment than rural areas, much more opportunity for establishing a household, more freedom and more culture. The larger the town, the more these advantages grow, and the greater its drawing power.

The establishment of an independent household and a family in the country requires the acquisition (by purchase or rent) of an independent agricultural enterprise. This is by no means easy where the large enterprise is developing, and such areas are marked by a particularly strong motivation to get off the land. But the establishment of a household also encounters difficulties in areas where the land is highly parcellised. House-servants, agricultural labourers and maid servants who lack sufficient savings have no chance at all. Not only are they condemned to a life in which they will never own any land, but also to a life of dependency as an appendage of another's household, excluded from marriage and a family. Their only road to freedom, to the marriage and family denied them by those protectors of the family, the pious big peasant or Junker, is – flight to the town, to the immoral Social Democrats, those enemies of marriage and the family.

How powerful this motivation is amongst those working in service can be gauged by a few extracts from a peasant's observations on the house-servants with whom he lived.

> No greater injury to human freedom and dignity matches that inflicted on servants or propertyless agricultural labourers in this respect. The difficulties associated with marriage are sufficiently well known not to need reiteration here: we therefore pass straight to the consequences. Since by far the bulk of humanity cannot completely suppress its sexual drive, and contemporary social circumstances do not allow it to be exercised within ordered limits, it is impossible to expect anything other than that the limits prescribed in the interests of maintaining the current social order will be repeatedly transgressed. Extra-marital sexual intercourse is an unavoidable consequence of this impasse: this has now gradually become so

entrenched in the ranks of rural servants that all the efforts to eliminate it by all the teachers of morals and religion put together would be utterly fruitless. Our present institution of marriage is for the most part unattainable for these classes: this is why they have to resort to lower forms of sexual behaviour. That the life of a servant or worker under such circumstances unavoidably becomes filled with the greatest humiliation, furtiveness, deceit, shame, duress and all manner of indignities is evident. Moreover, public feeling in rural areas is still highly moralistic: small wonder that so many prefer to escape this eagle-eyed *fama* in the hurly-burly of the town.

The vast bulk of those fleeing the land are simply driven by the lack of love or the limitations placed on it. Off they go to the towns, those dens of vice, only – with the exception of a fortunate few – to fall prey to poverty and complete degeneration. But the life of bliss awaiting the children of the rural proletariat in their homelands can also be summed up in very few words. Despite the urgent need for such human commodities, their existence is perceived, at best, as a burden by their creators. These can only rarely involve themselves with their children's upbringing, and have no idea of the real joys of parentage: in numerous instances their offspring face the dubious honour of being added to the burdens on the local exchequer. Their entry into life begins with distress and shame for their creators, it continues with a deficient upbringing, and their thorny path through life is crowned with the most gruelling wage-slavery – before coming to its loveless end. (Johann Filzer, *Anschauungen über die Entwicklung der menschlichen Gesellschaft*, pp. 161, 162)

The establishment of an independent household not only allows true marriage and a family, but also allows workers to conduct themselves as citizens outside work, to unite with those of common opinions – something favoured in urban large-scale industry by the concentration of large numbers of workers in a small area – and through the power of organisation and participation in local and national political life, to fight for better living and working conditions.

This also inevitably attracts rural workers into the towns. This, and other factors. The more intensive agriculture becomes, the more irregular the employment it can offer to its workers. Whereas some machines, such as threshers, can considerably reduce the number of workers employed and have been responsible for rendering the bulk of those employed in winter surplus to requirements, others require more labour, such as the drilling machine. Crop rotation also necessitates the cultivation of crops – so-called root crops, potatoes, turnips and so on –

which require regular attention in the form of weeding, hoeing and ridging throughout their growing period. Intensive farming generally tends *to reduce* the number of workers required in *winter* and increase the demand for labour for any given area in *summer*.

This leads both to a massive reduction in the number of servants and farmhands which the estate is obliged to keep on throughout the year, and greater fluctuations in the employment of free day-labourers. In areas where agriculture is often the only employment, this growing insecurity inevitably drives farm workers to the towns. And although employment is no more certain in the town, failure to find work in one trade can be offset by success in another.

Emigration into the industrial areas and towns grows in step with the development of the means of transport, the easing of links between town and country, and the discovery of town life by farm workers.

Easier transport between town and country, between the site of production and the market, is also an indispensable condition for the prosperity of intensive agricultural commodity-production. All farmers are eager advocates of improvements or extensions of the rail or postal system; but the same post that delivers reports on the state of the market and seed stocks, or business correspondence, also brings the rural worker letters from a relative in the town, a relative happy in freedom from rural slavery. It even brings newspapers, although admittedly only those with 'acceptable opinions'. But the more acceptable they try to be, the more they rail against the good living and excesses of urban workers, the more the yearning country-dweller's mouth will water. The same train which brings the farmer machines and fertilisers, and takes off their grain, cattle and butter to the urban consumer, also abducts the creators of these products.

Militarism has the same effect: it draws young people from the countryside into the towns and acquaints them with urban life. Anyone joining up is not only lost to agriculture for two years, but is gone forever. Strangely enough it is the large landowners and farmers, who suffer most from this state of affairs, who are the most energetic supporters of the military state.

Most susceptible to fleeing the land are propertyless labourers, and of these the unmarried. Yet the more the burden of taxation, indebtedness and soil exhaustion on agriculture grows, the more the peasant's farm has to compete with the large-scale enterprise (and with agriculture overseas, as we shall see below); the more the peasant is forced to fight the competitive struggle with overwork and the renunciation of every civilised need – sometimes including those vital to life itself – by descending of their own free will into the depths of barbarism, the less power the peasant plot will have to bind the owner to the soil, and the more the flight from the land will insinuate itself into the ranks of the small peasantry.

This flight already exceeds the natural increase in population, and is producing an absolute decline in the rural population. Between 1882 and 1895 the number of agricultural establishments in the German Reich grew from 5,276,344 to 5,558,317; in the same period the area in agricultural use increased from 31,868,972 hectares to 32,517,941 hectares. However, the population living from agriculture fell from 19,225,455 to 18,501,307 – by no less than 724,148 persons. This decline hit areas with predominantly small peasants as much as with big peasants and latifundia; it occurs in every province in Prussia, and all the larger states of the empire with the exception of Brunswick, which registered an increase from 120,062 to 125,411.

The number of wage-labourers in Germany was as follows in 1882 and 1895.

	1882	1895	Increase (+)/Decrease (-)
Agriculture	5,881,819	5,619,794	-262,025
Industry	4,069,243	5,955,613	+1,859,570
Commerce	727,262	1,233,045	+505,783

The same process can be seen in *France*, where the ratio of agricultural to non-agricultural population changed as follows:

Year	Agricultural population	Non-agricultural population	Percentage of population in agriculture
1876	18,968,605	17,937,183	51.4
1881	18,279,209	19,422,839	48.4
1886	17,698,432	20,520,471	46.3
1891	17,435,888	20,907,304	45.5

These figures also show an absolute drop in the rural population which is attributable to the reduction in the number of workers. The number of economically active persons in French agriculture was as follows:

	1882	1895	Increase (+)/ Decrease (-)
Independent	3,460,600	3,604,789	+144,189
Wage-labourers	3,452,904	3,058,346	- 394,558

The fall in the number of wage-labourers was even greater than in Germany.

The most glaring case of a drop in the size of the agricultural working population is that of *England*, the country with the most highly developed large-scale enterprises and the largest cities. In 1861 there were 1,163,227 agricultural wage-labourers, in 1871 996,642, in 1881 890,174, and in 1891 798,912. Within 30 years their number had fallen by 364,315, 31.3 per cent – *almost a third*.

But these figures do not reveal the full loss suffered by agriculture. We have already noted that younger independent people in particular tend to emigrate from the rural areas. Children and the elderly remain behind. This applies both for permanent and periodic migration. In practice, therefore, the fall in the rural population also means a fall in its capacity to work.

The most recent occupational statistics provide a good illustration of this state of affairs. In 1895 there were 8,281,220 workers in industry and 8,292,692 in agriculture in the German Reich. Both branches were almost equal. But the distribution of these numbers by age category shows a remarkable divergence:

	Under 14	14-20	20-30	30-40	40-50	50-60	60-70	70 years and over
Agriculture	135,125	1,712,911	1,761,104	1,347,206	1,232,989	1,149,404	702,268	251,685
Industry	38,267	1,770,316	2,321,139	1,750,933	1,206,624	759,403	336,256	98,282
Agriculture +/-	+96,958	-57,405	-560,035	-403,727	+26,365	+390,001	+366,012	+153,403

Agriculture has a deficit of a million workers in relation to industry in the 14–40 age group: and an equally large plus in the less able age groups.

Difficulties of Commodity-Producing 223

A table taken from Ballod's work *Die Lebensfähigkeit der städtischen und ländlichen Bevölkerung* shows an even more extreme situation. The distribution of the population in Prussia by age on 1 December 1890 was as follows:

Age	Number of persons per 1,000 inhabitants in each group		Rural +/-
	Rural parishes and manorial districts	Towns over 2,000	
0-15	379	313	+66
15-20	94	100	-6
20-30	143	210	-77
30-40	122	149	-27
40-50	100	105	-5
50-60	79	66	+13
60-70	54	38	+16
70-100	29	19	+10
Total	1,000	1,000	

Goldstein's work on occupational structures and wealth also provides a number of illuminating statistics. He examined the percentage of the population in the 15–45 age group in the English counties. In order not to be too long-winded we simply cite the most extreme figures here for the eight most and eight least agricultural counties.

County	Number of persons per 1,000 inhabitants in:	
	agriculture	15-45 age group
Huntingdon	232	400
Cambridge	199	419
Hereford	186	407
Rutland	183	417
Lincoln	181	421
Suffolk	177	406
Norfolk	167	410
Wiltshire	149	416
		Maximum 421

County	Number of persons per 1,000 inhabitants in:	
	agriculture	15-45 age group
London	5	494
Lancaster	20	479
Durham	21	455
West Riding	31	475
Stafford	34	446
Middlesex (E.)	39	464
Warwick	40	456
Monmouth	49	459
	Minimum	455

The differences in the age structure between the industrial and rural population are unmistakable. This is not only explicable through migration alone. The greater toughness of the agricultural population also certainly makes a contribution. At any event, however, these tables clearly show that with the same working population, industry has access to more of its stronger elements.

However, it is not simply the physically strongest but also the most energetic and intelligent elements who are most likely to leave the land: they tend to have the energy and courage to do so, and are also most sensitive to the contradiction between the growing civilisation of the town, and the growing barbarism of the countryside. Large landowners and peasants hope to cloak this contradiction by denying the rural population proper schooling. But the economic links between town and country are too close for the rural population to be fully protected from the 'seductions' of the towns. And however much the large landowners attempt to put a Great Wall of China around their people, their much-revered militarism will tear it down and lead off the young peasant men to the towns. Stunted school education, the obstruction of all attempts to obtain an education from newspapers and books, simply confuse rural people's ideas about town life. And the more intelligent country-dwellers are merely made all the more conscious of the barbarism of their surroundings and are therefore even more likely to flee to the town.

Statistically, this aspect of the flight from the land cannot be proved. But it is well known that farmers complain less about the absolute reduction in the number of workers available to them and more about the reduction in the number of intelligent workers.

This further widens the intellectual gulf between the countryside and the town, which has its roots in the greatly preferential treatment enjoyed by the latter as far as means for education and intellectual

Difficulties of Commodity-Producing 225

stimulation are concerned.

Physical degeneration often joins depopulation and intellectual sclerosis. This is not only confined to factory districts. Undernourishment, unhygienic housing, overwork, dirt and ignorance, unhealthy secondary employment (domestic industry) frequently lead to the physical degeneration of the rural population.

Statistics have recently come to light claiming that the industrial population is *generally* fitter for military service – that is, physically better developed – than the agricultural population. Nevertheless, the conclusiveness of these figures is still highly disputed, and we therefore refrain from using them here.

Although it may be premature to talk about the general physical inferiority of the rural population, it is certainly losing its superiority. They are no longer even particularly distinguished in a peasant country such as Switzerland. Of 241,076 persons liable for military service between 1884 and 1891, 107,607 were agricultural workers or peasants.

	Exempt	Per cent Fit	Unfit
Peasants	18.9	61.7	38.3
Overall sample	19.8	63.0	37.0

A higher percentage of peasants was unfit compared to the general population.

The agricultural population is not only experiencing an economic, numerical, and intellectual decline, but is also now waning physically.

Capitalist development is not only placing ever-growing burdens on agriculture, but also undermining the 'original sources of all wealth' (Marx, *Capital*, I, p. 636).

The farm itself cannot, of course, escape these changes. But in contrast to the towns the problem posed by the 'labour question' is not how to control the workers, but where to get them.

Chapter 7 noted that large-scale land-ownership set about the artificial creation of small farms wherever the land has been cleared of them. And the stronger the pull to the town, the more the landowners will try to bind the workers they need to the land. But often the mere creation of small peasant plots is not sufficient to overcome the attraction of industry: *legal compulsion* also has to be used to keep workers on the large estates. New smallholdings are created which are rented out by the landowner *in return for the obligation to perform certain labour services*. A new feudalism develops. But this does not last very long. The advance of industry brings it to an end. New tenancies carrying labour obligations only survive in the absence of local industry. Once this arrives, even the most tempting offers cannot induce workers to tie themselves down: they prefer to retain free disposition over their labour-power so as to be able to use every opportunity to sell it to advantage.

According to Kärger, his study of agricultural workers in North West Germany provides 'irrefutable proof' that

> the best working conditions for both employees and employers prevail where the bulk of agricultural labour is carried out by *Heuerlinge* as well as servant labour. Under such circumstances, employers always have sufficient labour to carry out all agricultural tasks in a proper fashion. Workers are also sufficiently well off to save as well as, ideally, to remain content.

Despite such a surfeit of contentment there are numerous localities in which workers are sufficiently eccentric to be discontented. Two factors work against the generalisation of the *Heuerling* system.

On the one hand a mood of defiant independence amongst the population, which rejects any lasting obligation as *serfdom*. This explains why it has frequently proved impossible to establish *Heuerling* farms in the Westphalian districts of Paderborn, Büren, Marburg and Hörter. On the other, the immediate proximity of substantial industrial activity; this eliminated the existing *Heuerling* system in the coal-mining districts of Bergen–Mark and in the Hamburg–Harburg area, and has prevented its re-establishment.

The reasons lie in the high wages which mining and industry can pay. Agricultural workers no longer consider it rational to conclude long-term tenancy and labour agreements if an increased demand for industrial workers could be met, to their own advantage, by the supply of their labour-power.

Industry therefore ensures that the feudal ideals of Herr Kärger will have no place in the future.

A more generally practical solution is to obtain workers from elsewhere, some of whom would be permanent and others periodic migrant labour. Whilst increasing proletarianisation of the peasantry stimulates the supply of such labour, the flow of rural workers into the industrial districts guarantees a rapidly rising demand for them. In many areas agriculture would cease to function without workers from outside. But as important as this type of labour has become, at most it can help in evening out the burdens which the shortage of labour imposes on agriculture over the whole nation, or, if foreign workers are used, over several nations: but it cannot add any new labour to agriculture as a whole. Labour drawn into one area deprives another: labour moves West, only to rob the East. The shortage of labour-power spreads to areas in which industry has not yet made its influence directly felt, and in the form of temporary migration prepares the ground for permanent emigration. Outside labour rarely fully makes up for those workers who have moved off to the towns. And as we have already observed, it is precisely the most energetic and intelligent workers who are most likely to turn their backs on the land. In contrast, the newcomers come from economically backward regions, regions in which both the level of popular education and often agriculture is much lower. The consequence is not merely a decline in the overall fitness and productivity of the agricultural working class, but often in the methods of agriculture as well. Kärger writes:

> What is unique about the whole labour situation is the fact that there is simply no indigenous class of agricultural workers. Virtually without exception, workers' children turn to mining immediately after confirmation. Almost all the labour used in agriculture comes from outside the region: East and West Prussia, Hesse, Hanover, Waldeck, and Holland. Recruitment has to be constant as most will not put up with agriculture for more than one or two years once they have got to know about, or experienced, the higher earnings that can be obtained in the mines. At harvest time, migrant workers arrive by themselves, mainly from the Minden district – the so-called Bielefeld Cutters. However, anyone who can avoid it tries not to engage these highly-paid migrant workers if they can scrape by with their own servant labour. Such harvest workers are therefore seldom seen in Schwelm and Hagen where the holdings are generally smaller, in particular Schwelm where smallholdings predominate.
> Although some reports state there is no shortage of agricultural labour in these areas, especially if industry is passing through a bad patch, there is nevertheless a complete lack of any permanent labour force, and a great shortage of *good* agricultural workers. Most reports conclude that it is difficult to obtain labour at all, and one official has claimed that the shortage of workers, in particular good workers, is so

acute that most farmers are utterly sick of farming. (Kärger, *Die Verhältnisse der Landarbeiter in Nordwestdeutschland*, 1892, I, p. 133)

A correspondent writes from the Grand Duchy of Hesse (Upper Hesse):

There was once a proper class of day-labourers who worked at their trade over many years and whose work showed their skill, experience and reliability. This group has now vanished. The large number of threshing machines deprived them of winter work; work was available all year in the industrial districts and in the mid-1870s they began to depart from Westphalia, Belgium and Paris, and in particular to 'seek their fortune' in America, Australia and Argentina. And to be quite honest, a good number of them have actually found it. Their friends, good workers, then followed. Their place has been taken by the so-called married servants, a collection made up of representatives of every nation: Swiss, East and West Prussians, Poles, Upper Silesians, and even Swedes. Some are indentured and imported, and others come of their own free will. In general they constitute a rough and completely degenerate mob, living in sin with the dregs of the female migrants, given over to drink and lacking in any occupational skill, intelligence or loyalty. But they always find work as grooms on tenant farms, or as so-called 'Swiss' cattle-feeders and milkers for high wages. At the same time, there are not enough local workers settled in areas with a heavy beet crop.

From early spring onwards large numbers of male and female migrant workers are therefore brought in from the Rhön area, Eichsfeld, Bavaria, the Black Forest, Upper Silesia, Poland and West Prussia. These have to be kept on at high wages until late in the autumn simply because the local population no longer likes to work for any length of time on tenant farms. (Auhagen, *Die ländliche Arbeiterverhältnisse in der Rheinprovinz*, 1892, II, pp. 230, 231)

Here is one final example to show how the advance of industry brings about the degradation of agriculture. In an article in *Die Neue Zeit* (XI, 2, p. 284), Dr Rudolf Meyer quotes from a number of reports prepared by the manager of a Bohemian domain embracing several thousand hectares of sugar-beet and corn.

We used to hoe the drilled grain several times with a horse-drawn hoe, but we no longer do this as an untrained worker could damage the crop. *Virtually none of the servants are now skilled in driving a team,* and those few who are soon leave. Once experience in the military has taught the young men something about the world, they no longer want to perform onerous duties for us at low wages. The only members of the indigenous population we can retain are therefore the elderly, children, women and tenant serfs from the Czechoslovakian Tabor area. They are very rough and uneducated and unfit to work the machines. As a consequence, our horse-drawn hoe is rusting away in the barn.

Such reports show how difficult it is to apply what seems to be the most obvious method of dealing with the shortage of labour in the age of steam and electricity – machines. Farmers cannot always find labourers skilled enough to use machines, and those that are soon leave agriculture. Despite this the machine is still making substantial headway on the land, although not quickly enough to offset the drain of workers. Reports of farmers being able to alleviate their problems by introducing machines are rare. We leave aside here the fact that although agricultural machinery always saves labour in relation to the volume of products produced, it does not always do so in relation to the area under cultivation. Many agricultural machines require more workers for the same area than more basic implements. 'In some instances, the application of more or of improved machinery increases rather than reduces the demand for human hands. A mechanical seed-drill requires more labour to sow the same area than a seed-broadcaster or hand-sowing' (Goltz, *Die ländliche Arbeiterklasse*, p. 168).

Finally, a fourth proposal has been made for combatting the shortage of workers: *a substantial increase in wages*, better treatment, better housing, and better food. Of the four methods discussed here, this is certainly the most effective; but it still does not seem to be enough to retain the labour-power needed by agriculture. Higher wages are not the only reason why workers move to the towns. The easier prospect of finding work in the winter, the greater independence, the greater ease of establishing a family and the cultural superiority of the town in general are all factors which could only be offset by an enormous increase in wages.

Grossmann writes:

Much complaint is made over the shortage of female servants in the Elbe Marshes, mainly because they have moved off to the towns. This is particularly astonishing since those who take up service in the neighbouring small towns earn, at most, half the wages of those who stay on the land. Even in Hamburg, wages are, on average, no higher but expenses certainly are.

Better treatment might also not be enough to keep workers on the land over the long term. 'How many instances', says one correspondent,

> do we know where employers barely regard or treat their servants as human; how often do servants have to tolerate a mediocre and often poorly prepared diet; how often do they lack even a modestly comfortable or heated room in which to spend their free hours; and how often do they have to clamber through all kinds of junk to find a room to sleep in in some remote corner of the house, a room frequently hardly even graced by a proper floor or somewhere to sit, let alone a table. In contrast, if servants are considered as members of the family in some respects, with whom matters affecting the farm can be discussed, who share the family's table – something customary in this area – who may spend their free time in the family's living room or have their own comfortable, suitable, well-heated parlour or bedroom, who are offered newspapers to read, then good servants will be happy with their lot. *However, even then, servants still seem in general to yearn for employment* as postmen, railway clerks, seamstresses or barmaids, or to get a job in one of the bigger cities: simply because life there is more agreeable than in the quiet, isolated simple village, which may not even have an inn. With the current high wages, good servants, assuming that they do not marry too early as often happens, can earn enough to buy a plot by the time they are thirty, especially where prices have fallen to present levels: and on this they can keep four cows with a few sheep. (Grossmann, *Zustände der Landarbeiter*, p. 419)

Neither higher wages, nor good treatment, nor the prospects of independent property can prevent the mass of agricultural workers from fleeing the land.

And how are agricultural workers supposed to obtain higher wages and better treatment? No class of entrepreneurs will ever voluntarily agree to an increase in wages: they must be forced into it. However, agricultural labourers are basically still too weak to be able to enforce this through the power of their organisations. Any increase in wages in the countryside will be the simple consequence of a growing shortage of workers. Higher wages and a plentiful supply of labour have been mutually exclusive on the land up until now.

Despite the good sense in recommending that a wage increase could bring the flight from the land to a halt, such a step cannot realistically be expected. The flight will continue unimpeded.

Anderson Graham's book *Rural Exodus* notes on this:

> If they get low wages, as in Wiltshire, then they emigrate. And if they get high wages, as in Northumberland, they also leave. If farms are small, as in the Sleaford District of Lincolnshire, they take their leave; and in Norfolk, where the farms are larger as a rule, the flight from the land continues to grow. The rural dweller seems to be utterly possessed of the desperate thought that there is no longer a bright future for him on the land. He simply puts down his hoe and spade and is off.

Where self-help fails, state compulsion steps in to assist. Tightening up the Servants Ordinance, punishing breach of contract, making marriage more difficult are all meant to ensure that the farmers can keep their servants. The elimination or obstruction of free movement by banning migration, measures making it more difficult for migrants to settle in towns, increasing the price of rail travel, and similar moves, are meant to keep the migrants at home.

Of these, the first will merely make rural life even more unbearable for the servants and contract workers, and will inevitably increase the flight from the land. Suppressing free movement, assuming the industrial population were to tolerate it and it was feasible, might help some farmers but not agriculture in general. It would rob numerous small peasants of the only opportunity they have for supplementary employment and throw them into acute poverty. And it would also make it impossible to practise any farming which needed wage-labourers in industrial areas: as we saw, such farming cannot manage without workers from outside. This would postpone the bankruptcy of agriculture in economically backward areas only to accelerate it in the economically more advanced districts.

No remedy for the shortage of agricultural workers has been found in capitalist society. Capitalist farming has now reached the stage which feudal agriculture arrived at in the late eighteenth century – a dead end, from which it cannot emerge by virtue of its own forces on the given social foundation.

One might imagine that one was reading a description from the last century:

> There is a shortage of labour which is especially noticeable on the large estates and peasant farms. The consequence is that large estates

and even peasant farms have to be leased off individually. The disadvantage of this practice is that it leads to a kind of depredation of the land since too few cattle are kept, and only latrine and other secondary fertilisers are used. This naturally impairs the long-term fertility of the soil. It has also been found that sandy fields, which were previously profitably cultivated, are now lying fallow, and *have not been cultivated for years*. These often belong to workers who earn more from wage labour at high wages than from tilling their own fields. (Grossmann, *Zustände der Landarbeiter*, II, p. 206)

Reports from Hesse and Bavaria note:

As the general reports state, the shortage of labour in some districts of Bavaria is not only reputed to have disrupted orderly farming, but also to have led to a general lowering in the intensity of farming. (Grossmann, *Zustände der Landarbeiter*, II, p. 110)

Compare this with the effects noted above of the use of imported labour. Despite every technical advance, an undoubted decline in agriculture has taken place in some areas. A continuing shortage of labour will mean this will become more generalised. '*A reduction in the labour-force must necessarily lead to a decline in the arable area cultivated each year, with an increase in pasturage*' (Goltz, *Die ländliche Arbeiterklasse*, p. 176).

All farms employing wage-labourers will be hit by the debilitating effects of the labour-shortage, but the smaller will be worse affected than the larger. These have least access to the means if not to overcome the shortage, at least to mitigate it to some extent. They have no land to rent out to wage-labourers in return for fixed labour-obligations; their need for labour is too small for it to be worthwhile importing labour from further afield, and they have to make do with those they can find in the vicinity; they are too small to mechanise and lack the resources to make any substantial increases in wages.

For this reason the smaller farms using wage-labour are precisely those which employ the type of worker most likely to migrate: unmarried workers, servants and serving maids.

Of farms engaged in commodity-production, rather than production exclusively or almost exclusively for the household, those least affected by the flight from the land are those employing only a few workers, and able if necessary to manage with family labour, but nevertheless large enough to bind the owner to the land. In general, such farms range from 5 to 20 hectares. They also benefit from the fact that the tendency towards parcellisation, from which they are most at risk, is reduced the more the flight from the land gets a grip on the agricultural population. The demand for land therefore falls, and the excessively high price for small farms comes down. Parcellisation ceases to be profitable, and the dismemberment of estates stops. It is, therefore, hardly surprising that such farms are the only ones in Germany to have noticeably gained in overall area. Between 1882 and 1895 the cultivated area in Germany increased by 648,969 hectares, of which 563,477 was accounted for by farms between 5 and 20 hectares; farms between 1 and 2 hectares *lost* 50,177 hectares, and those between 20 and 50 hectares 62,898. The overall distribution of land by farm size was as follows:

Number of hectares per 1,000 hectares of cultivated area on farms of:

	Under 1 ha.	1-2 ha.	2-5 ha.	5-20 ha.	20-100 ha.	100-1,000 ha.	More than 1,000 ha.
1882	24	33	100	288	311	222	22
1895	25	31	101	299	303	216	25
+/-	+1	-2	+1	+11	-8	-6	+3

Such figures warm the hearts of all good citizens who see the peasantry as the sturdiest bulwark of the existing order. Look, they exclaim, there is no movement – in agriculture that is: Marx's dogma does not apply *here*. And the figures do indeed seem to obliterate both the decentralising as well as centralising tendencies noticeable throughout agriculture up until the 1880s. The peasantry appears to be blossoming anew – to the detriment of all those socialist tendencies produced by industry.

But this blossom has its roots in a swamp. It is not a product of the *well-being* of the peasantry, but of the *distress* of the whole of agriculture. It has the same causes as the fact that machines which have been tried and tested in agriculture are now having to be abandoned, that feudal forms of labour contract are re-emerging, that arable land is giving way to pasturage, that some fields are beginning to be left fallow. The day that agriculture solves its 'labour question' and begins a new phase of expansion, will be the day that the tendencies currently favouring the medium-sized farm will turn into their opposites. Prosperity for agriculture and the continued existence of a peasant mode of farming are mutually exclusive within the developed capitalist mode of production. Proof of this cannot only be seen in Europe, but also in the Eastern states of the USA (see p. 137–8).

Nor should one expect a continuation of agriculture's current decline to lead to the displacement of the large enterprise and the dwarf-holding. The medium-sized peasants, described with such enthusiasm by Sismondi at the beginning of the century, will, therefore, neither come to dominate agriculture nor be able to proclaim to the whole of social development: Thus far, and no further!

Their reward for avoiding the worst effects of the shortage of labour out of all the agricultural commodity-producers is to suffer the most from the other burdens which afflict agriculture. The middle peasants are the main object of usurious and merchant exploitation; money taxes and military service hit them the hardest; and their land is most exposed to the threat of impoverishment and exhaustion. And since these farms are amongst the most irrational of those engaged in commodity-production, participation in the competitive struggle means superhuman effort and sub-human living. There is a peasant saying that as long as they avoid overwork, they will be relatively well off, and that 'misery starts with overwork'.

The size of their property still binds these peasants to the soil: but not their children. Like wage-labourers and dwarf-holders, the children of middle peasants are also beginning to be gripped by the flight from the land, and the nearer industry comes to them, the more they strive to escape. A report from Schleswig-Holstein, one of the provinces in which the peasantry has maintained itself in a healthy and vigorous state, observes:

> Servants, like *the sons of peasants*, who worked on the family farm up until their entry into the army rarely return to the land after completion of their military service unless they are learning a craft-skill; they move to the towns, since life in the open country no longer has any attraction for them. (Auhagen, Die ländliche Arbeiterverhaltnisse in der Rheinprovinz, p. 426)

But the more that the children of the middle peasant tire of being the worst kept and most oppressed wage-labourers, and the more they try to escape peasant barbarism, the greater will be the decline in the size of families. They will no longer be able to run the farm, even at a very low level of cultivation: the role of wage-labour will increase, and the labour question will also make its debut to add to the other problems weighing down on this class of farms.

The middle peasants are anything but true conservatives – that is, content with things as they stand. On the contrary, they are as eager to transform the prevailing order as the most radical Social Democrat, although, of course, in quite a different direction. Nevertheless, as obstreperously as they often might seem to behave, they will not act to overthrow the state. But they will stop being a pillar of the existing social order. The agrarian crisis extends to all commodity-producing classes in agriculture – and will not spare the middle peasant.

10
Overseas Food Competition and the Industrialisation of Agriculture

The Export Industry

Chapter 9 showed that although the capitalist mode of production has shattered the fetters of feudalism and given agriculture sufficient impetus to progress more in a few decades than it had managed over the previous thousand years, it has also generated forces which constrain and depress agriculture, creating a growing antithesis between the current mode of production's forms of appropriation and ownership and the needs of rational cultivation.

Such tendencies are nothing new in themselves: but they were not a particular burden to the farmer and landowner as long as their effects could be shifted on to the consumer. And as long as this proved possible, the period following the breakdown of the feudal state proved to be a golden age for agriculture: this lasted until the 1870s.

Meitzen, writing in the 1860s, commented:

> The memorandum on the state promotion of agriculture is quite correct in observing that 'hopes for the effects of the agrarian laws have not gone unfulfilled. In place of enervation, a welcome activation of the rural population has taken place. A coincidence and succession of fortunate circumstances has spread *general prosperity* amongst the owners of both peasant farms and Junker estates. The purchase price of estates of all types has risen, almost to excess, as a result of their free cultivability and unrestricted competition amongst buyers.' (Meitzen, *Der Boden und die landwirtschaflichen Verhältnisse des preußischen Staates*, p. 440)

Compare this with the present-day utterances of a Prussian Minister for Agriculture!

Food prices rose steadily up until the latter half of the 1870s, in marked contrast to the prices of industrial products. In many instances they rose faster than wages, leaving workers not only worse off as *producers*, through increases in the rate of surplus value, but also often as *consumers* too. Agriculture's prosperity rested on the back of proletarian impoverishment.

According to Conrad, wheat prices moved as follows in England, France and Prussia.

Price (in Marks) of 1,000 kilos of wheat in:

	England	France	Prussia
1821-30	266.00	192.40	121.40
1831-40	254.00	199.20	138.40
1841-50	240.00	206.60	167.80
1851-60	250.00	231.40	211.40
1861-70	248.00	224.60	204.60
1871-75	246.40	248.80	235.20

A kilo of beef cost the following (in Pfennigs) in:

	Berlin	London
1821-30	61	n.a.
1831-40	63	n.a.
1841-50	71	87
1851-60	85	101
1861-70	100	113
1871-80	125	131

This steady rise came to a halt in the 1870s.

A 1,000 kilos of wheat cost the following (in Marks) in:

	England	France	Prussia
1876-80	206.80	229.40	211.20
1881-85	180.40	205.60	189.00
1889	137.00	198.30	192.00

According to the latest report of the English Royal Commission on Agriculture, a quarter of wheat cost the following in England:

1888-91	32 shillings	11 pence
1890-92	33 shillings	1 pence
1891-93	31 shillings	2 pence
1892-94	26 shillings	6 pence
1894-95	24 shillings	1 pence

In the period 1881–5, a kilo of beef cost 119 Pfennigs in Berlin; between 1886 and 1890, 115 Pfennigs. In London the price was 124 Pfennigs between 1881 and 1885, and 101 Pfennigs between 1886 and 1890.

Prices have therefore reversed direction since the 1870s.

As with any other major change in modern agriculture the cause lies in *industry*, on which agriculture is becoming more and more dependent.

The capitalist mode of production causes the constant revolutionising of production. This has two main sources: accumulation, the increasing piling-up of fresh capital, and technical transformation, the product of the uninterrupted advance of science, now the servant of capital. The mass of products produced by capitalist methods grows year by year in the capitalist nations: and it is growing much faster than the population.

Curiously, this steadily growing wealth becomes a source of increasing problems for capitalist producers on account of the fact that their mode of production is the production of surplus-value; and surplus-value accrues to the class of capitalists, not their workers. At the same time, capitalist production is also production on a mass scale, the production of articles of mass consumption, goods for the masses. This is fundamentally different to the modes of production of feudalism or antiquity. Feudal lords and slave owners also squeezed a surplus-product out of their workers; but they, or their hangers-on, consumed it themselves. In contrast, the surplus-value appropriated by the capitalist usually initially takes the form of production which has to be bought by the mass of the population before it can take on the form of products suitable for capitalist consumption. Like the feudal lord or slave-owner, the capitalist has to try and hold down the consumption of the masses to increase their own. But the capitalist is also burdened with the novel worry of maintaining and increasing mass consumption. This contradiction is both one of the most characteristic, and one of the most uncomfortable problems which the modern capitalist has to solve.

Naive *Sozialpolitiker* and even zealous socialists have long tried to prove to the capitalist that mass consumption will be greater, the higher the consumption of the working masses; and that, as a consequence, all that has to be done to maintain and increase production is simply to raise wages. At best this might persuade an individual capitalist to welcome wage increases in other branches of industry, but never in his own. It may be in a brewer's interest for mass consumption to rise through increases in the wages of *other* workers but never through increases in the wages of his *own*. Of course, higher wages mean that capitalists can sell more. But capitalists are not in business to *sell:* they produce to make a profit. Other things being equal, profits will be higher the higher the surplus-value. In turn, this will be higher, for a given expenditure of labour, the lower the wage.

Capitalists have long been aware that there are quite different methods available for raising the mass consumption of goods produced under capitalist conditions than raising the consumption of the mass of their workers. Their first hunt for markets is not amongst the proletariat, but the non-proletarian masses, and in particular, the rural population. We have already seen how this ruins rural domestic industry and creates a large market for the sale of articles of mass consumption.

However, the greater the productive forces within the capitalist mode of production, and the more predominant wage-labour – that is, more numerous that class which in the nature of things can only consume part of the product it creates – the less this market suffices. The extension of the market beyond the confines of the nation, production for the world market and the constant expansion of this market, become a condition for the continued existence of capitalist industry. This is what lies behind the current urgency and struggle to extend markets; this is why our age is marked by the favouring of Africans with hats and boots, and the Chinese with battleships, cannons and railways. The internal market itself is now almost totally dependent on the external market. This determines, in the main, whether businesses succeed, and how much proletarians and capitalists, and with them merchants, craftsmen and farmers, can consume.

Once the external market, the world market, ceases to be capable of rapid expansion, the capitalist mode of production will have reached the end of the road.

The Railway System

The constant push to expand markets goes hand in hand with a revolutionising of the transport system.

The capitalist mode of production has always been based on mass production: and this necessitates mass transportation. This is not only for the export of its products. Capitalist large-scale industry consumes far more raw materials than are available in its immediate vicinity, and concentrates larger numbers of people than this area can feed. Raw materials and foodstuffs usually have a low value to weight ratio, and can only be economically moved over long distances by particularly inexpensive means of transport.

Only *water* could offer such cheap transport during capitalism's infancy. And this confined development to coasts or areas with suitable waterways. However, the capitalist mode of production not only requires *cheapness* but also *speed* and *certainty* of mass transport. The quicker the turnover of capital, the less capital had to be advanced for any particular undertaking in order to continue at a given scale: and consequently, the higher the scale that was attainable with a given capital. If I ship commodities from Manchester to Hong Kong, it makes an enormous difference whether I receive payment in three months or in a year. If my capital turns over four times in a year, then, other things being equal, my profit will be four times greater than if it turned over only once.

Moreover, the quicker the transport, the further I can look for customers, and the more I can expand my market without slowing down the turnover of the capital advanced or having to enlarge it.

Raw material stocks can also be kept to a minimum whilst maintaining constant production: more can be accomplished with a given capital, or the same with a smaller capital, and the range of raw material suppliers can be broadened.

Greater *certainty* of transport has the same effect. It reduces the mass of reserves of money and raw materials which the entrepreneur has to hold to cope with any disruptions in selling or the supply of raw materials.

As far as speed and certainty are concerned, water transportation by sail, oar, or draft-horse leaves much to be desired. Canals and rivers freeze in winter, the sea is made uncertain by storms, and calms or contrary winds can be even worse for the waiting merchant.

It was the taming of steam power which enabled the development of a form of mass transport which allowed the capitalist mode of production to become independent of the waterways, set down firm roots in the interiors of the continents and transform the entire world into a market for its enormously expanding large-scale industries.

Although steam engines and railways were invented at the beginning of our century [nineteenth century], their application remained confined to those areas dominated by large-scale industry. It was the great wars which put paid to the old Europe and America and cleared the path for the very rapid development of the railway system outside the regions of large-scale industry. Only then did the railway turn from being an upshot into a trailblazer of capitalist development. Strategic considerations were foremost in the widespread support for railway construction in Russia after the Crimea War, and Austria-Hungary since 1859, and even more since 1866. This also applies to the railways of Romania, Turkey and India. Commercial considerations also played a role, however. Governments needed money to compete with the capitalist powers. The only thing which their populations could bring to market were raw materials and foodstuffs. And these required means of mass transportation.

This was the essential reason for the railways built by the American capitalist class after the War of Secession which gave hegemony to the capital of the Union. The successes of these railways soon stimulated imitation, and one of the main activities of European finance currently consists in the establishment and financing of railways in regions outside Europe which are either economically backward or totally deserted. The construction of such railways not only offers welcome channels of investment for the flood of capital threatening to choke the European capitalist class, but also opens up and often creates new markets for Europe's rapidly growing industry, at the same time developing new sources of raw materials and food.

Giffen's recent figures show the expansion of rail mileage since 1850.

	1850	1860	1870	1880	1890	1895
Europe	14,551	33,354	64,667	105,429	141,552	155,284
America	9,604	33,547	58,848	109,521	212,724	229,722
Asia	-	844	5,118	9,948	22,023	26,890
Australia		350	1,042	4,889	13,332	13,888
Africa	-	278	956	2,904	6,522	8,169
Total	24,155	67,393	130,631	232,691	305,143	433,953

In 1870 the European rail network accounted for *half* the world mileage; by 1895 only a *third*. Route mileage increased fivefold between these two dates; but in America it increased sevenfold, and in the rest of the world *thirtyfold*.

Steam has also transformed shipping, if not quite as spectacularly as in the case of rail. According to Jannasch, the total tonnage of all inward and outward bound vessels in the major shipping nations was as follows:

	Total	Steam tonnage
1872 (38 nations)	137,226,600	52,908,900
1876 (45 nations)	189,785,300	100,754,700
1889 (41 nations)	360,970,800	287,965,100
1892 (41 nations)	382,480,600	313,393,100

The cost of both rail and sea transport is steadily falling. According to Sering average freight rates for the transport of wheat from Chicago to New York per bushel were as follows:

	By water	By rail
1868	24.54 cents	42.6 cents
1884	6.60 cents	13.0 cents

In 1868 the average cost of moving a bushel of wheat from New York to Liverpool by steamer was US$14.36; by 1884 it had fallen to $6.87.

Since then freight rates have fallen even further. According to the *Yearbook of the United States Department of Agriculture, 1896,* the cost of moving a bushel of wheat from New York to Liverpool changed as follows:

	January	June
1885	9.80 cents	5.00 cents
1890	11.13 cents	3.75 cents
1896	6.12 cents	4.00 cents

Transport of 100 lbs of wheat by rail from Chicago to New York cost 25 cents in 1893; by 1897 the cost was 20 cents.

This development has dramatically changed the position of European agriculture. Agricultural products – like potatoes, hay, milk, fruit and even wheat and meat – are characterised by their low value to weight ratio. In addition, many – like meat, milk and many types of fruit and vegetables – cannot tolerate long journeys. Under primitive means of transport, moving these products raised their price a great deal, and made it impossible to supply from anywhere more than a very short distance away. Supplying foodstuffs to the market, the town, remained an overwhelmingly local affair. The immediate locality had a monopoly on exploiting urban consumers and made thorough use of it. The level of transport costs from the furthest farms, whose products had to be brought in to cover urban food requirements, boosted the differential ground-rents of estates lying nearby. The increasing difficulties of extending the supply of foodstuffs beyond a certain area allowed a massive increase in absolute ground-rents.

Railway construction did not have any great impact on this situation as long as it remained confined to countries with a highly developed industry. Although urban markets were opened up to fresh sources of food, this was generally produced under similar conditions to those nearer the towns. The railway primarily served to bring about a massive expansion in the urban market, and it was this which facilitated the rapid and enormous growth in cities which has been the hallmark of our age. They did not reduce ground-rents. Quite the opposite: from the period of the beginning of the railway age until the 1870s ground-rents rapidly increased in Europe. And the railways increased the number of landowners who participated in this increase. They massively increased the volume of ground-rents accruing to large landowners.

Railways laid down in economically backward countries had a different effect. Although similarly hardly responsible for an overproduction of food, by increasing its supply they extended the urban market for it, and enlarged the size of the industrial population which could not have grown as rapidly as it did without the import of foodstuffs into Europe from overseas.

It was not the *volume* of imported food which threatened European agriculture, but rather the *conditions under which it was produced*. Such produce did not have to bear the burdens imposed on agriculture by the capitalist mode of production. Its appearance on the market made it impossible for European agriculture to continue shifting the rising burdens imposed by private property in land and capitalist commodity-production on to the mass of the consumers. *European agriculture had to bear them itself. And this is what is at the heart of the current agrarian crisis.*

The Regions of Food Competition

The countries able to undercut European agriculture can be divided into two major groups: the *regions of oriental despotism* and the free (current or former) *colonies*, on the condition that one can still include countries such as Russia in the former. As far as the rural population is concerned this is by and large quite valid.

Under oriental despotism, the rural population is completely at the mercy of the state and the ruling classes. Capitalism has not yet created a national political life; the nation – at least in the countryside – is still simply an aggregation of village communities, each of which lives out its own isolated life and is powerless in relation to the centralised state authority. As long as matters remain at the stage of simple commodity-production, the position of the peasant in such a state is not usually too bad. The peasants barely come into personal contact with state authority; the democratically organised village commune both protects them and represents their interests before the state, and in turn state authority has few means with which it can impose excessive demands on the commune, and little occasion to do so, since it can make only limited use of the payment in kind in which taxes are levied. The cruelties and exactions of oriental despotism are more visible in the towns in relation to the courtiers, higher officials and rich merchants than in the open countryside.

Matters undergo a dramatic change once state authority comes into contact with European capitalism – in whichever way this occurs. European civilisation makes its appearance in the forms of militarism, bureaucracy and state borrowing: both the state's need for money as well as its power vis-à-vis the rural commune suddenly increase. Taxes become money taxes. Existing modest money taxes are stepped up to intolerable levels and ruthlessly collected. As the nation's main branch of production, agriculture has to bear the brunt of taxation – all the more so, the weaker the rural population. The peasants' comfortable life comes to an end. Meeting their obligations forces them to undermine the physical basis of their own labour-power and of the land. Leisure, artistic activity – such as the fine wood-cuttings and embroidery of South Russian peasantry – become a thing of the past, rapidly followed by the peasants' own well-being. Although more is harvested than ever before, no time is allowed for the soil to recover; everything not absolutely indispensable for the most meagre level of survival goes off to market. But where to find buyers in a country in which almost everyone is a farmer seeking to sell food, and where no one needs to buy? The export of foodstuffs now becomes a matter of life and death.

Governments have to build railways from the interiors to the ports or national borders if they want to be able to collect money taxes from the peasantry.

The prices of such foodstuffs are naturally hardly regulated by the costs of production. They are not produced under capitalist conditions, and are sold under the pressure of the state and the usurer who enters the scene with the introduction of money taxes. The higher the taxes, and usurer's interest, the greater the distress and debt-servitude of the peasants; the greater their distress, the greater the need to get rid of their produce at any price, and hence the greater the amount of labour which has to be performed, unremunerated, to pay off their creditors – a rich peasant, village innkeeper or landlord. And the greater the volume of products which the peasant brings to market, the lower their prices – and hence the cheaper the products which are produced on their creditors' estates. The growing burdens on the peasant imposed by taxes and usurer's interest do not increase but in fact reduce the price of the product. The small peasant's ground-rent and wages, inasmuch as one can speak of such, are forced down to the absolute minimum.

A system of agriculture producing on a capitalist basis, with a given standard of living amongst the rural population, and a given level of wages and ground-rents – fixed in land-prices and mortgages – and which does not exhaust, but maintains the equilibrium of soil fertility, and additionally has to cope with an insufficient supply of labour, cannot match such competition.

Competition from the American and Australian colonies is quite different to that posed by those areas of oriental despotism which come into contact with European capitalism – Russia, Turkey and India.

Such colonies contain a vigorous democracy of free farmers, off the path of world trade, and free of militarism and the burden of taxes. Immeasurable tracts of unowned fertile land abound as the land's original rulers – the small number of indigenous peoples – have been exterminated or forced into small reserves. There is at yet no monopoly of land by individuals, no ground-rent, the land does not have a price. Unlike in Europe, the farmer does not have to use the bulk of his capital to purchase the land, but can use the whole amount for equipping the farm. Given the same expenditure of capital, and the same area, the farmer can therefore attain a much higher level of cultivation than is possible in Europe. Success is all the more probable since the colonists – if they are from Europe – are obliged to adapt to a completely fresh situation, in which the traditions and prejudices of the preceding age, which so hampered the European peasant, quickly disappear.

A further factor encourages the development of cultivation. The soil is not yet exhausted – it is still completely virgin. It does not require fertilising and crop-rotation, and will continue to produce a rich yield for years ahead with the same crop. The farmer does not need to buy or make fertiliser: he can stick to a single crop – such as wheat – and will be more inclined to do so, the more developed the transport system, and the more the farmer is exclusively involved in commodity production and no longer needs to produce for his own consumption. This one-sidedness of production allows large savings on labour-power and the means of labour, and at the same time means all the equipment can be fully adapted to the one end it is intended to serve. The wheat-farmer does not need stalls for cattle, apart from draught animals, and does not need barns for storing fodder. No labour is needed to tend the cattle; and there is no need to plant root-crops, thus saving on labour and implements. Like the absence of ground-rents, this one-sidedness enables the colonial farmer to attain a higher yield for a given amount of capital and labour on the same cultivated area, or with the same expenditure of capital and labour but over a much greater area, the same yield per hectare as in Europe.

The usual explanation for the highly developed technology of American farming is the shortage of labour and high wages, which made mechanisation a necessity. But without the other two factors noted above, this could not have been as influential as it in fact was.

For colonial agriculture there is no 'labour question' in the European sense. Nevertheless, the colonies are much more thinly populated than the European nations, and the number of workers for any given cultivated area is much less.

However, the number of workers available only determines the type of farming, and not its success. Farming is more extensive where there are few workers, and human labour is replaced by machines wherever possible. However, it is by no means irrelevant whether – with a given type of farming – the number of available workers *falls* or not, and whether their capacity to work diminishes or not. As far as the prosperity of agriculture is concerned, it is not the number or skill of its workers which is decisive, but the *direction in which these factors change*.

In this respect, the European colonies are far better off. The same flight from the land which is depopulating the European countryside not only leads to the towns, but also despatches new regiments of strong country folk to the colonies, the most intelligent and energetic of their type. And these will, and must, soon become even more intelligent and energetic in their new environment. Those who cannot adapt quickly will go under.

After a few years a completely uneducated immigrant will become a much more able individual since they can eat so much better. They are like a plant which one has transplanted from a poor to a better soil – this is still so today, and as long as labour is better remunerated here than in Europe will continue. (Meyer, *Ursachen der amerikanischen Konkurrenz*, p. 16)

There is no military service in the colonies to abduct labour from the land.

Sering (*Die landwirtschaftliche Konkurrenz Nordamerikas*, p. 179) states quite explicitly: 'One often hears complaints about the high wages in the farming districts, but rarely about the shortage of workers.' But even the high wages do not stay at their high levels.

Whereas the increasing difficulty in obtaining farm labourers in sufficient numbers is causing agricultural wages to rise in Europe, in the colonies – thanks to the constant influx of fresh labour – they show a tendency to fall. According to Sering (ibid.) monthly wages in the USA for farm labourers engaged for one year, in dollars, by region were:

Region	1866	1869	1875	1879	1881	1885 (May)
California	35.75	46.38	44.50	41.00	38.25	38.75
Eastern States	33.30	32.08	28.96	20.21	26.61	25.55
Central States	30.07	28.02	26.02	19.69	22.24	23.50
Western States	28.91	27.01	23.60	20.38	23.63	22.25
Southern States	16.00	17.21	16.22	13.31	15.30	14.25

There is an unmistakable downward trend. In view of all these facts, it is easy to see how laughable the advice given to European farmers by liberal economists really is: you only have to become as intelligent as the Americans, and American competition will be a thing of the past.

Nonetheless, it is curious that in the course of development the Americans themselves, instead of becoming more intelligent, are getting less intelligent – that is, they are beginning to farm using European methods.

The picture of colonial agriculture which we have drawn can only be applied to the United States to a limited degree. Agriculture there is based on robbing the soil (cf. p. 150) which it sooner or later exhausts.

This makes it necessary for the farmer to exchange fresh land for his exhausted land from time to time – either by having such a large farm in the first place that it can include both a cultivated and a non-cultivated part, or – if his entire holding is exhausted – by moving on to as yet uncultivated areas and making a new plot of land cultivable. The nomadic character of colonial agriculture resembles that of the ancient Germans – although with the difference that it is practised with all the aids of modern technology, and is for sale, not self-sufficiency. But this will mean that modern nomadic agriculture will inevitably exhaust the soil even more swiftly than the agriculture of the Germans. Abandoned land is left waste until it has recovered, or is taken over by a farmer who begins to farm using European methods, with manuring and crop rotation. At any event, sooner or later this old land will become unusable for extensive depredatory cultivation. Soils on which wheat can be grown uninterruptedly for 40 years without fertiliser (Sering, ibid., p. 188) are extraordinarily rare.

The fluctuating character of American agriculture is revealed in the following figures:

	Acres under wheat		
	Western states	Central states	Eastern states
1880	6,100,000	23,700,000	5,700,000
1890	11,400,000	17,600,000	4,600,000
+/–	+5,300,000	–6,100,000	–1,100,000

The cultivated area in the North Eastern states has been reduced even more markedly: from 46,385,632 acres to 42,338,024 acres, by more than 4 million acres.

With such a rapid exhaustion of the soil, the land hunger of the American colonists is inevitably greater even than that of the ancient Germans: and like Germany, the *vagina gentium*, the mother of peoples who over the centuries gradually pushed down as far as Africa, the East of America is becoming a new *vagina gentium*, a jumping-off point for settlers who have filled the whole continent across to the Pacific Coast within the space of a few decades.

This move westwards was encouraged by high immigration from Europe. The prospect of being able to farm without the burdens of the old capitalist civilisation – ground-rents, militarism, taxes – on fertile soils was too alluring. Countless numbers of farmers were tempted to leave the patriarchal plot to which – according to the assurances of our poets and politicians – they were inseparably wedded, and look for a new life over the ocean.

All the fertile land in the United States is now private property. The increase in the number of farms is steadily slowing down. Between 1870 and 1880 they increased by 1,348,922: 51 per cent; 1880-90 by only 555,734: 14 per cent. The land is no longer free: it yields a ground-rent and has a price. And with this begins the encumbering of agriculture with the burden of private property under capitalism. The American farmers now have to buy their farms. Working capital is reduced by the amount of the purchase price. The farms have to be smaller than would previously have been necessary, or alternatively, the farmers have to go into debt. Otherwise they have to rent land. And on their death they can no longer tell their children to look for free land in the West. The farms have to be divided up, or one heir must sell to the others: this cannot happen without increasing indebtedness or reducing working capital. Reduction in size and farm indebtedness, together with a deterioration in the quality of equipment are the consequences.

At the same time, the demands on the farmer are increasing. The soil is exhausted, and new land cannot be had for nothing. Fertilisers, crop rotation, stock-keeping become necessary – but all this requires additional labour and money. Since 1880 the costs of the amount of additional fertiliser used each year have been recorded in the Agricultural Census. In 1880 the cost was US$28,600,000; by 1890 this had risen to $38,500,000. This is yet another source of indebtedness and reduction in farm size.

Tenant farming and indebtedness begin to take root and expand. Renting accounted for 25.6 per cent of all farms in the United States in 1880; by 1890 the proportion had grown to 28.37 per cent. Farm indebtedness was first recorded for the Union as a whole in 1890. Of those farms not rented, 28.22 per cent were in debt in 1890, most of which were located in the states with the highest degree of capitalist development. Of the 886,957 indebted farms, 177,508 were in the North Atlantic States (34.22 per cent of farms in that region), and 618,429 in the North Central States (42.52 per cent). In contrast, only 31,751 farms were indebted in the Western States (23.09 per cent), 31,080 in the Southern Atlantic States (7.43 per cent) and 28,189 in the Southern Central States (4.59 per cent). The level of debt was put at $1,086 million, 35.55 per cent of the value of farms. For 88 per cent of the indebted farms, the cause of indebtedness was given as: purchase, improvements, acquisition of machinery, livestock and the like.

Such conditions are bound to dry up the flow of immigrants, whilst the transition from extensive to intensive farming is causing the demand for labour-power to grow. Immigration reached its high point in 1882, when 788,992 immigrants arrived. Since then it has steadily fallen, and in 1895 was only 279,948. Emigration from Germany which still ran at 220,902 in 1881 fell to 24,631 by 1897.

At the same time, industry and commerce are developing rapidly and absorbing a growing portion of the population. The number of persons employed in industry grew by 49.1 per cent between 1880 and 1890, with a 78.2 per cent increase in commerce over the same period. Growth in agriculture (including mining) was a mere 12.6 per cent over the same period.

American agriculture is also approaching the time when it will be faced with its own labour question. But the development of industry does not stop at directly poaching labour-power from agriculture – it also promotes militarism. Industry becomes industry for export, seeking to conquer the world market and clashing with rival powers. Militarism imposes great demands: state indebtedness grows, and taxes increase. Industry's rise is accompanied by crises which shake the whole country. Unemployment assumes threatening dimensions, class struggles intensify, and the ruling classes employ more and more drastic means to repress or prevent troublesome social movements – giving a further boost to militarism. In the process, the state itself increasingly becomes the prey of high finance, which plunders the population through its monopoly.

All this implies that agriculture in the United States will become increasingly burdened, and its competitiveness on the world market correspondingly reduced.

The competition from European Russia and India will also lose its edge with the passage of time. Depredatory agriculture will lead to the bankruptcy of the prevailing agricultural methods even sooner than in the United States, since reserves of land are smaller, the older cultivated areas already more exhausted, and the means of cultivation more exposed to deterioration with the increasing poverty of the peasants and the forced surrender of their livestock to the usurer and tax collector. The end result is chronic, and periodically worsening, famine.

Exports can therefore only grow as long as the rail system continues to expand into as yet unexploited and unexhausted areas. Such farming must eventually end – either in the complete desolation of the land, or in a transition to the capitalist farming of the large landowners and farmers, the first steps towards which are already evident in Russia.

The proletarianisation of the rural population, which casts

innumerable cheap workers and large alienable tracts of land on to the market, and the counterpart to this – the emergence of a class of rural usurers who pile up capital – supply all the preconditions for capitalist production. Conditions in Russia will converge towards those of Europe and ease the pressure on prices which its competition currently represents.

But it would be wrong to conclude from this that the agrarian crisis will soon be surmounted.

The process which it initiates continues without pause, opening up new regions, both colonies and areas of oriental despotism, to the capitalist mode of production. Unsettled land is still available in Australia, Canada and South America. Dr Rudolf Meyer, writing in 1894, noted:

> The London *Economist* of 9 September 1893 contained an extract from the report of the English consular official in Argentina which states, amongst other things, that in the current year only 12.5 million acres are being cultivated, against a potential cultivable area of 240 million acres. In addition, large areas with similar conditions for cultivation exist in the other Plate States and Venezuela, and parts of Brazil. The cultivable area suitable for wheat growing could be as much as *200 million hectares*. One can appreciate what this means when one considers that the area put under wheat, rye, oats and barley in the last few years has totalled approximately 56 million hectares in the USA, 13 million in Austria-Hungary, 4 million in Great Britain and Ireland, 14 million in Germany and 15 million in France – a total of 102 million hectares. (Meyer, *Ursachen der amerikanischen Konkurrenz*, p. 469)

The final report of the Royal Commission on Agriculture, 1897, comes to the same conclusion. Siberia, with its 100 million hectares of grain land, has been opened up by rail to the world market. Railways are encroaching on Central Africa from north, south, east and west: and the opening up of China by rail is expected imminently. However, as far as China is concerned, the coming of the railway will be more likely to increase imports rather than exports of food, although the economic structure of China shares too many common features with India to lead us to expect anything other than that it will share the same fate as the latter: the ruin of domestic industry, the rapid growth of peasant indebtedness, the slow emergence of capitalist industries, and alongside the increase in hunger and misery, a growth in the exports of agricultural products. India, in which famine constantly rages, customarily exports wheat and rice – approximately 20 million cwts wheat and 20-30 million cwts of rice.

The situation is not greatly different in Russia. According to the most recent calculations, the Russian peasantry annually produces approximately 1,387 million *puds* of grain (excluding seed-corn). Of this, 1,286 million *puds* of rye are needed for their own consumption, and 477 million for their cattle. This leaves a deficit of 376 million *puds* which peasants have to buy if they want to feed themselves and their stock properly. Instead – as is generally known – they continue to sell grain. The same factors will also compel the Chinese peasants to sell wheat and rice, regardless of how much they need for themselves.

Of course, not all countries are suitable for growing wheat. But then, wheat flour is not the only type of cereal flour. Attempts have been made to replace wheat and rye by other cereals, such as maize, rice and millet. Such experiments will not be successful, however, as long as wheat imports are increasing, and while there is no need to find a surrogate. But should the time ever come when all the wheat or rye lands are full, and grain prices inexorably begin to rise, the spirit of invention would immediately throw itself upon the problem of replacing customary cereals with surrogates made from tropical products. Those tropical countries which are not suited to wheat cultivation – Central America, Northern Brazil, large parts of Africa, India, South Eastern Asia – would then also join the ranks of the European grain farmers' competitors.

Eventually, this competition will have to lose its ruinous character. The surface of the earth is finite and the capitalist mode of production is expanding at a dizzy pace. As the product of the competition between the backward agricultural countries and the advanced industrial countries, the agrarian crisis must therefore eventually come to an end. But the end of this competition will also spell the end of the capitalist mode of production's possibilities of further expansion. Constant expansion is the life principle of capitalism: technical revolution and the accumulation of capital are unceasing; production becomes increasingly mass production, whilst the share of the masses in their own product steadily diminishes. The agrarian crisis can therefore only end with a general crisis of capitalist society as a whole. This point may arrive earlier or later; but as long as capitalist society continues, agrarian crisis will be its permanent accompaniment. And if the capitalist burdens which once depressed agriculture in Western Europe now begin to do the same to its competitors in the USA, Russia and so on, this is not proof that the crisis in Western European agriculture is coming to an end. It simply proves that the crisis is extending its grip.

Optimistic, and in particular, liberal economists have been prophesying the end of the agrarian crisis for 20 years; and for 20 years the crisis has been getting deeper and more widespread from year to year. It is not a passing phenomenon: it is permanent, embracing the whole of economic and political life.

We cannot consider the effects of the agrarian crisis on industry here, although its development has been extensively promoted by the crisis. The times are past when one could say *'Hat der Bauer Geld, hat's die ganze Welt'* (All's well with the peasant, all's well with the world).

Our task here is simply to observe the changes in agriculture which food competition from outside Europe has generated and fostered.

The Decline in Grain Production

The most obvious and simple method for landowners and farmers was to call for state assistance, and show their outrage at 'bleak Manchesterism'. That is, having lost the *economic* power to shift the burden of capitalist conditions of production on to the mass of the population, European land ownership will seek to have this accomplished through *political* power, through the imposition of tariffs on grain, debasing the currency (bi-metallism), and subsidies.

There is no need to rehearse the theoretical justification for these measures yet again; they have been discussed so often that the positions involved can be assumed to be known to all. And there is scarcely anything new to add. Such a discussion is all the more superfluous in that the agrarians themselves have begun to see that they are not going to advance very far with such 'petty means'. Their attempts to increase the price of food artificially are running head on into very determined opposition from the working class, those mainly affected. Grain duties have proved little help to agriculture. But were circumstances to arise in which they could become effective, and grain prices were to rise, this would bring about such intolerable hardship for the bulk of the population that concessions would have to be made in the face of popular resistance. The poor harvests of 1891 prompted an immediate reduction in grain duties in France (between July 1891 and July 1892); and they also gave rise to a reduction – if not an immediate one – of duties in Germany, not only temporarily but permanently.

In England no serious politician dare advocate an artificial increase in the price of food: the working class is too powerful. Moreover, competition with the free-traders of England does not allow other industrialised countries to hoist their food prices too high. England's insistence on the free import of food forces both workers and capitalists on the Continent to resist any increase in food tariffs which might negate the effects of external food competition. The fact that agrarian protective tariffs in Europe have not been put up to enormously high levels is primarily due to the power of English workers.

Our arguments in the previous chapter also suffice to show that were an energetic protectionist policy for agriculture possible, the sole beneficiaries would be the landowners, not agriculture. By holding up ground-rents such a policy would maintain the high price of land, and simply prolong the burden which this imposes on farming.

Attempts to protect European agriculture from external competition by duties and other 'petty means' cannot possibly succeed: their only achievement will be able to slow down the adaptation of agriculture to the new circumstances.

Yet despite this, adaptation is clearly going ahead.

One of the main advantages enjoyed by overseas competition is the abundance of available land; this allows it to select only the best soils, those most suited to crops, for cultivation.

The situation is different in Europe. As long as any rural economy is self-sufficient it has to produce everything which it needs, irrespective of whether the soil is suitable or not. Grain has to be cultivated on infertile, stony and steeply sloping ground as well as on rich soils. The replacement of self-sufficiency by commodity-production did not initially make a great deal of difference. In fact, the increase in the demand for grain as a result of rapid population growth forced a shift to increasingly infertile land, of which more and more was devoted to arable farming.

This changed once overseas competition entered the scene. It was no longer necessary to carry on producing grain on unsuitable soils, and where circumstances were favourable it was taken off the land and replaced by other types of agricultural production.

This tendency was also reinforced by the following factors. Overseas competition was firstly, and most acutely, felt in the grain market. The cultivation of grain is much simpler, and requires less preparation and human labour than intensive stock-rearing, the growing of root crops, or vegetables and fruit. Grain also has one of the highest value to weight ratios of agricultural produce, as the following table prepared by Settegast shows.

The table indicates the percentage of the value of the commodity per cwt/mile for transport by road and railway.

	Market price per cwt Pf.	By road @ 15 Pf per cwt/mile %	By rail @ 2.5 Pf %
Green fodder	50	30.00	5.00
Sugar beet	100	15.00	2.50
Straw	100	15.00	2.50
Potatoes	150	10.00	1.66
Hay	200	7.50	1.25
Milk, fresh fruit	400	3.75	0.62
Wheat	1,000	1.50	0.25
Livestock	2,000	0.25	0.25

Wheat is high up the scale. The transport costs of living animals have not fallen as a result of rail transportation, although the *speed* of their transport has naturally increased enormously. Their transport costs equal those of wheat. However, wheat can stand extremely long journeys, storage, transhipment and sea voyages without damage; living animals suffer greatly on long journeys, especially passage by sea. It is, of course, impossible to store them. Grain's insensitivity to the duration and rigours of transportation makes it far superior to most other mass products of agriculture – meat, milk, fruit, vegetables and eggs.

Given that foreign competition is most likely to emerge in the field of grain production, it would seem that any European farmers not committed to grain production should seek their salvation by switching to the other products cited above, but they cannot do so simply at will. A market has to exist. And in many instances economic development can be quite obliging in this respect. A number of historical and physiological factors mean that meat consumption is much greater in the towns than in the countryside. And since the urban population is growing much faster than the population as a whole, the demand for meat must also be growing at an equally rapid pace. Moreover, the production of milk, vegetables, fruit, eggs and similar products for the market was confined to a small number of districts neighbouring on the towns until well into this [nineteenth] century. And nearly every household in villages and small towns in rural areas – including non-farming households – produced food for their own requirements. This is impossible in the large town or city. As soon as a large proportion of the population begins to live in such towns, demand for these products will grow strongly. Their production for market will expand, to the advantage of the peasant's *purse* if not their *health*. The peasant family used to consume the milk and eggs which the farm produced; now they go off to market, to be replaced by coffee-extract, brandy and potatoes. Even an increase in meat eating can be damaging if potato eating increases at the same time and the consumption of milk and cereals falls (Weber, *Die Verhältnisse der Landarbeiter*, p. 777). However, statisticians assure us that the increase in the consumption of these 'luxuries' means an increase in popular welfare.

The same developments in transport which make grain growing unprofitable can enable some areas to begin producing meat, milk, and so on for large-scale sale by providing access to markets from which they were previously excluded.

Such factors strengthen those tendencies favouring the small-scale farm and weaken those favouring the large-scale farm. As the latter is superior in the sphere of grain production, these are the most hard hit by overseas competition. And those fields in which farmers driven out of the grain market have sought refuge are – with the exception of the production of meat – exactly those in which small farmers are better able to defend themselves than the large.

Such factors should not be overestimated, however. They are not universal. There is not a market for milk, vegetables and meat everywhere. And increasing the stock of capital requires additional capital and labour-power which are not available to every farmer.

These factors were felt most strongly and earliest of all in England, where the climate is very favourable to pasturage and where the urban population has rapidly grown. By 1851 as many people lived in towns in England as did in the countryside; in contrast, in 1849 slightly over one quarter (28 per cent) of the population of Prussia lived in towns; only now is the urban population equal to the rural population in the German Reich.

Moreover, capitalist tenant farming also prevailed in England: the farmer had to pay rent punctually every year, and could not use indebtedness to perpetuate unprofitable farming methods. Such a system was most likely to force the farmer to adapt to new circumstances.

England's geographical location and intensive commerce placed it most prominently in the firing line when overseas competition emerged. Net imports of wheat and wheat flour into England were, on average: 1873–5, 12,191,000 quarters; 1883–5, 17,944,000; 1893–5, 22,896,000. This amounted to 50.50 per cent, 64.20 per cent, and 76.92 per cent of the total amount of these products available in England. Only a quarter of the wheat consumed in England comes from local sources.

English farmers had to recognise that the age of the Corn Laws was over. England is much too democratic, its rural population too weak, and its industrial population too strong for anyone to dare to increase food prices artificially.

Agriculture was faced with an alternative: either imminent bankruptcy or a rapid transformation of its operating conditions. In most instances the latter occurred. Landlords had to reduce ground-rents – in Ireland under the pressure of legislation, and in England under pressure from a powerful class of tenant farmers. In recent years rents in the best areas have fallen by 20 to 30 per cent, and in the poorer areas by 50 per cent or more. At the same time, the outlays which the landlord has to make for improvements and buildings have increased. The English Royal Commission on Agriculture gives numerous examples, one of which we cite here by way of illustration – that of a farm in Norfolk. Income and outgoings were as follows (in pounds sterling):

	1875	1885	1894
Gross income	4,139	2,725	1,796
Total outgoings	1,122	1,166	1,216
Percentage of income accounted for by outgoings	27.1	42.8	67.7
Net income	3,017	1,559	580

(Royal Commission on Agriculture, 1895, p. 22)

The owner's net income thus fell from £3,017 to £580 over 19 years.

But this reduction in the burdening of agriculture from ground-rents is not enough. It is accompanied by the shift from grain growing to stock-rearing. Average wheat harvests in the United Kingdom (net of seedcorn) were as follows:

1852-59	13,169,000 quarters
1860-67	12,254,000 quarters
1868-75	11,632,000 quarters
1889-90	8,770,000 quarters

Since then production has slumped to an average of seven million quarters.

Area under wheat was as follows:

1866-70	3,801,000 acres
1889	2,545,000 acres
1894	1,985,000 acres
1895	1,417,403 acres
1896	1,692,957 acres

In contrast, pastureland has increased. In 1875 it covered 13,312,000 acres, in 1885 15,342,000 acres, and in 1895 16,611,000 acres.

Matters have taken a different course in Germany. Its continental location, grain duties, and the conservative character of the peasantry serve to hold back development. At the same time we see an advance from primitive to intensive farming, the abandonment of fallow, and the transition from the three-field system to crop rotation – advances which are by no means completed everywhere. These latter also, of course, favour grain production. The decline in grain cultivation, its displacement by stock-rearing, vegetable and fruit growing has been confined to a few regions of Germany thus far, and is not a general phenomenon.

Within Germany the harvested area of cereal crops has changed as follows:

	\centering *Hectares*				
	1878	1883	1893	1896	Increase(+)/ Decrease (-) 1883-1896
Wheat and spelt	2,222,500	2,306,100	2,398,200	2,249,900	- 56,200
Rye	5,950,200	5,817,100	6,016,900	5,982,100	+ 165,000
Barley	1,623,300	1,754,300	1,627,100	1,676,300	- 78,000
Oats	3,753,100	3,773,800	3,905,800	3,979,600	+ 205,800

The area under these main cereal crops has hardly changed. In 1883 cereals and legumes were planted on 15,724,000 hectares; and in 1893 on 15,992,000 – an increase of 268,000 hectares. In the same period the area of pasturage and fallow was reduced by 576,483 hectares from 3,336,830 to 2,760,347 hectares.

Whilst the area under grain more or less remained constant, the animal stock increased markedly.

	Cattle	Pigs
1873	15,776,700	7,124,100
1883	15,786,800	9,206,200
1892	17,555,700	12,174,300
1897	18,490,800	14,274,600

Thus, whereas the number of cattle increased by a mere 10,000 between 1873 and 1883, in the following decade the increase was nearly two million, with almost a further million added over the subsequent five years. The increase in pig numbers is also much greater in the period since 1883 than in the preceding period.

Despite its high tariffs, France is in a worse position as far as grain growing is concerned. The areas under the principal crops changed as follows between 1840 and 1892 (in hectares):

	1840	1862	1882	1892	Increase (+)/ Decrease (-) 1862-1892
Grain crops	14,552,000	15,621,000	15,096,000	14,827,000	- 794,000
Planted grass	1,577,000	2,773,000	3,538,000	3,532,000	+ 759,000
Natural pasture and meadows	4,198,000	5,021,000	5,537,000	5,920,000	+ 899,000
Fallow	6,763,000	5,148,000	3,644,000	3,368,000	- 1,780,000

The area of grain crops has been considerably reduced since 1862. One important part of this was the loss of territory in 1871 (1,415,000 hectares): but this was more than made up for by the reduction in fallow and the decline in cereal growing continued from 1882 to 1892, whereas despite the loss of territory, the meadows and pastures continued to increase.

The number of cattle also increased, whilst horses fell in number.

	1862	1882	1892
	(89 Départements)	(86 Départements)	
Horses	2,914,412	2,837,952	2,794,529
Cattle	12,011,509	12,997,054	13,708,997

Optimistic economists who believe that European agriculture will be able to fend off overseas competition by switching from grain to the production of milk, meat and fruit are mistaken, however. The technical revolution and the accumulation of capital will not stop; transport will become cheaper and quicker, and preserving methods increasingly effective. Overseas competition will therefore progressively invade those areas in which hard-pressed European agriculture has sought refuge.

Twenty years ago almost all the livestock imported into England came from Europe. Today this has virtually completely stopped, and most comes from North America. Livestock will soon be able to be transported from South America.

The change in the source of English livestock imports has been as follows:

	Europe %	USA %	Canada %	Argentina %
1876	99	-	1	-
1886	43	36	21	-
1891	16	67	21	1
1895	-	67	23	9

Head of cattle imported were as follows:

	Country of Origin				
	Canada	USA	Argentina	Others	Total
1895	95,993	276,533	93,494	3,545	415,565
1896	101,591	393,119	65,699	2,143	562,552
1897	126,495	416,299	73,867	1,675	618,338

The countries of origin of sheep imported into England were as follows:

per cent

	Belgium	Denmark	Germany	Ireland	Holland	USA	Canada	Argentina	Others
1876	24	5	30	-	40	-	-	-	-
1886	-	9	32	3	45	-	9	-	1
1891	-	12	-	7	61	3	9	6	2
1895	-	-	-	6	-	42	21	29	2

As far as the supply of live sheep is concerned, the displacement of the European countries from the English market by overseas territories began later, but increased very quickly.

Twenty years ago meat could only be transported by sea in the form of conserves, tinned meat, salt-meat, and smoked meat. Since then methods for keeping fresh meat edible for weeks by refrigeration have developed to such an extent that the import of fresh foreign meat into England has constantly risen. In 1876, 34,640 cwts of fresh beef imported; by 1895 this was 2,191,037, and by 1897 3,010,387. The largest quantities came from the USA.

Fresh mutton was first recorded separately in the English statistics in 1882. Imports at that time were 190,000 cwts; by 1895 this figure has risen to 2,611,000, and by 1897 to 3,193,276. Of this latter figure, 1,671,000 came from Australia and 715,000 from Argentina.

As with wheat production, the USA has probably already gone past its peak exports of meat. The extensive pasturage needed for profitable livestock production for export requires enormous tracts of land which are steadily being encroached upon by a growing population. In the USA the development of population and livestock was as follows:

	Population	Cows	Oxen and other cattle	Sheep	Pigs
1870	38,558,000	10,096,000	15,389,000	40,853,000	26,751,000
1880	50,156,000	12,027,000	21,231,000	40,766,000	34,034,000
1890	62,622,000	15,953,000	36,849,000	44,336,000	51,603,000
1895	69,753,000	16,505,000	34,364,000	42,294,000	44,166,000

Only dairy cattle are increasing in number: beef cattle are falling. The beneficiaries of this process have not been located in Europe, but in Argentina and Australia, where enormous areas still exist for extending grazing. These two countries now account for the bulk of mutton and sheep imported into England, and their exports of cattle and beef are growing rapidly.

In 1890, 150,000 head of cattle were exported from Argentina: by 1894, this had risen to 250,000.

In addition to meat production, there are also proposals to enlist dairying, fruit and vegetable growing, and poultry farming in support of Europe's ailing agriculture.

But these fields will also not go untouched by overseas competition for very long. In fact, the competition has already arrived in some areas. Fruit growing, for example, is already so threatened by American competition that the Germans have found it necessary to elevate the San José shield-louse to the status of their patron-protector, to hold its shield over the German apple.

Overseas competition is also arriving in the field of fresh vegetables. England imported 1,893,000 bushels of onions in 1876/78, and 5,232,000 bushels by 1893/95. Spain alone supplied 41,000 bushels in the first period, rising to 1,300,000 in the second. Substantial imports also came from Holland, France, and Egypt.

Other fresh vegetables to the value of £227,000 were also imported into England in 1876/78, rising to more than £1,100,000 by 1893/95.

England obtains its eggs from an orbit embracing Italy, Hungary and Russia. And in the last few years successful attempts have been made to bring in fresh milk from Holland and Sweden.

The technical preconditions for opening up egg, vegetable and milk production to overseas competition are therefore already present. And this competition will grow in strength in the older agricultural export countries, as well as in Europe, the more that grain-production is forced back by the rise of the newer exporting countries. Until now, improvements in the transportation of these products of the secondary branches of agriculture have only damaged English agriculture. Farmers in the non-industrial parts of Europe have gained as England's suppliers. But eventually European agriculture will cease to export even within these fields, and overseas competition will spread, with the exception of those branches of production too insignificant to be seized on by the foreign farmer. And although competition has so far mainly affected spheres occupied by large farms, it will then get a grip on those in which the small farm is predominant.

No further argument is needed to appreciate the extent to which this will exacerbate the agrarian question. But European agriculture still has a few devices available for defending itself against its overseas enemies.

The Unification of Industry and Agriculture

Our main example so far in this chapter has been England. But when it comes to looking at the methods employed to defend agriculture and fight off overseas competition we can remain on the Continent as this aspect is little developed in England. In fact, conditions are much more favourable on our side of the Channel, and in particular in Germany.

Tenant farming initially permits the burdens of overseas competition to be shifted on to land-ownership. Where the landowner and farmer are one and the same person, the fixing of the price of land through mortgage indebtedness hinders this process. Such farmers are forced to look for a means of reducing their costs of production more quickly than tenants; and they are finding one which is more favoured by the system of proprietor farming than tenant farming, since the former renders the agricultural populations more stable, and exposes cooperation between farmers to less disruptive interruptions.

As we already know, agricultural produce generally has a low value to weight ratio, restricting the radius within which it can be profitably sold. With a given method of transportation, this radius can be extended enormously if the product concerned is exported in a processed rather than in a raw state.

Returning to Settegast's table, the percentage of the value accounted for by transport costs per cwt/mile is as follows:

	Market price per cwt Mk.	By road @ 15 Pf per cwt/mile	By rail @ 2.5 Pf
Sugar beet	1.00	15.00 per cent	2.50 per cent
Sugar	35.00	0.43 per cent	0.07 per cent
Potatoes	1.50	10.00 per cent	1.66 per cent
Spirit of wine	20.00	0.75 per cent	0.12 per cent
Livestock	20.00	0.25 per cent	0.25 per cent
Meat extract	600.00	0.03 per cent	0.0004 per cent

The higher specific value of many products of the foodstuffs industry is joined by an additional advantage: they keep better than raw products. Examples are butter and cheese, and preserved meat, vegetables and fruit.

Some agricultural industries also offer a further, very important, advantage: the product contains little or none of the constituents needed to retain the fertility of the soil. Their export does not remove anything of significance from the soil. Conversely, industrial residues contain material which can serve as excellent fertiliser, either directly or indirectly, as animal feed, enriching the soil. The distillation of brandy and sugar-beet processing are good cases in point: their residues, exploitable as feed and fertiliser, have considerably increased grain production and stock-rearing, and become the indispensable foundation of intensive rational farming wherever they have become established.

Agricultural industry also provides winter employment for people and draught animals. And the steam engine used in the large industrial establishment also provides a handy source of motive power for the running of the farm (for threshing, grain-cleaning, malt-milling, pumping, sawing and the like): these will inevitably grow in importance once electrical power transmission establishes a firm footing on the land. The steam-engine in the factory will then power the plough, the thresher, the dung-cart on a field railway, and the reaper.

Where suitable conditions existed, such factors encouraged farmers to set up industrial establishments on their farms to process their raw products. The arrival of foreign competition gave a powerful boost to this by forcing down ground-rents and the prices of raw products. Farmers had a double reason to win back as industrialists what they were losing as farmers: the drop in ground-rents could be compensated for by a rising industrial profit, and an expensive product could be processed from cheap raw materials.

As with any economic advance of our age, large enterprises were in the forefront, and derived the greatest benefit from this innovation.

Small firms do not usually possess sufficient capital or produce sufficient raw materials to be able to set up a plant for processing their own products. Small farmers are also slower to adapt, more conservative and less knowledgeable about technical progress and the needs of the world market than large-scale farmers and capitalists. It was the large landowners, in particular latifundium owners, who first introduced the large industrial establishment on to their estates, along with capitalists who set up agricultural industries and bought up the land needed to supply the raw materials. The link between industry and agriculture was forged from both sides. Distilleries and sugar-factories were joined on the large estates by starch factories and breweries, although the latter were not on a large scale as beer production was more profitable as an urban industry. Some of the raw materials for brewing have the same specific value as the end-product (barley), and some a higher (hops), and both are more easily transportable than beer. Brewing-barley and hops also only do well in certain areas. Apart from the agricultural industries already mentioned, dairies and factories for preserving vegetables, fruit and milk were also established.

One of the latifundium's greatest advantages over the smaller farm was that the farmer could establish a productive and broad connection between industry and agriculture. This advantage is at its greatest where the latifundium not only supplies the raw materials but also industry's motive power – water power, wood from nearby forests, coal. Consider the savings on transport and middlemen.

The successes of these agricultural industries inspired smaller farms to try and emulate them. The most appropriate form for this was found to be the cooperative – a form already prepared by some individual capitalist enterprises which were too large to obtain all their raw-material requirements from their own land, and which therefore had to conclude agreements for the supply of raw materials from farmers in the surrounding area. If such an enterprise was a joint stock company, the suppliers merely had to buy shares to complete the cooperative.

Such cooperatives have developed rapidly in recent years, especially in Germany. The growth of agricultural cooperatives (excluding lending, purchasing and marketing cooperatives) has been as follows:

	1891	1892	1896	1897
Dairy cooperatives	729	869	1,397	1,574
Other cooperatives	131	150	273	484

The latter are mainly engaged in distilling, milling, baking, wine-producing and similar industries.

We are in no doubt that this cooperative movement, which is still in its infancy, will have a significant effect and bring about a major transformation in agriculture.

But whereas one individual might see this as a transitional stage on the way to socialism in agriculture – the other favoured transitional stage being the remnants of the feudal common pasture – and another as a means for preserving an independent vigorous peasantry, we see it as neither of these.

Modern socialism is characterised by the ownership of the means of production by the workforce – and in a socialist communal system this means everyone. For a producers' cooperative to serve as a transitional stage to such a state, it would have to be an organisation of producers who own the cooperative's means of production. One of the most important objections to the view that present-day producers' cooperatives of workers represent a transitional stage to socialism consists in the fact that in capitalist society, a flourishing cooperative of this type will eventually reach the point at which the cooperators will take on wage-labourers, proletarians, who do not have a share in the ownership of the means of production and who are exploited by the members of the cooperative: that is, any producers' cooperative in modern society – if it is thriving – will tend to become a capitalist enterprise.

Whereas this is a mere tendency in producer cooperatives established by wage-labourers, it marks those set up by farmers from the very beginning: and these are the subject of our discussion here. Workers in a cooperative sugar-factory, distillery, dairy, conserving factory, mill, etc., are not members of the cooperative but wage-labourers hired and exploited by the members. Amongst the benefits which the farmer derives from the cooperative – alongside saving on transport and handling expenses – is the pocketing of a *profit on capital*. Such agricultural production cooperatives of this type – and there are not yet any other types – are not a transitional stage to *socialism, but to capitalism*.

But what about the role of the cooperative in rescuing the small peasant? The first observation to be made here is that they are not available to the dwarf-holder, to the proletarian peasant, who is most in need of help: an industrial establishment takes money and this is precisely what the small peasant is lacking. Most small peasants are also unable to produce raw material of the appropriate quality for processing. It is the 'middle strata' of peasants who stand to gain the most from producers' cooperatives.

But here too, the large farm will always enjoy considerable advantages over the small farm. There is nothing to stop the large landowner with the necessary cash from setting up a lucrative industrial enterprise: compare this with the difficulties involved in setting up a cooperative! The large landowner will quite naturally adapt their agriculture to the requirements of the factory: but think how difficult it is to get large numbers of small farmers to coordinate and standardise their supplies.

The large farm is the ideal partner for large-scale agricultural industry. In fact, the latter often creates a large farm where none existed before. Sugar-making, the classic example of large-scale agricultural industry, has greatly encouraged the development of large-scale farming. And Paasche has observed that one of the reasons holding back the spread of agricultural industry in Southern Germany and some parts of France and Northern Italy is the local fragmentation of land-ownership.

Dr Ihne's article on German sugar factories in America, published in *Zukunft* (V, p. 382), refers to the 'cheap and rational manufacture of sugar in some parts of East Prussia, where the owners of large estates have built sugar-factories and supply them with their own beet, produced by their own workers on their own land, independently of the fickle and often bloody-minded beet-growing peasants and cottagers. In this they resemble the big plantation owners of Louisiana with their cane sugar factories.'

Some agricultural industries also offer the large farm a number of benefits.

If a distillery is attached to an estate, all the residues of the process can be used on the farm, progressively improving the land. The opposite occurs where potatoes are supplied to the distillery from a number of farms. 'The high water content of the residuum makes it difficult to transport: it is only worthwhile using as feed on the distillery's own farm. The enrichment of this farm will be at the expense of the other farms, since the soil nutrients supplied via the potatoes are unlikely to retrace their steps' (Krafft, *Lehrbuch der Landwirtschaft*, p. 101).

According to Settegast's now familiar table, the transport of distillery residuum costs 30 per cent of its value per cwt/mile, compared to only 10 per cent for potatoes. With cooperative distilleries, those farms nearest to the distillery will increase their soil's wealth, whilst those more distant will be drained of it.

The same applies with sugar-factories.

In addition to the large farmer, it is large-scale capital which gains the most and is most likely to avail itself of the closer connection between agriculture and industry in a number of industries.

At the most recent congress of German agricultural cooperatives in Dresden, farmers were warmly recommended to establish cooperative bakeries and mills. Large-scale cooperatives, offering not only their members but also the public considerable benefits, were to replace the former, often very inadequate, small enterprises.

The idea of elevating the position of the agricultural small-scale enterprise by feeding it with the profits of large-scale baking and milling is, of course, a fine one – at least for the small farmer. Less so for the small miller and baker. But this is no embarrassment to the farmers – as they readily admit. And if uniting milling, baking and agriculture in one hand really does yield such great advantages, as is claimed, and we have no reason to doubt it, isn't it more likely that the large, well-capitalised power-mills rather than the slow-moving undercapitalised small-farmer cooperatives will be first to grasp the advantages? The large mills will take control of the small farmers and bakers before the small farmers take control of the large mills.

How matters stand between the peasant and the large power-mills is revealed in the following letter from the grain region of Upper Bavaria, which appeared in the press in the summer of 1897.

> Two power-mills dominate the entire area for a day's journey around. The peasants are completely dependent on them. Saturday is cornmarket day in the small provincial town: but only oats are sold there now as the peasants don't dare to bring wheat and corn to market. The two millers are the only buyers, and anyone who goes to market instead of selling to them is punished by being offered 10 Pfennigs less per cwt. The free sale of grain has completely stopped: peasants simply have to turn up with their wares and wait quietly to see what they get. If they refuse to play along, all they get is the answer: Go back home then – I've just bought in 1,000 cwts of Hungarian wheat.

Although the large farm may have a number of advantages over the small farm in the industrialisation of agriculture – as in other fields – this does not of course prove that the small farm will not derive some considerable benefits from the only form of agricultural large-scale industry available to it – the agricultural producers' cooperative. Where such a cooperative can be established, it allows the farmer to become a capitalist, enrich his agriculture with the fruits of capitalist exploitation, organise it more rationally and generally raise its level.

But how long can a conjuring trick which overnight converts a peasant heading towards the proletariat into a capitalist last?

The establishment of a cooperative does not alter the relationship between the peasants and any outside factory which they supply: they have to adapt their farming to its requirements. The sugar-factory instructs the farmers as to which seeds to use and how to fertilise: the dairy tells them which feed to use, when to milk and even the type of cattle to buy.

Farmers used to shy off heavy nitrogen manuring since this was held to reduce the sugar content of the beet. The factories therefore mostly prescribed a 1:2 ratio of nitrogen to phosphoric acid, and completely forbade a top dressing of Chile saltpetre and the planting of beet in fresh dung. Of these instructions only the ban on top dressing and the planting of beet in fresh dung, which was put out on the fields after Christmas, has been retained. The proportion of nitrogen to phosphoric acid has gradually shifted to the advantage of the former, so that some factories now demand a proportion of 2:3 or 3:4, and many even 1:1. (Kärger, *Die Sachsengängerei*, p. 14)

Such instructions cease to be necessary once agriculture has fully adapted itself to the sugar industry.

Stöckel's work on the establishment, organisation and operation of dairy cooperatives (*Errichtung, Organisation und Betrieb der Molkereigenossenschaften*) provides a model management plan for such an institution.

Paragraph Four reads, for example:

This paragraph contains all the instructions necessary for feeding. Certain binding instructions on feeding are an absolute necessity for the sale of fresh milk, and, in particular, the sale of so-called mother's milk. It can also become necessary to establish feeding rules for processing cooperatives, in particular the restricting of feeds which affect the taste and life of the butter.

Paragraph Five. Milking times should be arranged so that milk is delivered directly from the stall to the cooperative.

Paragraph Six. The greatest cleanliness is to be observed during milking.

Paragraph Seven. The members of the Board of Supervision (and the Board of Management) have the right to inspect the stalls and milk storage rooms of members at any time without notice, to be in attendance during milking and to take samples of the milk being obtained. These agents are entitled to demand fully accurate and detailed information from members as to the feeding of the cattle, their treatment, and similar matters. (Stöckel, ibid., pp. 102–4)

In Denmark the creamery societies make regulations for the feeding and management of cattle in order to ensure uniformity of quality and the absence of unpleasant flavourings from particular kinds of food, together with a steady supply of milk in winter. (Royal Commission on Agriculture, 1897, p. 126)

The farmer is therefore denied the final say in how his own farm is run. The farm becomes an appendage of the factory, and has to adapt to its requirements. And the farmer becomes a specialised worker of the factory.

Technical dependence can grow to such an extent that the factory supplies the farmer with feed and fertilisers.

And technical dependence is soon followed by economic dependence. The cooperative not only supplies the means for improving the farm and covering any deficits which may arise, but also – the more the farmer adapts his farming to its requirements – becomes the sole buyer of the farmer's output. Agriculture then ceases to be possible without industry: industry becomes agriculture's backbone. Industry's collapse would be agriculture's ruin.

And such a collapse can happen all too easily.

The greater the profits obtained from agricultural industry, the greater the number of capitalists who apply themselves to it. Large profits can only usually nowadays be made by enterprises with a far-above-average capitalisation, enabling them to defeat any competition both technically and commercially. And they can only be earned either in fields conducive to monopoly by their very nature or open to artificial monopoly, or in fields newly created by technical or economic revolutions and freshly opened up to capitalist exploitation, such as electrical engineering. This type of profit does not persist: the new field is quickly filled up, and chronic overproduction sets in. The first arrivals get the cream, and the latecomers are left with skimmed milk – and often not even that.

In agricultural industry, the large landowner – in particular when also a capitalist – therefore has an advantage over smallholders and their cooperatives. The larger landowner is more flexible, enterprising, far-seeing and less ponderous than the smaller; and where the necessary preconditions are there, can more quickly set up an agricultural industry, as long as it is profitable.

All agricultural industries – like all other industries – eventually reach the stage where they are overcrowded. Wherever competition rages, prices will be put under pressure, and the weakest and less competent eliminated. Finally, the branch is convulsed by periodic crises, some of which are more generalised, coinciding with the general alternation of economic prosperity and crash, and some of which are specific, the result of particular technical, economic and legislative changes.

The more the state steps in to help these industries, the more agriculture profits at the expense of the population as a whole, the sooner this moment will arrive. The European alcohol and sugar industries are clear illustrations of this fact. Both have been widely stimulated in Germany, Austria, Russia, France by all manner of concessions and privileges, in particular export premiums, which take the form of a rebate on taxes.

Between 1872 and 1881, the number of distilleries processing molasses or farinaceous materials in the Reich tax area increased from 7,011 to 7,280: but the number of distilleries paying over 15,000 Marks in spirits tax increased from 789 to 1,492 – almost double.

Between 1880/81 and 1885/86 the quantity of potatoes used for spirits increased from 1,982,000 to 3,087,000 tonnes.

The upshot of this amazing increase was a crisis, which began in 1884. The first response was for Bismarck's government to take the ailing industries under its wing. The government finally succeeded in pushing through the 1887 Tax Act which ensured the distilleries their annual 'gift' of 40 million Marks, and was a vigorous counter to overproduction. In 1895 this was supplemented by a new law even more restrictive to the overproduction of alcohol, which raised the domestic price of spirits: the ensuing tax revenue was used to pay an export premium of 6 Marks per hectolitre. But despite this, the ghost of the spirits crash refuses to be laid.

Sugar has also been the happy beneficiary of the state's goodwill – like alcohol it is produced by the high and mighty. The consequence has been an enormous growth in sugar production. The figures for the German

Reich are as follows:

	Factories processing sugar	Processed tonnage	Volume supplied by factories	Tonnage of raw sugar produced
1871/72	311	2,251,000	1,504,000	186,000
1881/82	343	6,272,000	3,432,000	600,000
1891/92	403	9,488,000	4,644,144	1,144,000
1896/97	399	13,722,000	5,782,051	1,739,000

Compare these figures with those for the export and internal consumption of sugar in the German Reich.

	Consumption of Sugar	Export of Sugar
	tonnes	
1871/72	221,799	14,276
1881/82	291,045	314,410
1891/92	476,265	607,611
1896/97	505,078	1,141,097

Although sugar consumption, and in particular sugar exports have grown enormously, they have recently slipped far behind production. In 1896/97 sugar consumption and exports totalled 1,640,000 tonnes against total output of 1,740,000 – an overproduction of 100,000 tonnes. It should also be borne in mind that the sugar industry greatly benefited from the Cuban War which completely blocked Cuban sugar exports. In 1894/95 overproduction had reached 300,000 tonnes.

Conditions for the sugar industry cannot be expected to improve; they are more likely to get worse. The pressure of overseas competition which necessitates the development of agricultural industries, and the encouragement of such industries by the ever-growing volume of subsidies, is also felt in other countries. In round figures, beet production, expressed in tonnes of raw sugar, was as follows in the early 1890s (figures taken from Schippel, 'Zuckerkrisis, Ausfuhrprämien und

Zuckerring', *Neue Zeit*, XV, 1, p. 622).

	Germany	Austria	France	Russia	Belgium and Holland	Other European countries	Total
1891/92	1,200,000	780,000	640,000	550,000	230,000	90,000	3,490,000
1893/94	1,370,000	840,000	570,000	650,000	310,000	110,000	3,850,000
1894/95	1,830,000	1,060,000	780,000	620,000	370,000	150,000	4,810,000

An increase of almost *one million tonnes* in the supply of raw sugar, against an annual increase in world demand of a *quarter*, at best a *third*, of this figure.

The best customer for German sugar after England is the United States of America. Exports of raw sugar, and sugar products from the German Reich were as follows:

	Total	To Great Britain	To the USA
1891	784,000	454,000	140,000
1896	974,000	513,000	316,008
1897	1,120,000	564,000	376,000

In the meantime the Americans have been devoting no small amount of effort to establishing their own sugar industry. F.W. Ihne, President of the Polytechnic Society of Chicago, recently invited German engineering companies to take the opportunity to set up sugar-beet factories in America. How patriotic! The Americans' efforts will increase in proportion to the drop in wheat profits. However, as the above figures show, the sugar industry is capable of extremely rapid growth, and the Americans are just the people to push it sky high.

In the sugar-producing countries of Europe, export premiums are being increased rather than reduced: they were doubled in Germany in 1896 (from 1.25 Marks to 2.5 Marks). The premiums are following the same course already trod by protective tariffs and militarism: once underway, they can't be stopped – even if the wish to do so is there. It is widely acknowledged that the premiums are pushing overproduction towards a fearful crisis – but each individual country thinks that it will suffer the worst should it be the only one to abandon these premiums: and each hopes that it can hold out longer than their rivals. The population is bled more and more, at the same time as beet cultivation continues to expand, and wider and wider circles of agriculture become chained to the fate of the sugar industry.

The number of hectares planted with sugar-beet increased as follows:

	Germany	Austria	France	Russia	Belgium/Holland
1891	336,000	328,000	223,000	310,000	75,000
1892	441,400	369,000	272,000	331,000	103,000

But the bankruptcy of the sugar industry is becoming increasingly unavoidable: and the devastation which this eventual breakdown must inevitably cause is becoming ever greater.

Dairying in Germany is promoted somewhat less energetically than sugar-processing. Nevertheless, it has grown rapidly under the pressure of foreign competition as grain cultivation becomes less lucrative, as the figures from the dairy cooperatives noted above show. Unfortunately, no detailed statistics of dairying in Germany are yet available. Evidently, only part of the rapid growth in dairying is associated with higher milk production. The number of cows is increasing much more slowly than the production of butter and cheese. The rapid expansion of dairying is more attributable to another factor. Because of difficulties in transportation, milk produced at some distance from the towns could not formerly be brought to market and become a commodity. It was consumed on the producer's farm – by the family and wage-labourers, if any were employed. Going over to dairying allowed the producer to make butter and cheese which could stand more extended transport, and not only make an appearance as a commodity on the domestic market but also on the world market. Nevertheless this deprives farmers of the milk which they and their household once consumed. The expansion of dairying in the country and rural milk consumption took divergent paths.

Apart from being able to work in the fresh air, the superior strength and stamina of the rural population compared with the urban – despite overwork and poor living conditions and the lack of meat in their diet – was principally due to their high consumption of milk. Working in the fresh air ceased once domestic industries became established, and milk consumption came to a stop once dairies began to take the milk from the rural population. These preferred means for saving the small peasant economically turn out to be *highly effective methods for ruining them physically*.

Matters are at their worst where the dairies produce cheese. But it seems rather optimistic to hope that if the dairies confined themselves to producing butter as mostly happens in Württemberg, and gave the skimmed milk back to the farmers, the disadvantages of the dairying system for the rural diet would be eliminated: this has been suggested by Landauer-Gerabronn, for example, at the Forty-Second Congress of Württemberg Farmers, held at Hohenheim in 1897. He noted,

> Such a type of milk use might cause our doctors to be better disposed towards the dairies than was the case when all milk was delivered to the cheese-makers, without the farmer taking any of the sweet skimmed milk home. Quite correctly, this gave rise to some concern on health grounds amongst doctors and also occasioned one military doctor to make public his disastrous experiences in mustering recruits in some areas.

Skimmed milk can never replace full-cream milk since it lacks the latter's fat content. Full-cream milk contains 2.8–4.5 per cent fat, skimmed milk only 0.2–0.5 per cent. This writer can also recall coming across reports which were no less unhappy about the use of skimmed milk, and found it very pernicious that it was given to babies in dairying regions. Of course, the return of skimmed milk would be least beneficial to the rural population if farmers abstained from drinking it themselves and made commercial use of it by feeding it to pigs, which then thrive quite magnificently and fetch a good price. The more the products of the small peasant become commodities, the more they are transformed into money, the poorer the peasant's diet.

If the dairying system inflicts indisputable *physical damage* on the dairy farmer, the economic *boost* which it is claimed to provide is far from indisputable, aside from the most immediate considerations.

Whilst German butter production is growing rapidly, butter exports are falling and imports rising. The movement of imports and exports was as follows between 1886 and 1897:

	Exports	Imports
	kilogrammes	
1886	12,309,000	5,119,000
1891	7,649,000	7,950,000
1895	6,857,000	6,890,000
1896	7,101,000	7,857,000
1897	3,716,000	10,326,000

Cheese imports and exports were as follows over the same period:

	Exports	Imports
	kilogrammes	
1886	3,409,000	5,216,000
1891	1,883,000	8,392,000
1895	2,212,000	9,348,000
1896	1,840,000	10,196,000
1897	1,373,000	11,937,000

Here the picture is also one of falling exports and rising imports.

Competition in dairy products on the world market is also rapidly increasing. The supplanting of grain is stimulating dairying in virtually every European country. Denmark in particular has expanded its butter production enormously. The excess of exports over imports increased from 18 million kilos in 1881 to 119 million kilos by 1896. The ratio of cows to the human population has not substantially changed.

	Cows per 1,000 population	Absolute number
1871	448	807,000
1881	452	899,000
1893	449	1,011,000

The dairying system has also been growing swiftly outside Europe. *Canada* for *cheese*, and *Australia* for *butter* are particularly relevant.

Canadian cheese exports grew from 106,200,000 lbs in 1891 to 146,000,000 by 1895.

Apart from falling wheat prices, dairy production has also been encouraged by export premiums (2 pence per lb of butter and 1 penny per lb of cheese) in Victoria (until 1893), South Australia (until 1895), and Queensland (until 1898). The 1897 Royal Commission on Agriculture reported on the situation in Australia in the following terms.

One feature of the progress of dairying in Victoria has been the extension of the factory system. According to the latest official information there were 155 butter and cheese factories in operation in the colony, as compared with 74 in 1892, and out of an estimated total production of 35,580,000 lbs of butter in the former year, nearly 27,000,000 lbs were manufactured in the dairy factories. The increase in the exports of butter from Victoria since 1889 has been as follows:

1889/90	829,000 lbs
1890/91	1,700,000 lbs
1891/92	4,794,000 lbs
1892/93	8,094,000 lbs
1893/94	17,141,000 lbs
1894/95	25,948,000 lbs
1895/96	21,024,000 lbs

(Royal Commission on Agriculture, 1897, p. 80)

There are similar reports of rapid growth in dairy production from Queensland and New South Wales; in the latter colony, butter production rose from 15,500,000 lbs in 1889 to 27,359,000 lbs in 1895.

The following extract from the report on New South Wales is of particular interest:

It seems that dairying is not now, as formerly, wholly confined to farmers, since many graziers in a large way of business, especially near the coast, have lately turned their attention to the industry. When the factory system was first introduced, the factories were mostly cooperative and the process of cream separation and butter-making were carried on together. This arrangement is gradually dying out, and central butter factories, fed by numerous separating establishments called 'creameries' are taking the place of the others. The advantages gained from this change are said to be considerable; a butter of more uniform quality is made in each centre, and there is a reduction in the cost of manufacture owing to the greater quantity made and the use of improved appliances, such as refrigerators, which the larger establishments can profitably provide. (Royal Commission on Agriculture, 1897, pp. 80-1)

As with exported German sugar, England is the largest consumer of German exports of butter. Of the 7,101,000 kilos of German exports in 1896, 5,570,000 went to England; and of the 3,716,000 kilos in 1897, 2,766,000. But these figures also show that German butter is rapidly losing its place in the English market. Butter imports into England in per cent were broken down as follows in the period between 1887 and 1895:

	Denmark	Norway and Sweden	France	Holland	Germany	Australia	Other countries
1887	32.3	11.3	27.5	10.7	10.3	0.4	7.5
1890	40.7	11.3	25.9	7.7	5.1	2.0	7.3
1893	40.2	12.4	20.1	6.1	7.1	7.3	6.8
1894	42.8	11.0	16.5	6.4	5.4	11.3	6.6
1895	41.1	11.5	16.1	6.8	4.0	11.1	9.4

Australia's rapid rise is especially noticeable. The Danish dairies are being hard-pressed by Australian competition, which forces down prices and threatens their markets.

Nevertheless, German cooperative members are busy, eagerly trying to increase the number of dairies. They are proud of the rapid growth seen over the last few years, as if the lucrativeness of a business was to be judged by the number of competitors. Of course, as saviours of the peasantry they are forced to strike such an attitude. Irrespective of how many dairy cooperatives there might be, it will never be enough when set against the number of peasants who await their salvation by this brilliant method. But butter and cheese production will have fallen victim to overproduction and crisis long before any major portion of the peasantry will have been rescued by dairying cooperatives.

In Denmark, the promised land of dairy cooperatives, many are already in dire straits. The gloomiest reports were given on the position of the butter producers during the committee stage of the German Margarine Act. But this did not inhibit the conference of agricultural cooperatives at Dresden from triumphantly announcing that 175 new dairies had been established in 1896, and a further 177 in 1896. And the fever seems likely to continue to rage ever more strongly. The more perceptive cooperatives are already beginning to raise warning voices. Landauer-Gerabronn noted:

> An extraordinarily powerful movement for the founding of new dairies had made itself felt over the last year. If this continues it cannot be ruled out that the number of dairies could double within two or three years, and might even triple. In the Gerabronn district no new dairies had been established in the 16 years since the first, but no less than ten new dairies have appeared in the last six months and more are expected in the immediate future. Plans are on such a grand scale that even enthusiastic admirers of cooperative activity are beginning to shake their heads and wonder if the setting up of so many dairies might not be indirectly exposing agriculture to very serious dangers.

Along with an alcohol and a sugar crisis, a dairying crisis is also now inevitable. In fact, this goes without saying for any large-scale industrial enterprise.

Sering also complained about the bitter competition between the dairy cooperatives. At a lecture to the Royal Prussian State Agricultural Board in February 1897 he offered the consolation that

> there are now hopes that these problems can be surmounted by a further extension of the cooperative idea, or more likely by the same method now uniquely reshaping our large industries, the *cartel system*. Individual dairies are being urged to join the large retail butter cooperatives in larger numbers than before, and to commit themselves to the exclusive sale of a portion of their output through these retail cooperatives. The enlarged and strengthened retail butter associates will then seek to divide the market amongst themselves, and hence overcome the ruinous and unpredictable competition which formerly prevailed; surpluses should be disposed of abroad [to England] even if this means sacrifices.

Interestingly, Professor Sering's recommendation of this splendid approach occurs in the same speech in which he shortly beforehand indignantly declared: 'Retail cooperatives are most indispensable in a period in which industrial cartels are growing: there is no other protection against the misuse of the economic power which association confers on manufacturers than an association of consumers' (Sering, in *Thiels landwirtschaftliches Jahrbuch*, 1897 Supplement, pp. 223, 225).

So, whilst the agrarian cartel is 'an extension of the cooperative idea', the industrial cartel is a 'misuse of economic power' which can only be combatted by extending the cooperative idea. The cooperative is praised as the means of dealing with the cartel, and the cartel is praised as the means of avoiding the otherwise inevitable bankruptcy of the cooperative. The Professor's logic is at about the same level as his moral indignation.

But this is not the most interesting thing about his arguments. What is noteworthy is that they confirm the difficulties experienced by the dairies and preach the cartel as the only way out – a strategy made impossible by the constant increase in the number of dairies. And this has to be admitted by a luminary of agrarian science in a hymn of praise to the miraculous workings of the cooperative system!

The same applies to the other agricultural large-scale industries which have not been of such significance for the cooperative system.

Of course, the coming crisis does not have to ruin the industry which it afflicts. In fact, this is a rare occurrence. The usual outcome is a transformation of the prevailing property relations into a more capitalist shape – carrying out exactly what the cooperative is supposed to prevent.

The small, inadequately-equipped and under-capitalised enterprises will go under in a crisis. But the ruin of a factory in an agricultural industry is not confined to that enterprise alone: it drags down, or at least undermines, very many dependent agricultural existences with it. And the greater the prop offered by the industry, the more farmers relied on it, the more devastation its bankruptcy will unleash.

The larger, better-equipped, enterprises can survive, although they will be forced to pass through a difficult period in which profits will dry up and production will only be sustainable through increasing amounts of subsidy. Cooperative members who cannot afford to make such advances lose their rights in the cooperative. If the insolvency of the cooperative members becomes generalised, nothing remains but to sell the undertaking to a capitalist; if it is not generalised, the crisis will lead to the undertaking becoming the private property of a few rich cooperators who will run it on purely capitalist lines.

This process does not mean the inevitable proletarianisation of the former cooperative members: if they are lucky they can hang on to their peasant holdings. But even then, their economic dependency on the former cooperative undertaking will remain intact – being transformed from dependency on an association whose members, as farmers, shared equal rights and interests, into dependency on one (or several) dominant capitalists with antagonistic interests. The *specialised workers of the cooperative factory become wage-labourers of a capitalist factory.* And matters are not improved by the fact that, as in domestic industry, this form of wage-labour is a hidden one. This is the inevitable end to agricultural producer cooperatives.

As everywhere else in capitalist society, industry finally wins out over agriculture, and capital over individual producer cooperatives.

Because such cooperatives hold out the prospect of immediate benefits to farmers, they in fact prove to be a powerful means for furthering the industrialisation of agriculture and hence for clearing the path for domination by capital – a path on which capital might otherwise have encountered difficulties.

We do not mean to underestimate the significance of these cooperatives. They are important for the revolutionising of agriculture: but they are not a means for saving the peasant.

However, the cooperative system has its limits.

The laws that apply to every other industry also apply to the agricultural industries. Concentration and centralisation of enterprises, which encounters so many strong counter-tendencies in agriculture, is making rapid progress: as with other industries, the tendency towards the large undertaking dominates the agricultural industries.

This is most evident in the, admittedly state-fostered, field of sugar-processing. The number and size of enterprises grew as follows in the German Reich between 1871/72 and 1896/97.

	Sugar factories	Processed tonnage of beet	Average tonnage per factory
1871/72	311	2,250,918	7,237
1881/82	343	6,271,948	18,286
1891/92	403	9,488,002	23,543
1896/97	399	13,721,601	34,389

This represents virtually a *five-fold* increase in the average tonnage of beet processed by the individual factory within a space of 25 years.

The same trend can also be seen in the field of potato distilling, albeit on a less dramatic scale, up until the passing of tax laws designed to curtail the growth of production. The Reich Statistical Yearbook shows that the number of distilleries processing potatoes, grain or molasses increased from 7,011 in 1872 to 7,280 by 1881/82. However, the number of those paying a spirits tax of less than 15,000 Marks annually fell from 6,222 to 5,788, whilst those over this level increased from 789 to 1,492.

Moreover, the scale of production changed as follows:

	Potato distilleries	Processed tonnage of potatoes	Average tonnage per distillery
1882/83	4,180	2,392,000	572
1886/87	4,069	2,719,000	668

After 1887/88 the output per distillery within the Reich tax area has remained at the same average level, although it should be noted that the smallest distilleries have shown a marked decline in numbers.

	1890/91	1894/95	Increase/Decrease
Up to 50 litres	1,300	513	-787
50-500 litres	731	720	-11
500-5,000 litres	632	657	+25
5,000-50,000 litres	1,931	1,983	+52
Over 50,000 litres	1,793	1,758	-35

The dairies are also naturally subject to the laws of development of modern large-scale industry. Technical progress will not stand still just for them. Hand-operation is being replaced by steam-power, machines increase in number and size, and with this their productivity; processing and storage areas grow, markets expand, and with them the need to employ commercially trained staff, who can only be properly utilised by a large enterprise.

We saw above how the dairies in New South Wales are steadily increasing in size. The same is also reported from Belgium. A report from Colard Bovy to the 1885 International Agricultural Congress confirmed that inadequate and poorly managed small cooperatives were steadily retreating before the larger cooperatives, 'which can process large quantities of milk at the lowest prices and under better conditions, and can supply produce of constant uniformity. These advantages are maximised if the establishment is in the charge of a diligent official' (cited in Vandervelde, 'Agrarsozialismus in Belgien', *Neue Zeit*, XV, 1, p. 755).

The development of the foodstuffs industry in the German Empire is shown in the following figures, based on data from the 1882 and 1895 occupational statistics.

Number of wage-labourers and clerks per 100 managers (owners and employed managers)

	Grain mills	Sugar processing	Production of other vegetable food products[1]	Production of animal products (except meats)[2]	Malting and brewing	Brandy distilling, liqueurs	Sparkling wine, cider, perry, wine-conditioning	Vinegar
1882	101	2,831	688	141	364	299	256	162
1895	237	5,764	1,231	315	759	413	315	237
Increase	76	2,933	543	174	395	114	59	75

[1] Conserves, vegetable compresses, coffee substitutes, cocoa, starch, noodles.

[2] Salt-fish, conserved milk, butter and cheese processing.

The growth in the size of establishments is visible everywhere: the number of wage-labourers is increasing much more quickly than that of owners and managers in all the agricultural industries. The increase is over 100 per cent in beet-sugar processing, dairying and brewing, and 400 per cent in the production of vegetable conserves.

The Nestlé company provides a good example of such expansion. The company owns two large factories in Switzerland for the production of condensed milk and one factory for producing cereal foods for infants. The latter, in Vevey, has a daily throughput of 100,000 litres of milk, the produce of 12,000 cows from 180 villages – 180 villages which have lost their economic independence and become subjects of the House of Nestlé. Although their inhabitants are still the nominal owners of their land, they are no longer free peasants.

As this development proceeds and the capital sum needed to set up a competitive undertaking increases, the number of farmers able to take the step of setting up a producers' cooperative declines: the likelihood increases that any new undertaking will be capitalist from the outset, as can already be seen with sugar-beet processing and potato distilleries. Those cooperatives which are established in these branches of industry are almost entirely composed of big peasants and Junkers.

If every rural producers' cooperative is inevitably threatened with falling into the clutches of a capitalist every time a crisis occurs, sooner or later the time will come when the small peasant will no longer have access to such institutions, and the industries will become the monopoly of capitalists and large landowners. This development also generally leads to small-scale agriculture being supplanted by large. Again the sugar industry provides us with the best demonstration of this. The advantages of agricultural mechanisation are most evident where the motive power for the machine does not have to be specially obtained but can be supplied by a factory located on the estate itself.

When this does not lead to the decline of the small farm, the industrialisation of agriculture sets the seal on the small farmers' dependence on the factory, the sole buyer of their products. They become fully subordinated to industrial capital, and their farming is directed solely to meeting its requirements.

This is the salvation which agricultural industry offers to the peasant.

The Displacement of Agriculture by Industry

Although the development of agricultural industry may offer farmers some new, if temporary, support, the advance of technology sets in train developments which put them under great pressure and ruin individual branches of farming. One element in this is greater economy in the use of raw materials: with constant consumption of the end-product, the demand for raw materials will fall, and with increasing demand for the end-product demand will not rise as fast. Industrial progress also tends to replace high-value raw materials by low-value ones, especially via the use of waste and the production of surrogates. Finally, industry may even advance so far that it can begin to produce materials previously supplied by agriculture, or can make such effective substitutes that the agricultural product is no longer required.

A few examples will serve to illustrate this point. The major loss of nutrients caused by imperfect grinding of corn is well-known. Advances in milling are constantly reducing these losses.

> In the seventeenth century, Vauban estimated the annual consumption of a man at nearly 712 lbs of wheat, a quantity which now suffices nearly for two men; and by the improvements in mills there are now gained to the population immense masses of nutritious matter, of the annual value of many millions, which were formerly used for animals alone; whereas for the feeding of animals the bran may be far more easily replaced by other food, not in the least adapted for the use of man ... Wheat does not contain above 2 per cent of woody indigestible

fibre, and a perfect mill, in the most extended sense, should not yield more than that proportion of bran; but practically the best mills always yield, even now, from 12 to 20 per cent (10 per cent coarse bran, 7 fine bran, 3 per cent bran flour); and the ordinary mills produce as much as 25 per cent of bran, containing 60 or 70 per cent of the most nutritious constituents of the flour. (Liebig, *Familiar Letters of Chemistry*, pp. 464–5)

In 1877, a Herr Till, the owner of a power-mill, claimed to have invented a milling process which yielded 92.6 per cent flour and only 7.4 per cent bran and waste (Till, *Die Lösung der Brotfrage*). We have not come across any greater reduction in bran. Trials are also currently underway to make the nutrients in the bran, in particular the protein, digestible through chemical means.

Clearly, if flour consumption remains constant, any advance in milling must result in a reduction in the demand for grain. The same result as an actual fall in demand will occur even with rising demand if the mass of grain coming on to the market is increasing as fast, or even faster, than the consumption of flour. The displacement of primitive mills by power-mills is bound to exacerbate the effects of the crisis on the grain market.

Attempts to transform the nutrients in bran into a form digestible by humans is one example of the use of waste and the production of surrogates.

The increasing use of waste is one of the most fundamental and unique features of the modern mode of production. It is the natural outcome of large-scale production, which accumulates waste in enormous amounts at particular points. The need to dispose of it stimulates experiments in finding industrial applications – transforming a source of problems and unproductive expenditure into a source of profit.

These wastes have become very important for agriculture. The waste products churned out by large-scale industry – such as distilling, sugar-making, brewing, oil-mills, together with 'Thomas powder' and wood ash – supply agriculture with animal feeds and fertilisers and function as a powerful force binding agriculture to industry. Conversely, industry also appropriates the wastes from agricultural products and uses them to compete against agriculture.

The production of oil from cotton-seed is a good example: this was previously thrown away, or at most used as a fertiliser in the cotton plantations. Having discovered how to extract oil from the seed, this industry is rapidly stepping up its competitive challenge to the European oil-producing plants. In Germany oil imports have advanced as follows:

	Cotton-seed oil tonnes	Linseed oil tonnes
1886	8,067	39,743
1891	21,366	37,385
1895	34,460	19,863
1896	27,047	19,693
1897	30,227	15,548

Cotton-seed oil is used in particular in the adulteration of *olive-oil* and the production of *synthetic butter*, margarine, which is manufactured from *ox-tallow*, milk and cheap oils – especially cotton-seed oil – and is scarcely distinguishable from butter in terms of taste and physiological effect. The first synthetic butter factory was established in Germany in 1872, and there are now approximately 60.

Such a development will obviously not do much to improve the already crisis-stricken butter market. The escalating complaints of the agrarian lobby, which won them new limitations on the margarine industry in 1896, are certainly exaggerated: but the counter-claim that farmers have not been damaged by synthetic butter is also equally overstated. It is little consolation to the farmers to point out that the manufacture of synthetic butter is itself in difficulties. This fact is not so much expressed in losses for individual factories – the same phenomenon can be found in the poorly managed, unfortunately located or inadequately equipped plants even in prospering branches – as in the statistics of that country in which competition between margarine and butter is least restricted: Great Britain. Imports into Great Britain developed as follows between 1886 and 1895:

	Butter cwts	(of which Australian) per cent	Margarine cwts
1886	1,452,000	–	870,000
1892	2,107,000	4	1,293,000
1895	2,750,000	11	922,000

Cheap Australian butter is not only putting pressure on the producers of natural butter, but also those of synthetic butter. This will not, of course, lead to the demise of synthetic butter production but rather to improvements in production methods, something from which the producers of natural butter have nothing to gain.

Even if we did not dispute the fact that dairies are being damaged by margarine production, this would not imply that we ought to approve of attempts to hinder the production of the latter to the advantage of the former. Evidently, it is a matter for regret when the bankruptcy of a cooperative dairy propels large numbers of hard-working peasants into the proletariat: but it is no less cause for sadness when equally hard-working proletarians lose their livelihoods because of a new machine. This is how technical progress takes place in present-day society. Anyone wishing to do away with this method of progress must also be prepared to do away with this social order in its entirety. It is sheer nonsense to use all means available to maintain this order on one hand, yet seek to suppress its consequences on the other. And such nonsense actually becomes a disgrace if, in seeking to put it into practice, passing or sectional interests dictate that a small number of producers are accorded the privilege of being sheltered from any technical progress which might impinge on their profits at the expense of society in general.

In a modern state the mass of the population will not tolerate such a privilege indefinitely: and it is therefore utopian to protect agriculture from the onward march of industry by these means. The agrarians' desperate efforts to do so merely expose the extent to which they are threatened by capitalist large-scale industry in the food sector, and the importance of industry relative to agriculture.

Of all the surrogates produced by large-scale industry, synthetic butter along with synthetic cheese have had the greatest impact on agriculture so far. But they are not the only ones working in this direction.

Beer brewing has gone through an enormous upswing in almost every country in Europe in the last few decades.

Germany		Great Britain	
Year	Hectolitres	Year	Hectolitres
1872	32,945,000	1873	35,700,000
1882/83	39,250,000	1881	44,774,000
1890/91	52,730,000	1891	52,675,000
1895/96	60,563,000		

	Austria		Belgium
Year	Hectolitres	Year	Hectolitres
1870	9,303,400	1870	7,794,000
1880	10,530,000	1880	9,238,500
1890	13,570,000	1890	10,770,000

	France		Russia
Year	Hectolitres	Year	Hectolitres
1872	7,131,000	1866	2,200,000
1885	8,010,000	1884	4,212,000
1890	8,490,000	1890	8,490,000

In Denmark beer production grew from 1,200,000 hectolitres in 1876 to 2,185,000 by 1891. In Sweden production increased from 419,815 to 1,240,811 between 1880 and 1890; beer production in Switzerland increased from 280,000 in 1867 to 650,000 by 1876, 1,004,000 by 1886 and 1,249,000 in 1891.

One might think that *hop production* would have increased at the same rate. Nothing could be further from the truth. It has only increased very slightly. In 1867 the European hop harvest was put at 50,000 tonnes. The figure was still the same in 1890 (of which 24,705 was produced in Germany and 15,000 in England). In 1892 the harvest amounted to 57,550 tonnes (of which 24,150 was produced in Germany and 19,000 in England).

In England annual beer production rose from 35 million hectolitres in 1873 to 52 million by 1891, an increase of almost 50 per cent. In contrast the area under hops fell from 24,000 in 1871 to 23,000 in 1892. And according to the Royal Commission the import of hops, 'has remained practically stationary throughout the last 20 years. Taking the period 1876-78, the average annual importation of hops from all sources was 195,000 cwts, and in 1893-95, it amounted to 203,000 cwts' (Royal Commission on Agriculture, 1897, p. 83).

Developments in Germany are illustrated in the following table:

	1884	1896
Hop harvest	28,870 tonnes	25,325 tonnes
Hop imports	1,340 tonnes	3,041 tonnes
Total	30,210 tonnes	28,366 tonnes
From which hop exports	11,514 tonnes	9,868 tonnes
Remaining quantity	18,696 tonnes	18,498 tonnes
	1884/85	1896/97
Beer production	42,287,000 hectolitres	61,486,000 hectolitres
Hectolitres of beer per tonne hops	2,260	3,324

Rising beer production has therefore done absolutely nothing to help hop producers. It has simply encouraged the production of hop surrogates.

The development of chemistry has afflicted vine-growers even more seriously than hop growers in showing how to manufacture *grape-sugar*, the best known method for improving low-quality wines from potato-starch, rag or wood fibres. And chemistry has also shown how wine can be manufactured from draff or raisins using sugar and other products of agricultural industry.

Even so-called 'natural wines' are now increasingly obliged to pass through a number of processes requiring scientific knowledge and expensive equipment, making natural wine more and more a product of capitalist large-scale industry, to which the vine-grower merely supplies the raw material.

In other words the wine-cellar is becoming a wine-factory.

In his speech 'The Position of Legislation on Wine Preparation', given to the Royal Prussian State Agricultural Board in February 1897, Professor Märcker noted:

> Wine is not a fully natural product; it does not grow ready for the bottle on the vine, but has to pass through a lengthy process in its treatment once in the cellar until a noble wine has been obtained from the sweet must ... The preparation of wine has occasioned many scientific studies in recent years. Much progress has been achieved in that we are gradually learning how to produce natural wine from low-quality grapes. Of prime importance is the rise of selective yeast breeding.

Many types of yeast fungus cling to the peel of the grapes and cause fermentation.

It is known that there are various strains of yeast, and that the yeast which grows on the Johannisberg in Geisenheim produces a wine of a quite specific character: attempts have been made to breed a pure yeast strain in order to obtain a specific type of wine. Those of a sanguine disposition thought that once positive results had been obtained, grape growing could be eliminated together. All that would be required would be to add yeast to sugar solution, and produce the finest Johannisberger or Steinberger.

Clearly, one ought to be enthusiastic about such a prospect: not only *sugar-plums* for the masses but now Johannisberger too. Wouldn't this be the beginning of heaven on earth?

This is how a socialist might think – but not an agrarian. Good fortune for the population at large – a plentiful supply of foodstuffs and luxuries – would be a disaster for ground-rents. If anyone can make their own Johannisberger out of sugar-solution, think of the catastrophic effects this would have on those vineyards currently producing such wines. Professor Märcker continues, somewhat relieved:

Thank God, this has not yet happened. But we have succeeded in producing a much better wine with the pure yeast than without it, and we can get much better prices for our products. And this only a few years after pure yeast was first used.

The yeast fungi have respectfully refrained from encroaching on ground-rents. But might not these microscopic young blades one day abandon their loyal posture and turn rebellious? Producing Johannisberger from scrapings is just the beginning: why not go on and make wine out of sugar-solution?

The improvement of wine cannot be prohibited – this much is admitted by Professor Märcker himself in his speech. Statistics tell us that only one vintage in ten is really excellent, three good, three average, and three poor. Such sour wines cannot be drunk by educated palates. To put a ban on the improvement of wine would cause serious damage to the growers themselves.

In addition to draff and improved wines, we also have raisin-wines.

Raisins, stirred in water, chopped and left to ferment can produce quite excellent wines when used in conjunction with pure yeast strains.

It is a very good and drinkable wine, having all the character of a wine and representing serious competition to our German wines. It is immune to analysis and enormously cheap: 100 litres can be produced for 12 marks. This is therefore competition which has to be combatted by legislation.

Imagine the calamities which would befall the German people were raisin-wine to displace potato hooch!

Pure yeast strains can also be used to produce wine-like drinks from malt. A large factory is currently producing such malt-wine in Hamburg. We note here one observation made during the discussion of this speech by Privy Councillor Thiel who, amongst other things, said that the small vintners are not in a position to undertake the necessary improvements themselves and that only the large vineyard owners and wine-traders could do it. Meitzen wrote in similar vein in the 1860s:

Only the larger owners and prosperous growers can actually press, treat the wine in the cellar and then wait to sell it at a favourable moment. The number of poorer growers who do not possess the means to do this is currently 12-13,000 (in pre-1866 Prussia). They sell the grapes immediately after picking to obtain ready money quickly, and have often sold off the profits from the grapes against advances. The mass of grapes ceded to the dealers and wine-producing manufacturers by this class of grower in the autumn of 1864 was put at 69,405 cwts by the tax authorities. (Meitzen, *Der Boden und die landwirtschaftlichen Verhältnisse des preußischen Staates*, II, p. 275ff.)

The dependence of small growers on the dealers is bolstered by the uncertainty of grape yields. Not only, as Märcker noted, are there fluctuations in quality, so that only one crop in ten will produce an excellent and three in ten a poor vintage, but *quantities* vary equally as much.

Meitzen cites wine yields (in pails) for the period 1821 to 1864 in his above work (p. 277). Extracting some of the salient figures gives the following picture:

1821	24,868	1854	91,299
1822	469,211	1855	212,358
1828	816,228	1856	175,663
1829	271,088	1857	546,545
1830	41,970	1858	576,205
1834	850,467	1864	320,471

Under such conditions wine growing is a game of pure chance, in which the ultimate winner is the one with the largest – and annually replenishable – purse. A poor year will bankrupt a small under-capitalised grower, or drag him into hopeless debt-servitude.

The cooperative system is also supposed to be the saviour here. Cooperative cellars are intended to enable the small grower to pocket the profits both from improved wines and from trading in wine. But like the agricultural producers' cooperatives, these are inaccessible to the very small grower lacking in capital, and, like any other producers' cooperative, sooner or later degenerate into a capitalist form or become capitalist property. As such they merely accelerate the development by which the grower becomes increasingly dependent on the factory, on the cellar, and is transformed into a specialised worker within the wine industry.

But the same technical development which makes the grower ever more dependent on the manufacturer also makes the latter increasingly independent of the indigenous grower. Rapidly rising quantities of cheap foreign wine can be imported and improved: and increasing amounts of cheap raw material of other sorts from which wine can be made can also be obtained.

The revolutionising of wine production can be followed most clearly in France. Phylloxera and other blights caused the grape yield of the country to fall precipitously. Annual production was as follows:

Ten year average	Area of grape cultivation	Yield per hectare	Total	Consumption	Surplus or Deficit	Export of Wine
	hectares		hectolitres	hectolitres	hectolitres	hectolitres
1870-1879	2,364,175	22.4	52,935,956	38,100,000	+14,800,00	3,283,419
1880-1889	2,052,897	16.3	33,499,782	36,400,000*	-3,000,000*	2,538,198*
1887	1,919,878	13.6	25,365,441	34,000,000	-9,000,000	2,402,216
1891	1,763,374	17.0	30,139,000	not known	not known	2,044,000
* 1880-1884						

Although wine consumption has far exceeded production since the beginning of the 1880s, exports have barely fallen at all. This is partly explicable by the accumulated surpluses of previous years, and partly through the import of lower-quality wines which are improved and then either consumed in France itself or exported as fine French wines.

Wine imports (in thousands of hectolitres) were as follows:

From	1878	1889
Spain	1,347	7,052
Algeria	1	1,581
Portugal	16	875
Austria-Hungary	9	422
Turkey	8	194
Greece	0	146

The manufacture of synthetic wine has increased over the same period. According to official figures the total production of synthetic wine was as follows:

	Dried grapes hectolitres	*Draff* hectolitres	*Total* hectolitres
1880	2,320,000	2,130,000	4,450,000
1890	4,293,000	1,947,000	6,240,000

The true figures may be considerably higher. Only part of this industry is conducted above board.

The import of raisins into Germany increased from 12,994,000 kilos in 1886 to 32,846,000 in 1895. The lion's share of this increase is accounted for by wine manufacture. In addition, the import of fresh grapes rose from 3,381,000 in 1886 to 19,371,000 by 1895.

Moreover, foreign competition was also readying itself in this field, notably in Africa (Algiers, Tunisia, the Cape), in the USA (in particular California), and in Chile, Uruguay, Argentina, and Australia. In Algiers 17,600 hectares were planted with vines in 1878, 96,624 in 1889, and 116,000 in 1893 with a total yield of 3,800,000 hectolitres. In the USA 1,500,000 were produced in 1889, the same in Argentina, and

1,000,000 in Chile.

The surrogates and waste products dealt with so far are still raw materials – if of low value – produced by agriculture. However, industrial development has advanced so far in some areas that it can now fully produce materials which once had to be obtained from agriculture.

The best-known of these are the successes registered by chemistry in the processing of *tar*. This is not only used to obtain an uncommonly large and daily increasing number of completely new materials, which are especially important in medicine, but can also very cheaply produce materials previously furnished by agriculture.

Madder, for example, was an important commercial crop until the 1870s in some parts of Europe, especially Holland, Southern France and South Germany. The extraction of alizarin from coal-tar by Graebe and Liebermann in 1868, a substance increasingly used in aniline factories since 1870, spelt doom for madder cultivation.

Saccharin, another product of coal-tar, discovered in 1879 and produced en masse since 1886 was also initially expected to have a similar impact on sugar-beet cultivation. This has not come about, however. Although saccharin is 500 times sweeter than cane-sugar, it can only replace sugar as a sweetener, not as a nutrient. Nevertheless, it has pushed sugar out of a number of former uses, and thus acts to put a brake on the expansion of its consumption.

Alcohol can also be obtained from tar, although not yet in a form suitable for industrial exploitation.

The advances of *electrical engineering* appear to be of greater – and more disagreeable – significance for agriculture. It seems to have managed what steam-power never did – the almost complete expulsion of the horse from economic life.

Steam-power is best fitted to move large loads with little interruption to the operation. It has displaced the horse from the movement of loads over long distances. But the growth of large towns, stimulated and in fact caused by the railway system, required increasing short haulage which until recently could only be met by the horse. And despite its value in carrying out many tasks on the farm, steam-power has not been able to push the horse out of agriculture.

Electricity, whose power is easily divisible and transmissible over long distances, which can be switched on and off at will, whose motors are compact and easy to operate, is able to take over the functions of the horse as motive power both in transport and agriculture, and has already done so in many instances. Other technical advances are also working towards the displacement of the horse from transportation.

Electric trams, electric cars and buses are being joined by another type of motor vehicle: and the spread of human-propelled bicycles is making advances whose speed is not only an inexhaustible source of material for jokes and moral outrage, but also of fat profits for cycle manufacturers and dealers.

The effect of all this is clear: the demand for horses must fall, the production of horses must become unprofitable. In the USA, where the electric tram has already displaced the horse-drawn coach to a greater extent that in Europe, this has already happened. An English farmer, who knows the situation in America at first hand, writes:

> One has recently been hearing numerous complaints about the horse business. The production of horses seemed particularly unprofitable in America: horse producers told me that they often could not sell their own raised stock at all because of lack of buyers: the supply was bigger than the real need. This did not surprise me, since every small town in America now has an electric or cable railway instead of a horse-drawn way. The practical American has long since discovered that electricity is cheaper than the expensive keeping of horses. I was often astonished at the spread of electricity to even the smallest villages. (König, *Die Lage der englischen Landwirtschaft*, p. 408)

As a consequence, the number of horses is falling in America – despite agricultural expansion, population increase and urban growth. The price of horses has fallen even more swiftly than their number.

Horses and their value have changed as follows in the Union:

	Number	Value (US dollars)
1892	15,498,140	1,007,593,636
1893	16,206,802	992,225,185
1894	16,081,139	769,224,799
1895	15,893,318	576,730,580
1896	15,124,057	500,140,186
1897	14,364,667	452,649,396

The present value of the stock of horses in the Union is now less than half its 1892 value.

Growth in exports has accompanied the fall in domestic demand.

	1892	1896
Total	3,226 head	25,126 head
To England	467 head	12,022 head
To Germany	28 head	3,686 head

These figures are taken from the Yearbook of the United States Department of Agriculture (pp. 574, 580). According to the German Statistical Yearbook import figures of horses from the United States were as follows: 1890, 19; 1896, 4,285; 1897, 5,918. Imports from America have easily overtaken those from England, which themselves grew from 1,070 in 1890 to 2,719 in 1897.

At the same time technical progress in transport in Europe will also inevitably first limit the increase in the keeping of horses, and then bring about a reduction.

First affected are the horse-breeders, mostly large farmers; but breeding also remains an important source of income for middle and large peasants in some areas. In contrast, *small* farmers are barely threatened by the overproduction of horses. In this instance too, the smaller have the advantage over the larger – though not on grounds of technical superiority.

However, they are indirectly affected by the cut in the keeping of horses since this naturally implies a cut in the demand for feed. Bicycles, electric trams, motor vehicles and electric ploughs eat neither hay nor oats. And of the main grain crops, oats have so far been the least hit by overseas competition. In Great Britain the area under the main cereals has changed as follows (in acres):

	1867-72	1878-82	1895
Wheat	3,563,000	2,965,000	1,417,000
Barley	2,289,000	2,460,000	2,166,000
Oats	2,746,000	2,777,000	3,296,000

A slight drop in acreage was recorded in 1896, when the total area under oats fell to 3,095,000 acres. Whether this decline will be temporary, or already represents the beginnings of a progressive decline in the cultivation of oats is not yet decided. In any eventuality, such a development must occur sooner or later.

What is spared from overseas competition is threatened by industrial development at home.

The transformation of agricultural production into industrial production is still in its infancy. Bold prophets, namely those chemists gifted with an imagination, are already dreaming of the day when bread will be made from stones, and when all the requirements of a human diet will be assembled in chemical factories. Of course, such fantasising is not strictly relevant to our concern here.

But one thing is certain. Agricultural production has already been transformed into industrial production in a large number of fields, and a large number of others can be expected to undergo this transformation in the immediate future. No field of agriculture is completely safe. Every advance in this direction must inevitably multiply the pressures on farmers, increase their dependence on industry and undermine their security.

This does not mean that the time has arrived when one can reasonably speak of the imminent demise of agriculture. But wherever the modern mode of production has taken root, agriculture has lost its conservative character forever. Keeping to the old ways threatens farmers with certain ruin: they have to follow the development of technology, and adapt their farming to the new circumstances. There is no time to pause for breath. Farmers may think they have defeated one foe, but another will quickly rear its head. Economic life even in the open countryside, once trapped in such eternally rigid routines, is now caught up in the constant revolution which is the hallmark of the capitalist mode of production.

All those lacking either in extraordinary luck, extraordinary ruthlessness, extraordinary business acumen or extraordinary amounts of money will be sucked into the whirlpool.

The revolutionising of agriculture is setting in train a remorseless chase. Its participants are whipped on and on until they collapse exhausted – aside from a small number of especially aggressive and thrusting types who manage to clamber over the bodies of the fallen and join the ranks of the chief whippers, the big capitalists.

11
Prospects for the Future

The Mainsprings of Development

When bourgeois economics looks at agricultural development, it tends to focus on the ratio between large and small farms, as defined by area. And since this proportion has only minimally changed, it concludes that, unlike industry, agriculture is essentially conservative in character.

In contrast, the prevalent socialist position perceives the revolutionising element in agriculture in usury, in the indebtedness which divorces the peasant from his land and drives him from home and hearth.

We hope that we have succeeded in showing how inaccurate the first view is; but it would also be wrong to accept the second without qualification.

Peasant indebtedness is not unique to the capitalist mode of production. It is as old as commodity production, and was of importance as early as the era of Greece and Rome, when history ceased being legend and became verifiable in written records. Usurers' capital, on its own, can only make the peasantry discontented and rebellious; it does not represent a driving force towards a higher mode of production. Capitalism, the development of the competitive struggle between large and small farms and the advantages of large-scale production conferred by the ownership of more money, are required before usury can become credit, significantly raise the efficacy of capital and accelerate economic development. Nevertheless, this still applies more to industry than to agriculture. In agriculture, the credit system generally retained its pre-capitalist character. Most indebtedness on the part of land-ownership is still, by and large, not the product of the desire to extend or improve the farm; for the most part it is the consequence of distress and changes in ownership either by sale or inheritance. As such it not only fails to promote economic development but, by subtracting from the means available for making progress, actually obstructs it. Peasant indebtedness is not only not revolutionary, it is conservative. It is not a means for raising the peasant to a higher mode of production, but serves to trap the peasant mode of production in its previously unsatisfactory state.

Debt is not only more of a conservative than a revolutionary force as regards the *mode of production* in the countryside: it also has this effect on *property relations*. Naturally, the appearance of a new mode of production which disrupts peasant property can mean that indebtedness becomes a means for hastening its expropriation. This happened in Ancient Rome, when the surplus of slaves taken as prisoners of war favoured the development of a plantation economy. It was the case in England at the time of the Reformation when the rise in the wool trade led to the extension of sheep-grazing. However, the fact that indebtedness is merely a *lever* of expropriation, and not its driving force, can be seen from the fact that at the time of the Reformation in South Germany, the outcry over peasant indebtedness was even louder than in England. Nevertheless, this did not lead to any marked expropriation of the peasantry. The individuals owning peasant farms changed, but the farms themselves remained. Usury was more an instrument for sucking wealth out of the peasantry than reducing its numbers.

The transformation of rural relations of production which followed the French revolution and its offshoots also gave usurer's capital numerous opportunities to overturn property relations. It gave support to the tendency both towards the large farm, and towards the fragmentation of holdings. Peasant indebtedness helped large landowners to consolidate their estates and extend woodland. On the other hand, the growing rural population's increasing demand for living space and land led to the carving up of estates and the parcellisation of indebted farms – a process systematically pursued by many usurers. Both processes are still under way – although they have slowed down since the onset of overseas competition hit agricultural profitability, and the increase in the rural population lost momentum or stopped completely. Ground-rents and estate prices are no longer rising; and apart from a few favoured locations, such as near towns or factories, they have started to fall, and are threatened by even further falls. The advantage to be gained by expropriating indebted peasants diminishes. Forced sales not only threaten to lose usurer-capitalists their interest, but even part of their capital. Instead of hastening this moment, they try to postpone it by granting more time to pay interest, and often by advancing fresh loans – just as in England, where the agrarian crisis forced even the greediest and most callous landlords to allow time for the payment of rent arrears, to reduce future payments, and to assume direct responsibility for improvements.

The *Verein für Socialpolitik's* enquiry into peasant conditions included the following report by a Westphalian estate owner, a Herr Winkelmann:

Given the tenacity with which local peasants cling onto their birthright, many usurers find it more worthwhile to employ rural dwellers directly and divest them of everything above bare subsistence rather than go in for the dubious benefits of carving up the estate. In many of our poorer mountain districts, there are already simply no buyers. (Verein für Socialpolitik, *Bäuerliche Zustände in Deutschland*, II, p. 11)

Peasant indebtedness, in the main an obstacle to the revolutionising of rural relations of production, does not always imply the revolutionising of property relations. In fact the agrarian crisis is tending to push any revolutionary aspects into the background. But every major new change in the relations of production will find that the indebtedness of land-ownership will act as a lever to adapt property relations to the conditions of production.

But where should we look for the motive force necessitating such a change in the mode of production?

Our whole argument so far points to only one answer: *industry*. Industry is not only the motive force of its own development, but also of the development of agriculture. It was urban industry which destroyed the unity of industry and agriculture in the countryside, turning country dwellers into mere farmers, commodity-producers dependent on the vicissitudes of the market, and creating the possibility of their proletarianisation.

We also found that feudal agriculture had run into a blind alley from which it could not escape by its own efforts. It was urban industry which created the revolutionary forces capable of tearing down – in fact, forced to tear down – the feudal regime, opening new paths not only to industry but also agriculture.

It was industry which produced the scientific and technical conditions for the new, rational agriculture, revolutionised it through machinery and synthetic fertilisers, through the microscope and chemical laboratory, and in doing so established the technical superiority of the large capitalist farm over the small peasant farm.

This same economic development added a further distinction to the qualitative difference between the large and small farm: the distinction between farms simply providing for the subsistence of their attached household, and those producing mainly or substantially for the market. Although both became subordinated to industry, the process took different paths in each case. For the former, the need to acquire money developed through the sale of labour-power, either as wage-labour or in domestic industry: the small farmer became more and more dependent on industry and found himself more and more in the position of an industrial proletarian.

Commodity-producing farms were also increasingly forced to seek out a supplementary industrial occupation. Although the tendency towards reducing the costs of production is inherent in technical progress, this is more than offset by counter-tendencies in capitalist agriculture, tendencies which impose an increasing burden on it: the growth of ground-rents and lease prices, mortgage indebtedness, and its increase, or the fragmentation of holdings via the law of inheritance, the increasing exploitation of the country by the town as a result of militarism, taxation, absentee landlordism and so on, soil exhaustion, the growing susceptibility of cultivated plants and refined animal breeds to disease, and finally the increasing absorption of the rural labour-force into industry. Despite technical progress, these factors combine to raise production costs in agriculture. This initially leads to a general and steady increase in the price of food, but also to a sharpening of the antagonism between town and country, between land-ownership and the mass of consumers.

The same industrial development which creates these agricultural conditions effects a further transformation by expanding world trade and creating overseas food competition. Wherever land-ownership lacks sufficient power it receives the full force of such competition, as happened in England. But this also mitigates the antagonism between land-ownership and the mass of consumers.

Where land-ownership can recruit state power to its side, it will seek to restore production costs to their former levels by artificially increasing the price of food. Given the present level of world trade and international competition, this can never fully succeed and merely sharpens the already high degree of antagonism between land-ownership and the mass of consumers, especially the proletariat.

Agriculture also suffers alongside the landowner, especially where farmer and landowner are one and the same person. A great variety of methods are resorted to in an attempt to adapt production to the new circumstances – in one situation extensive pasturage, and in others intensive horticulture. But eventually, they come to see that the most rational means is the unification of industry and agriculture.

The modern mode of production – admittedly in two forms, industrial wage labour by small peasants and agricultural industry by the large farmer – therefore completes its dialectical process by returning to its starting point: *the transcendence of the division between industry and agriculture.* But whereas agriculture provided the central and leading force in primitive peasant farming, the roles are now reversed.

Capitalist large-scale industry now has the upper hand, and agriculture has to be the obedient and accommodating partner. What agriculture does is determined by the direction of industrial development. Should industry turn towards socialism, then agriculture must follow suit.

The number, the abilities, the intellect and the welfare of the population all decline in those areas which remain purely agricultural and closed to the incursions of industry, either because of inadequacies on the part of the localities themselves or of their inhabitants. And this is followed by the impoverishment of the soil and the degeneration of agricultural activity. In capitalist society, agriculture pure and simple ceases to constitute a prospering element in the community. And this extinguishes any hope that the peasantry could ever again recover its golden age.

And as with the agricultural population of the feudal period, these elements have also reached an impasse from which they cannot escape through their own efforts, and within which they cling together in ever greater anxiety and desperation. As at the end of the eighteenth century, their deliverance, and their path to further development, will be brought by the revolutionary population of the towns.

Whilst the capitalist mode of production hampers the formation of a revolutionary class in the countryside, it fosters one in the towns: it concentrates workers in one place and creates favourable conditions for their organisation, intellectual development and class struggle. It depopulates the open countryside, disperses rural workers over wide areas, isolates them, and robs them of the means for intellectual development and resistance to exploitation. In the towns, its concentration of capitals in fewer and fewer hands forges the conditions for the expropriation of the expropriators. In agriculture the concentration of enterprises is only one aspect: the capitalist mode of production also produces fragmentation. The advance of the capitalist mode of production sooner or later converts all industry into export industry in every country in which the domestic market is insufficient: industry produces for the entire world market. By the same token, it reduces pure agriculture to a trade which cannot even maintain the home market, and whose importance dwindles in relation to world production.

The more that capitalist forms of property and appropriation and capitalist interests come into contradiction with the needs of agriculture, the more they burden it, crush it down and the more desperate becomes agriculture's need to destroy capitalist forms and overthrow capitalist interests, the less agriculture is able to develop the forces and organisation needed to do this – the more it needs the impetus of the revolutionary forces of industry.

And such an impetus will not be lacking. The industrial proletariat cannot liberate itself without, at the same time, liberating the agricultural population.

Human society is an organism, not animal or vegetable in character but of its own specific type, although no less an organism. It is not merely an aggregation of individuals. And as an organism, it must be organised in a uniform manner. It would be absurd to imagine that one part of society can develop in one direction, and another part, of equal importance, in the opposite direction. Development can only go in one direction. However, each part of the organism does not have to generate the necessary force for its own development. It is enough that one portion of the organism produces the forces necessary to sustain the whole.

If the development of large-scale industry is proceeding towards socialism, and if it is the dominant power in present-day society, it will win over for socialism those areas unable to produce the preconditions for this transformation themselves and adapt them to its requirements.

Industry must do this, both in its own interests and in the interests of the uniformity and harmony of society.

No one could offer a worse prognosis for modern society than those bourgeois economists who triumphally proclaim that although the path of industry may lead to socialism, the path of agriculture leads to 'individualism'. Were this to prove correct, and agriculture were to become strong enough to defend itself from socialism and industry lack the strength to sweep this 'individualism' aside, this would signify not the salvation but rather the destruction of society: it would mean a state of *permanent civil war*.

Fortunately for human society, this sheet anchor of capitalist exploitation has no foundation on which to fasten itself.

The Elements of Socialist Agriculture

We begin from the axiom that the development of modern industry necessarily leads to socialism. It would require an entire book to provide the proof of this: and such proof has already been furnished in the great basic works of scientific socialism, and in particular in Marx's *Capital*. Our intention here is simply to indicate a little more concretely how the conquest of political power by the proletariat, and the consequent socialisation of industry, must affect agriculture.

Our choice of the term socialisation rather than nationalisation of industry is quite deliberate. We disregard the question here as to whether a socialist society can be a state. Initially, it certainly will be a state: in fact, state power should function as the most powerful lever of social transformation. However, to be exact, this transformation does not imply the *nationalisation* but rather merely the *socialisation* of production as a whole together with the means of production. They will cease to be private property and become social property; but which type of social association they will be employed in depends on their social significance. Means of production serving local needs, such as bakeries, power stations, trams, are more suitable for municipal rather than state ownership. Some means of production (including, of course, the means of transport) have an international significance and can become international property – the Suez and Panama Canals for example. The decisive means of production will naturally pass into state ownership, since only the modern state can create the framework for a socialist society, and produce the conditions within which municipal or cooperative establishments can become the limbs of socialist production.

If socialisation only initially embraces large-scale capitalist industry, then those farmers unable to live solely from agriculture and forced to take up a supplementary occupation will evidently be transformed into workers for society, without the slightest encroachment on their property. For example, the socialisation of mines and brickworks will transform hundreds of thousands of dwarf-holders, forced to work in these industries to cover their agricultural losses, from capitalist wage-labourers into workers for society. On the other hand, the simple socialisation of sugar-factories will transform beet growers from being the specialised workers of a capitalist into the specialised workers of a social establishment without any direct expropriation. The same applies to the relationship between dairy producers and the butter and cheese factories which are currently having to assume an increasingly capitalist character. However, by concentrating large industrial establishments in a single hand, socialisation must also transform farmers who presently, under free competition, come independently to market into social specialised workers. The unification of beer breweries into one hand will place the hop and malt producers in the same relationship to the breweries as beet growers will be to sugar-factories. The same will happen to the relationship between the grain producers and socialised mills, and between wine-growers and socialised wine cellars.

The dependence of rural producers on large-scale establishments of this type is already considerable; their transformation from capitalist into social property must, therefore, represent as much a deliverance for the farmer, especially the small farmer, as the socialisation of mines will for the dwarf-holder who performs wage-labour.

The growing industrialisation of agriculture is accompanied by the increasing independence of ground-rents vis-à-vis capital-profit, and of landed property in relation to agriculture, on one hand in the form of the tenant system and on the other in the form of mortgage debt. A proletarian regime must, of necessity, socialise landed property in both these forms. The greater the development of large-scale land-ownership (in countries with tenant farming) and the more that mortgage debt becomes concentrated in a few hands, the more this process will be welcomed as a deliverance by farmers – just as is the case with the socialisation of the agricultural industries.

Finally, a proletarian regime must also socialise large-scale agricultural establishments based on the exploitation of wage-labour. Although the large establishment is not as dominant in agriculture as it is in industry, it would be utterly misplaced to expect the peasant farm to supplant the large farm. In capitalist agriculture, large and small farms provide the conditions for each other's existence.

The independent peasant farm has become untenable: it can only continue by being associated with a large establishment. If a nearby large industrial enterprise employs peasants as wage-labourers, or specialised workers, they will become its slaves. Where no such establishment exists, the peasant needs a large agricultural enterprise to avoid sinking into extreme poverty. Although the large farm suffers more from the flight from the land than the small farm, the same process is beginning to break up the peasant family, which lacks the means to compensate for the loss of labour by mechanisation. And although the agrarian crisis tends to expropriate the undercapitalised large landowner before the peasant, the constantly accelerating advance of the accumulation of capital will supply sufficient capitalists able to make a profit by combining agricultural and industrial exploitation – something only possible within the context of a large, not a peasant, farm.

So, although we should not expect small farms to be rapidly swallowed up by large, there are fewer reasons to expect the opposite process to take place. In fact, statistics show only a minimal shift in the proportions of individual farms by size, shifts often explicable by changes in the mode of farming – greater intensity for example – rather than economic decline. While the proportion of establishments with more than 50 hectares of agriculturally used land fell from 33.00 per cent to 32.56 per cent in Germany between 1882 and 1895, that is not quite half a per cent, in France the proportion of establishments with more than 40 hectares of cultivated area increased from 44.96 per cent to 45.56 per cent between 1882 and 1892, that is by over half a per cent.

These are insignificant differences. But in both France and Germany the large farm occupied a very substantial share of the land – almost a third in Germany, and almost a half in France. However, only 142,000 farmers (out of 5,672,000, 2.51 per cent) had an interest in such establishments in France in 1892; by 1892 the figure had fallen to 139,000 (out of 5,703,000, 2.42 per cent). In Germany the figure for 1882 was 66,614 (out of 5,267,000 farmers, 1.20 per cent) and for 1893 67,185 (out of 5,558,317, 1.21 per cent). There is no doubt at all that such establishments would pass into social ownership when the continuation of the wages system becomes impossible. This alone would put over a third to a half of agricultural land at the disposal of society.

The large area occupied by large farms, whose capitalist character is steadily becoming more and more developed, the growth of the tenant and mortgage system, and the industrialisation of agriculture, are the elements preparing the ground for the socialisation of agricultural production which is just as certain a product of the rule of the proletariat as the socialisation of industrial production with which it is progressively merging into a higher unity.

The unfolding of the technical aspects of socialist agriculture is proceeding in step with the social. We have seen how modern science and modern technology have taken hold of agriculture and are transforming it; and how the modern large farm has reached its apogee in the capitalist latifundium which we considered in detail in Chapter 7. But just as the perfected techniques of English agriculture in the last century could only flourish on those few estates not subject to the destructive force of feudal property, so modern techniques can also develop only on a small number of isolated estates. Their generalisation requires another social revolution to sweep away those obstacles to development which so stunt agriculture after any short upswing. The victory of the proletariat will mean the suppression of militarism and centralisation in large cities. The socialisation of large farms will release them from the burdens of the law of inheritance and absentee landlordism. The replacement of wage slavery by the labour of free cooperators will also provide the large agricultural establishment with that crucial element of prosperity whose current absence is the greatest obstacle to their development: *sufficient, intelligent, willing and careful workers.*

The flight from the land will cease once workers find sufficient work on the land able to match the level of cultural conditions and welfare found with work in the towns. And its cessation will be all the more likely, the stronger the link between industry and agriculture, and the more that the commodity-production and commerce which gravitate towards centralisation in the cities are replaced by production by and for society, creating a more even spread of the means of production and allowing an end to be put to the murderous concentrations of population in the cities. The unity of industry and agriculture, which finds its first miserable renaissance in the industrial labour of small peasants and cottagers, which appears more fully developed in the supplementary industrial occupation of the farmer who processes their own raw materials, and which reaches its present high point in the modern latifundium, will become the general law for social production as a whole.

The independent small agricultural establishment is now losing its last foothold. We have seen the three forms under which it has persisted: supplementary industrial work, wage-labour on a large farm, and where neither of these is available and the small peasant remains a mere farmer, with the large farm existing not as an opportunity for work but as a competitor, through overwork and underconsumption – as Marx puts it, through barbarism. The passage of capitalist enterprises into social property will mean the dependence of the small farm of both the first and second types on social production. They will either be absorbed by it or become appendages to it.

Independent, purely agricultural establishments will then lose any attraction for their owners. The position of the urban proletariat is already so superior to that of small peasant barbarism that the younger generation of peasants is just as susceptible to the flight from the land as rural wage-labourers. Once socialist latifundia start emerging all around them, cultivated not by poverty-stricken wage slaves but by prospering cooperatives of free and happy individuals, the flight from the parcel-holding into the town will be replaced by an even more rapid flight from the parcel into the large cooperative establishment. Barbarism will have been driven from its last bastions, where it still rules in splendid isolation in the midst of civilisation.

The large socialist establishment will not bring about the expropriation of small peasants but rather their deliverance from the hell in which private property now chains them.

Social development is currently proceeding in the same direction in agriculture as it is in industry. Social needs and social conditions are pushing in both areas towards the large social establishment, whose highest form unifies agriculture and industry in one cohesive unit.

Part II
Social Democratic Agrarian Policy

12
Does Social Democracy Need an Agrarian Programme?

Off to the Land!

If there is any clear conclusion to be drawn from the developments presented in Part I, it is that industry will become the determining force in society as a whole: that agriculture will lose in significance relative to industry, will increasingly have to concede territory to industry and will become more dependent on industry in those spheres left to it. Social Democracy is not only entitled to draw its hopes for victory from the growing power of the proletariat, but also from the growing power of industry in society.

But to conclude from this that Social Democracy, or if one prefers, the proletariat struggling for its emancipation, can afford to ignore agriculture would be to go too far. The proletariat is the heir to present-day society and has every interest in ensuring that its inheritance is as rich as possible. Irrespective of the relationship between industry and agriculture, the land will always remain the basis of human existence; its productivity will always be a decisive factor in determining how much labour a society has to expend in order to maintain itself; and its character will always be crucial in determining the physical and intellectual character of the population.

The well-being of the society of the future is not the only reason why the proletariat should direct its attention to agriculture, however. The demands of the present are even more pressing. The proletariat cannot be indifferent to rises or falls in the price of food as wages do not follow these fluctuations quite as precisely as the iron law of wages might lead one to suppose. And the tempo of the proletarian class struggle is by no means unaffected by whether the rural population has a poor standard of living or represents an ignorant and obtuse mass.

Even if Social Democracy wanted to confine itself to industrial matters alone, the growing importance of agrarian issues for the whole of public life in all modern nations would make this impossible. It is a curious phenomenon that agriculture's *political significance* is in inverse proportion to its *economic significance* relative to industry, not only in areas dominated by Junkerdom, but also in peasant areas; not only in East

Elbia, but also in Bavaria – both where absolutism and where democracy reign, not only in Russia, Austria and Germany but also in France and Switzerland. This apparent contradiction between economic and political significance is explained once we recall that private property in land enters into an irresolvable contradiction with the existing mode of production much earlier than private property in the other means of production, generating unsustainable and unbearable conditions long before the latter. The classes affected by this process are precisely those who were once the former most solid pillars of the prevailing political and social order; some of these are members of the ruling class directly, whilst others are preserved by the ruling classes in their own interests. Hardly surprising, therefore, that agrarian issues number amongst the most taxing questions occupying the politically most influential sections of the civilised nations. Such elements are not concerned with saving agriculture so much as with saving those 'loyal classes' whose conditions of existence can no longer be reconciled with modern conditions of production. Their salvation of course implies reconciling the irreconcilable, and does not gain in rationality by the fact that the intellectual and economic conditions for a higher mode of production are notably less developed in agriculture than in industry.

In view of this, it is hardly surprising that the more the agrarian movement grows, the more it tends to spawn fanciful quack remedies which are taken more and more seriously by the ruling classes. Anyone who wants to give practical help to the rural population needs great clarity and strength of conviction to remain firm when confronted with this agrarian witches' dance. Social Democracy, for this reason alone, needs to possess an unequivocal view on agrarian questions: indifference would mean abandoning the proletarian masses in the countryside to the agrarian tricksters and conjurors.

It is this concern which explains the increasing attention paid to agrarian issues by Social Democratic parties in all the civilised nations over the last few years. But the unique lack of ripeness of the situation in agriculture has also made itself felt here too. Social Democracy did not initially take up agrarian issues for reasons of fundamental principle, but for reasons of political practice – considerations of electoral agitation. It needed to offer the rural population something, needed to make practical demands which might enlist the interest of the country-dweller in the socialist movement. Attempts were made to propose Social Democratic *agrarian programmes* before coming to terms with fundamental principles of any Social Democratic *agrarian politics*. And the search for a programme in the absence of clearly understood principles will always be a tentative, groping affair, producing short-lived and unreliable results, regardless of the skill and perception of its instigators.

The need for Social Democracy to adopt a clear position on its agrarian policy has been generally acknowledged in its ranks. By contrast, there is no unanimity as to the necessity for an agrarian programme.

A specific agrarian programme is usually regarded as a programme of measures in the interests of the *peasantry*. No particular programme is needed to advance the interests of the agricultural wage-labourer: all previous Social Democratic programmes already encompass this. But making the specific interests of the peasantry into an issue for Social Democracy requires a specific agrarian programme.

This issue is widely known to have caused deep divisions of opinion within Social Democracy.

The *protection of the peasantry* [*Bauernschutz*] has been advocated as a necessary complement to the *protection of the worker* [*Arbeiterschutz*]. The proletarian in the countryside is the peasant: and Social Democracy is the party of the proletarian class struggle against capital. The roots of its strength are not in its ultimate objectives but its immediate demands. Just as Social Democracy defends the urban proletariat against its capitalist exploiter, the *entrepreneur*, it also has the task of protecting the rural proletarian from its exploiter, the *usurer*. It must oppose the impoverishment of the peasant no less vigorously and with just as much purposive engagement as it does the impoverishment of the town labourer.

We now consider this argument.

Peasant and Proletarian

The peasants' standard of living is often undeniably proletarian, and sometimes sub-proletarian. But this is far from implying that their class interests have become proletarian.

The modern proletarian is not characterised by poverty. Although the poor have not always been with us, they have been with us for many thousands of years. In contrast, the Social Democratic proletarian movement is a specific product of the last century, the product of a proletariat never before seen in world history, at least as a mass phenomenon.

One hallmark of the modern proletariat is its important role in the production process. The proletarian is the foundation of what is now the decisive mode of production, the capitalist mode. This distinguishes the proletarian from the lumpenproletarian of both ancient and modern times.

Modern proletarians are also by no means as utterly lacking in means as lumpenproletarians. The latter are lacking in everything, but this is most acutely felt in the shortage of food and other means of consumption. They are not overbothered by the lack of means of production. Lumpenproletarians are excluded from the sphere of production anyway, and often exhibit little enthusiasm to be admitted to it. But although they don't want to work, they do want to live – and can only do so if those owning the means of production will share with them. What social aspirations lumpenproletarians have tend towards an ideal of communism of the means of consumption, not of means of production, a communism of division, not combination – an aim which, in reality, leads to plunder where social circumstances facilitate acts of violence, and to beggary where this is impossible.

In contrast, the lack of means which marks out the modern wage-proletariat is simply that of the *means of production*. This can, but does not have to, be associated with a lack of means of consumption. Modern wage-labourers remain proletarian so long as they are not in possession of their means of production, regardless of how satisfactory their status might be as a consumer, and what they – as a consumer – might own, be it jewellery, furniture or even a small house. In fact, far from making them unfit for proletarian class struggle, improving their position as a consumer enables them to struggle all the more vigorously. Proletarian class struggle is not the outcome of poverty, but of the antithesis between the proletarian and the owner of the means of production. The establishment of social peace will not be brought about by the overcoming of poverty – even if this were to prove possible – but by overcoming this antithesis. And this can only occur when the working population regains possession of its means of production.

This brings us to an additional characteristic of modern wage-proletarians. They work not on individual but on social means of production, means of production of a scale which can only be utilised by a society of workers. Two types of ownership of such means of production are possible. Ownership by individuals who necessarily exploit the workers they employ: this is capitalist ownership. Or cooperative ownership. But under the rule of private property in the means of production, the cooperative form can never become general. Assuming that they succeed, all such attempts sooner or later take a capitalist direction. Cooperative ownership of the means of production can only become general in the form of social, that is socialist, property in the means of production. Other factors also push towards the socialisation of the means of production. However, we confine ourselves here to those arising out of the class interests of the proletariat and which cause proletarian class struggle to take a socialist direction by its very nature.

Finally, we should also mention a fourth characteristic of the modern wage-proletarian, already referred to elsewhere in this work: separation from the employer's household. Wage-labourers of earlier epochs usually constituted an appendage to their employer's household, and belonged to their family, not merely as workers but as human beings. They were dependent on the employer in all their activities, even outside work. In contrast, the modern wage-proletarian belongs to no one once outside work. And the more that the capitalist mode of production develops and sweeps away such feudal remnants, the more proletarians are able to confront capitalists as free and equal individuals outside work.

It is these factors which have made the modern proletariat into the powerful driving force of the socialist movement.

These characteristic features are by no means all present when we turn to the peasantry. Reference is sometimes made to the mortgage creditor who is the real owner of the peasant's farm: but the relationship between peasant and mortgage creditor is not that of capitalist to wage-labourer, but of landowner to entrepreneur. Mortgages no more make peasants into proletarians than renting a factory, rather than buying it, makes the manufacturer into a proletarian. The peasant remains the owner of their means of production, their tools and implements, and stock – in short, their inventory. This can of course be pledged against a debt: nevertheless, the peasant still has to exercise the functions of an entrepreneur, and as such consequently remains in an *antithesis* to the proletariat, in the same way that any manufacturer producing with borrowed capital, and not owning any of their means of production, still functions as an industrial capitalist in a relationship of conflict to the proletariat.

This antagonism is most marked amongst peasants reliant on the exploitation of wage-labour, the big peasants.

In fact, as long as workers' movements confine themselves to the towns and direct their efforts against urban capitalists, large farmers are inclined to be sympathetic to them. English and later Prussian large landowners took a benevolent attitude towards the socialist movement in its earlier days and preached an alliance of wage-labour and ground-rent against profit on capital. This changed once the socialist movement threatened to gain a foothold amongst agricultural workers, in fact once the increase in industrial wages began to draw rural workers into the towns, leaving those left behind more demanding. Today the Prussian Junkers are more implacable opponents of Social Democracy than even the 'Manchester Men'. They no longer follow the colours of

Wagener, but of *Stumm*. And the big peasants are not far behind.

And even if we were to find districts in Germany in which the larger peasants still took a benign attitude to the workers' movement, and believed that each had some interests in common, this would not prove that these strata could be won for Social Democracy if only the right approach were used. It would merely show that the workers' movement is still too weak to have any positive effect on the position of rural workers in such districts. It would be a proof of backwardness, not of the first signs of progress.

The contradiction between proletarians and middle peasants who do not employ wage-labourers, or at least not in any great numbers, and who essentially maintain their farms with family labour, but still produce food for market, is less acute than that between the larger peasants and proletarians. Although there is no contradiction between exploiter and exploited another contradiction nevertheless remains: that between the waged proletariat and all those who produce for the market – the contradiction between *buyer* and *seller*.

Despite this, one area of harmonious interest has been unearthed inasmuch as the worker is said to be the best customer for rural produce. And the higher their wages, the more they can consume. Peasants therefore have an interest in high wages, and share identical interests with the proletariat.

Such arguments are not new: they are repeatedly employed to discover harmonies of interest. Elements friendly to workers' interests advise manufacturers to raise wages as the best method of extending their internal market and avoiding problems in selling their output. At the same time elements friendly to manufacturers advise workers on the idiocy of wanting to force manufacturers into paying higher wages. This would either raise food prices, so that workers will lose with one hand what they gained with the other, or it will reduce profits. And the higher profits are, the more capital will be accumulated, and the more that is accumulated, the faster the growth in the demand for labour – the most powerful means for raising wages. Workers therefore have good reason to avoid anything which might lead to a diminution of profit, such as strikes and so on. Both workers and manufacturers share an identical interest in higher profits.

Both these arguments are right, inasmuch as capitalist society, like any other society, is a unitary organism in which damage to one part inevitably produces some disagreeable effects in the other parts. But this fact does not abolish class contradictions: it does not absolve any class of the necessity to assert its own interests and attack the interests of its opponents in the struggle against the opposing classes. The contradiction between the harmony of interests of the various classes, undeniable to some extent in the final analysis, and the much more crucial and decisive antagonistic clash of class interests simply shows that capitalist society is an extremely imperfect organism which requires the squandering of much effort for it to fulfil its task.

The relationship between the individual classes and the moving force in capitalist society is not a product of the highly mediated harmony of their interests, or is so only a very limited extent, but is rather, and primarily, determined by their direct class antagonisms.

This also applies to the relationship between the sellers and the buyers of food. Their antagonism is too immediate to be softened by the much more remote interests of the seller in the purchasing power of the buyer.

Country-dwellers want to sell their products as dearly as possible, and workers want to buy them as cheaply as possible. What does it profit the former, if the latter use their high wages to buy margarine, American bacon, Australian meat and conserves of every description! Meanwhile farmers try to suppress any competition which might be welcomed by the worker, and artificially push up the prices of their products.

No amount of preaching of, albeit, an intelligently devised but nonetheless intangible harmony of interests can bridge this conflict of interests.

What decides whether a farmer is ready to join the ranks of the proletariat in struggle is not whether he is starving or indebted, but whether he comes to market as a seller of labour-power or as a seller of food. Hunger and indebtedness by themselves do not create a community of interests with the proletariat as a whole; in fact they can sharpen the contradiction between peasant and proletarian once this hunger has been stilled and debts repaid, should food prices rise and make it impossible for workers to enjoy cheap food.

Nevertheless, the peasantry and the proletariat do have some interests in common, alongside those antagonistic interests, as we shall discover later. And occasionally their common interests can outweigh their antagonisms and lead to political cooperation between peasants and proletarians. But irrespective of how often they might fight together, as a rule they must march separately: and the allies of today can become tomorrow's enemies.

But isn't it the case that the antagonism between the sellers of food and the sellers of labour-power inevitably spells disaster for the latter? Won't the events of 1848 be repeated and the hobnailed boots of the peasants and sons of peasants turn against the proletariat and trample it underfoot?

Let us consider this hobnailed spectre a little more closely. Perhaps, like many other phantoms, it will lose its nightmarish character once we tackle it head on.

The memory of 1848 may be conjured up. But 50 years of capitalist rule have passed by since then. Have they had no effect?

In 1848 the agricultural population accounted for around three-quarters of the total population of Germany: it now amounts to just over one third, to be more precise 35.7 per cent, 18.5 million out of a population of 51,800,000. As late as 1882 it was still 700,000 more, amounting to over two fifths, 42.51 per cent of the population, 19,225,000 out of 45,222,000.

In the Kingdom of Saxony, it does not even amount to 14 per cent (in 1882 it was 19 per cent): and in the country of Zwickau it is only 10 per cent of the population as against 14 per cent in 1882. It is most strongly represented in North Germany in Posen (58 per cent as against 64 per cent in 1882), and in Southern Germany in Lower Bavaria; the German Vendée, the only major district of the German Empire in which it has not fallen, or only barely perceptibly since 1882. In 1882 it amounted to 61.5 per cent of the total population, and in 1895 61 per cent.

The agricultural population is larger in France, but there too it fell from 51.4 per cent to 45.5 per cent of the population between 1876 and 1891.

	Total population	Percentage of agricultural population
1876	36,906,000	51.4
1881	37,672,000	48.4
1886	38,219,000	46.6

We are rapidly approaching the situation in England where the number of those employed on the land in 1890 only amounted to *10 per cent* of all economically active persons.

A relative, if not absolute, reduction in the number of those employed in agriculture has also taken place in the United States, although unfortunately agriculture is counted together with the fishing and mining industries. Were it to be recorded separately, its decline would certainly be more marked. In 1880, it accounted for 50.25 per cent of all economically active persons (7,405,000), and in 1890, 44.28 per cent (8,334,000). In the North Atlantic states, only 22.6 per cent of all economically active persons was engaged in agriculture in 1890, although the proportion remained at over 60 per cent in the Southern states.

Not all those employed in agriculture are sellers of food. A good number also sell labour-power. In 1895 the situation in agriculture was as follows in the German Reich.

	Economically active	Dependants and servants	Total
Self-employed farmers	2,576,725	6,900,096	9,476,821
Wage-labourers (hands, maids, day-labourers, clerks etc.)	5,715,967	3,308,519	9,024,486
Total	8,292,692	10,208,615	18,501,307

The population living from wage-labour in agriculture equals that of self-employed farmers and their dependants.

And not all the independent producers live solely from the sale of produce. Of the 2,530,539 independent producers in agriculture proper (excluding horticulture, forestry etc.) 504,465 had a supplementary occupation.

The position of the independent farmer looks no better when we turn from occupational to farm statistics. Out of 5,558,317 owners of agricultural establishments, only 2,499,130 are independent farmers: 717,037 are non-independent farmers, and the rest belong with other occupations, including no less than 1,495,240 in industry.

Two and a half million independent farmers are therefore set against 6 million agricultural wage labourers on one hand; and 3 million owners of agricultural establishments, whose main interest is in an area other than agriculture.

The peasants therefore no longer constitute the majority in the countryside: they are counterbalanced by a large stratum of agricultural workers, whose interests on all essential points are identical with those of wage-labourers.

Of course, the independent peasantry is still much stronger in some areas than these average figures indicate. For example, of the 20 German Administrative Districts with the highest middle peasant holdings (5 to 20 hectares), 13 are in Bavaria alone. Whereas only 30 hectares per 100 hectares of agricultural land are accounted for by holdings of middle peasants in the German Reich as a whole, such holdings account for 60 to 70 per cent in these localities. The peasants' hobnailed boots can unquestionably still sometimes tread very hard on the toes of the proletariat in such areas. But they are a long way from trampling it down completely or even getting near to seriously endangering it once it begins to march in full strength, unified under one banner. The proletariat not only has all the advantages of high intellect conferred by town life, better organisation and training of its forces and the economic preponderance of industry over agriculture. It now also has numerical superiority.

The proletariat is now the most numerous class in the German Reich. Disregarding the army, public officials and so forth, and the unemployed, in 1895 there were 20,674,239 economically active persons and servants. Of these the following can be counted as being in the proletariat:

Service	1,339,318
Wage-labourers in agriculture, industry and commerce	10,746,711
Domestic servants	432,491

Of the remaining 8,155,719 economically active persons, many still fell within the scope of the proletariat; the 2 million employed family members, the 600,000 white-collar workers and the 5.5 million self-employed, who are often only nominally independent and in reality serve as wage-labourers for capital, as in domestic industry for example.

In the face of such figures, still rapidly moving to the advantage of the proletariat, it is simply anachronistic to conjure up the memory of 1848. Once Social Democracy has 'landed' the entire mass of the proletariat, together with those apparently independent farmers and industrialists who are, in fact, wage-labourers for capital, no power will be able to withstand it. The main task of Social Democracy is, and remains: to win over this mass, to organise it politically and economically, to elevate its intellectual and moral level and bring it to the point where it can assume its inheritance – the capitalist mode of production.

This 'landing' is no easy task, however, especially in the countryside.

The development of the proletariat, the growth in its political and economic power, its intellectual and moral elevation, will not take place, and cannot take place, as swiftly in the open countryside as they can in the centres of industry.

The *Communist Manifesto* already spelt out the factors working in this direction, and we do not need to dwell on them here. Pre-capitalist commodity-production begins by herding together large masses of propertyless wage-labourers in a few towns. Their power and intellectual development grow along with the power and intellectual development of the towns. But the journeymen were still half unfree; they belonged to their master's household, and their work and the boundaries of the household isolated them from each other. Only the conviviality of holidays and feast days brought them together. In contrast, the capitalist mode of production unifies wage-labourers in large masses, not only in individual towns, whose size far exceeds those of the feudal period, but also in enormous places of work within these towns: the capitalist mode of production itself organises and disciplines its wage-labourers. But they no longer belong to their employer's household. Outside of work they are economically completely independent free individuals with their own household.

Capitalist development has a different effect in the countryside. Instead of bringing people together, it disperses them. At a certain stage of its development, it not only leads to a relative but also to an absolute depopulation of the countryside. And those who are abducted are precisely the land's most assiduous, capable, energetic and intelligent elements. The weakest and most helpless remain behind. Depopulation is accompanied by intellectual desolation.

Improvements in education, very problematic in the countryside, and advances in the means of communication which bring books and newspapers to the country dweller, can only offset this process to a limited extent. Although the rural population now reads more than they used to, especially in winter, the newspapers which they get hold of are usually of the most reactionary type, judging modern society against long-outmoded models, and able to do more violence to those facts which do not fit in with these models, the more naive and ignorant their readership. Apart from the Bible, the product of long-gone millennia, their reading matter consists of the worst kind of penny-dreadful, distorting reality in the crudest way imaginable.

Such literature is not only utterly unfitted for clarifying anyone's perception of reality or for unlocking the essence of modern society: it can actually produce total confusion, reinforcing rather than reducing the effects of isolation.

This alone makes it difficult to organise the rural proletariat and teach it an understanding of and interest in the aspirations of the urban proletariat. But these more superficial hindrances are joined by much more massive, and deeper rooted, obstructions.

Although the rural proletariat may share the same interests as the industrial proletariat on all essential matters, it by no means exhibits all the characteristics of the modern proletariat. This applies, in particular, to house-servants (*Gesinde*), and to the *Instleute, Heuerleute* and *Einlieger*.

All these types of rural wage-labourers still live under feudal conditions, as members or appendages of another's household. They are subject to the discipline of their master outside of work: their pleasures, their reading and even their associations are subject to his control. They have no right of combination, even where this is not actually denied them in law; they are not allowed to read a newspaper which their master finds disagreeable, and are often instructed what to choose. Not even the possibility of eventual independence once they have saved enough serves to distinguish them from the serfs and slaves of preceding periods, since these too could also buy their freedom.

Excessively bad treatment may lead such a class to outbreaks of desperation and rebellion but its situation does not favour the waging of an organised, resolute and tenacious class struggle.

Agricultural labourers with property are better off in this respect. Possession of their own farm does not put them above the proletariat, since it is only an appendage of the household. And we already observed that the hallmark of the modern proletarian is not lack of the means of consumption, but of means of production for the market for commodities. A miner remains a proletarian, even though he may have a small house, a little potato plot and cow, as does the dwarf-holder as long as his farm merely serves his own household.

Although possession of a farm does not prevent dwarf-holders from *being* proletarians, it certainly makes it much more difficult for them to feel like proletarians. Their past, their present and their future conspire to bombard them with reasons why they should stand on the side of the independent farmers. Tradition alone, which has much greater force in the country than in the town, will incline a small cottager and cow owner towards an ancestral peasant class consciousness rather than the novelty of proletarian class consciousness. But peasant consciousness also draws strength from the present.

In theory the small farmer produces for his own consumption; his need for money is met through the sale of labour power, not agricultural produce. But although this is by and large correct in theory, life itself does not deal in the sharp distinctions we require for science. Any theoretician attempting to investigate the fundamental laws underlying these phenomena may, in fact has to, neglect a number of gradations: needless to say, the application of such laws to practical life demands that such gradations be taken into account. Small farmers whose farm is sufficient to supply the household with necessary food, and even farmers whose farm is not completely able to do so, will usually sell part of their produce; pigs or geese are fattened, eggs, milk, vegetables sold if there is a nearby market such as a town or factory. Such farmers are by no means indifferent to the price of food and have a strong interest in high prices for the produce they sell.

Where workers are paid in kind, agricultural workers also have an interest in high food prices even as wage-earners. If they receive part of their wages in rye, which they sell, they have an interest in high rye prices and hence high rye duties too. They appear on the market not only as sellers of labour-power, but also as sellers of food.

But alongside all these past traditions and current interests, the interests of the future are perhaps the most powerful force for instilling peasant feelings and thoughts into the dwarf-holder. Although individuals live in the present, they work for the future, and Social Democracy, the party of the future, is only too well aware of how massively this can influence their thoughts and actions.

The industrial wage-labourer who still believes that handicrafts have a future, or the journeyman who fancies himself as a future master, is different to one who has abandoned any hope of ever becoming independent within the present-day mode of production. Similarly, the dwarf-holder who has given up hope of prospering and becoming independent on his own farm is different to the one who harbours hopes of one day ceasing to be a dwarf-holder, of saving enough out of his wages to buy sufficient land to become a fully independent peasant. Although he might still be a cottager who has to buy food, he regards himself as a prospective peasant who will sell it.

Bourgeois economists therefore regard the nourishing and sustaining of this hope as an important task: it is the most powerful bond tying the most numerous of the working classes on the land to land-ownership and separating them from the proletariat. Such economists therefore plead with even the large landowners not to buy up all available plots in their blind greed for land but to leave sufficient, if not to allow all agricultural workers to become peasants – where would one get wage-labourers from otherwise? - but to nurture the hope that each might one day become an independent peasant. It is just this hope which makes them all the more eager, willing and subservient.

One of the most eager advocates of large landowners giving workers opportunities to buy land is von der Goltz. However, he notes,

> My view is by no means that one should seek to make all agricultural workers into landowners: or at least this is an aim which does not need to be seriously considered for the present in the Eastern Provinces. The *prospect* of one day becoming a landowner makes the *Instleute* industrious, thrifty, economical, holds them back from excesses, and also benefits the employer. (Goltz, *Die ländliche Arbeiterklasse und der preußische Staat*, p. 215)

Roscher echoes this view.

> The existence of small farms is particularly useful in that it offers an unbroken ladder filling the gaps between day-labourers and large peasants. The prospect of advance which such a ladder offers if one is industrious, skilled and thrifty both appeases and stimulates. (Roscher, *Nationalökonomie des Ackerbaus*, p. 176)

Two souls inhabit the breast of the dwarf-holder: a peasant and a proletarian. The conservative parties all have cause to strengthen the peasant soul: the interest of the proletariat runs in the opposite direction – along with the interests of social development and the dwarf-holders themselves. Consider the numerous examples of peasant underconsumption and overwork in Part I: the fact that the agricultural wage-labourer is better off than the independent small farmer, that misery begins when the peasant shackles himself to the land, should leave no doubt that we should not seek to elevate dwarf-holders as *persons*, to raise them from barbarism to civilisation, by lifting them out of wage-labour and into the peasantry. In fact, nothing could be more dangerous and cruel than to awaken illusions amongst them as to the future of the small peasant farm.

But an agrarian programme which promises effective protection for the peasantry does just this. Such a programme inevitably strikes a death blow at the proletarian soul in the dwarf-holders, and leaves the field free for the peasant in their heart. It severs the bond linking them to the industrial proletariat, and gives new life to all those factors which separate them from the wider mass of the proletariat. This type of rural proletarian agitation will inevitably achieve the exact opposite of what it was intended to. The basis of real proletarian class struggle in the countryside – as opposed to mere electoral agitation – is undermined for the sake of a few transient moments of success.

Class Struggle and Social Development

Social Democracy is the party of the proletariat in class struggle. But it is not *just* this. It is also a party of social development: it seeks the development of the whole of the body of society to a higher form beyond that of its present capitalist stage.

Social Democracy is characterised by the fact that it has joined together these two aspects into a cohesive unity. The establishment of this unity constitutes the immortal historical service rendered by Marx and Engels. The workers' movement and utopianism originally developed independently of each other, and not infrequently antagonistically. Their unification had, in part, been achieved prior to the work of Marx and Engels as in the socialist wing of the Chartists, the egalitarian French Communists, and Weitling's sects. Theory has never yet raced ahead of practice in any new major social development. Its accomplishment was merely to discover the main outlines of the new formation amongst the scattered and hesitant experiments, which had not as yet intellectually detached themselves from their inherited foundation, and discern their general necessity. And this was what in fact Marx and Engels achieved in the unification of the workers' movement and socialism. They replaced empirical trial-and-error and sentimental yearnings with the clear perception that the highest form of the workers' movement is the socialist movement, and that socialism can only be realised through the workers' movement; that the workers' movement must, of necessity, strive to advance beyond capitalist society, and that the only class which has the power to struggle for a higher social stage beyond that of capitalism is the class of wage-labourers.

Their work firmly established the inseparable link between socialism and the proletarian class struggle. Resurrecting the issue of whether the final aim or the movement is the more important, whether theory is more important than practice – questions which are no more than vague variations on themes already resolved 50 years ago in the *Communist Manifesto* – is a sign of theoretical regression, not advance.

The aim and the movement belong together in Social Democracy: they are inseparable. But should they ever come into conflict, it will be the movement which will have to give way. In other words: social development takes precedence over the interests of the proletariat. Social Democracy cannot protect proletarian interests which stand in the way of social development.

This is not, of course, generally the case. The theoretical basis of

Social Democracy consists in the recognition that the interests of social development and those of the proletariat coincide, and that the proletariat is therefore destined to act as the mainspring of social development.

However, an excessively close observation of the maxim 'charity begins at home', or a tendency to 'put the immediate before the longer term' can mean that quite significant special interests of specific sections of the proletariat can emerge which do indeed stand in the way of the development of society.

The proletariat consists of many diverse strata. Unless these are united within the overall mass of the proletariat in the struggle for its major objectives, the proletarian elite can all too easily come to feel that its interests are opposed to those of the broad masses. At the same time, these individual labour aristocracies are seriously threatened by the revolutionising of the prevailing conditions through technical and economic developments: these introduce mechanisation, replace men by women, skilled workers by unskilled, they render whole categories of workers superfluous, draw backward workers from the countryside or abroad into the towns and so on. The *Social Democratic* method for fighting this involves activating the *solidarity* of the proletariat as a whole – organising women, unskilled workers, foreign workers, introducing a legally regulated normal working day, and so forth. The *guild* method, which apes bourgeois conceptions, consists in the *exclusion* of other workers from work, and in arresting economic development. The labour aristocrats imagine themselves to have an acquired right for employment in those areas in which they wish to remain, and proceed to fight off the introduction of new machinery, women's labour and and so on – in vain, as experience shows. Economic development is more powerful than they are; they are obliged to give way, step by step, but not without first suffering serious losses.

The first method is that of Social Democracy: the second, that of those worker' movements which are not led by a higher aim, by a 'theory' – which are purely pragmatic movements. Can there be any doubt as to which movement is preferable?

Social Democracy is only too well aware that every economic advance in the capitalist mode of production is initially a source of degradation and decline for those layers of the population affected; but it also recognises that obstructing progress will result in even more disagreeable consequences. Progress does not simply degrade the working population: it also lays the basis for their subsequent elevation and emancipation. The advance of the machine system was accompanied by untold miseries inflicted on the working population. Their general position fell below that of the heyday of handicrafts. But if those branches of industry in which the machine ultimately prevailed are compared with those in which production is still carried out using handicraft methods, on average the former will be seen to have shorter working hours, higher wages and more hygienic conditions.

The above discussion has been restricted to proletarians, since they provide the clearest illustration of the relationship between class struggle and social development. Applying these arguments to the question of the protection of the peasantry requires no special effort.

Social Democracy clearly cannot offer peasants what it denies to proletarians – the protection of their *occupational position*. The protection of workers demanded by Social Democracy is not aimed at preserving the occupations of individual workers, but rather their capacity for work, and for life: it protects their *humanity*, not their particular job. The proletariat does not demand this protection as a privilege for itself; it is to be shared by anyone who needs it, and should the peasantry ever demand the extension of worker protection to their own workplaces and their own selves, they will find no more eager helper than Social Democracy. But, as is well known, this is not what they want: in fact they resist it quite desperately. What they demand is the protection of their specific type of cultivation against the advance of economic development – and this Social Democracy cannot provide.

But aren't conditions in agriculture different to those in industry; doesn't economic development in agriculture merely lead to the ruin and pauperisation of the peasantry, rather than the supersession of the small enterprise by a higher mode of production? Protecting the peasantry would not therefore retard economic advance, but would simply put a brake on the physical degeneration of the agricultural population. Although the methods may differ, in essence this is no different in aim to steps made to protect workers.

The reply to this is as follows. Protection of the peasantry does not primarily mean protection of the individual peasant, but rather of *peasant property*. And this is, in fact, the main cause of the peasant's poverty. We have already noted that agricultural wage-labourers are often better off than small peasant proprietors, and that the propertyless wage-labourers are much more likely to escape their native misery than the peasants, whose property binds them to the soil. Peasant protection does not, therefore, protect the peasant from impoverishment: it protects the fetters which chain the peasants to their poverty. Protection of the peasantry also implies the protection and encouragement of the sale of peasant produce. The commodities which the peasants sell are food. The more they sell, the less they consume themselves. Promoting the sale of milk, eggs and meat in the towns means reducing their consumption on the land, and their replacement by potatoes, schnapps and coffee essence. Improvement of their position as peasants is bought at the cost of ruin as human beings.

Attempts to combat peasant impoverishment by shifting the burden on to industry and the proletariat are naturally ruled out from the start – in fact, they should be vigorously opposed.

Such methods of protecting the peasantry mean food tariffs on the one hand, and the law of entail, the binding of workers to the land, the strengthening of the Servants Ordinance, the payment of peasant debt interest and insurance premiums by the state, and the like, on the other. Attempts to ward off the impoverishment of the peasantry by any of these methods will either fail utterly or pauperise industry and the proletariat long before their goal is attained. But industry is the crucial mode of production in a capitalist polity: whether the population thrives, or not, depends much more on its fortunes than on the state of agriculture. As the case of England shows, a capitalist polity can sacrifice agriculture to industry without damaging its well-being. The reverse procedure leads to the ruin of both industry *and* agriculture. Nowhere is the rural population more poverty-stricken than in those modern agrarian states lacking in developed industry: one only has to look at Galicia, Italy, Spain and the Balkan countries to discover what undeveloped industry means for the peasantry.

On the other hand, it is the proletariat, not the peasantry, which is the bearer of modern social development: elevating the peasantry at the expense of the proletariat means arresting social progress.

Moreover, it is not quite correct to say that agriculture does not exhibit any progress. Although this may be true of pure agriculture, which eventually runs into a dead end, the relations of production on the land are revolutionised in a variety of ways once industry breaks out of the towns and spreads into the countryside. Any agricultural activity linked with and dependent on industry passes into a phase of uninterrupted transformation, constantly creating and recreating new forms – just like industry itself. This process of the revolutionising of agriculture is still in its infancy, but it is advancing rapidly. Protection of the peasantry, the attempt to maintain the old independent peasant agriculture, can only impede this development. It will not prevent the transformation of agriculture, and will prove just as impotent as measures to protect the handicrafts within industry. In fact, it will inevitably increase the suffering and sacrifice incurred in development, and its ultimate bankruptcy will inflict a serious wound on the moral reputation of those parties which advocate it.

Nationalisation of the Land

A Social Democratic agrarian programme conceived as protection of the peasantry would not only be futile: worse still, it would prove deeply damaging to Social Democracy, since it would stand in contradiction to its character as both a proletarian and evolutionary, or if one wishes, revolutionary party. The price it would have to pay for these very questionable, short-lived successes would be the disruption of its internal character, a reduction in its capacity to go on the offensive and the loss of its reputation as the party with the farthest horizons.

However, Social Democracy could adopt a different type of agrarian programme. Agriculture is claimed to display much slower development than industry: it will act as a brake on our advance. We therefore need measures to accelerate this development. This would be the right type of agrarian programme.

This is quite correct. Human society is a unitary organism, but – and this is what particularly distinguishes it from animal organisms – it is not an organism whose parts all develop at the same speed. Some remain backward, are overtaken by others and must, in the interests of uniformity, be driven onwards artificially by external forces in order to adapt to the whole. This applies as much for individual tracts of land as for individual classes. Nothing could be more mistaken than to suppose that recognition of the principle of social development rules out any leaps forward, anything artificial – that is, *conscious* intervention in social processes. It only rules out *arbitrary* intervention – intervention which contradicts the tendencies of social development, intervention inspired not by social insight, but merely by our whims and wants.

The civilised countries of Europe became ripe for capitalism long before feudalism had become obsolete in every branch of production and in every locality – we still find many vestiges of it today. And modern society will also be ripe for socialism long before the last handicraft worker and peasant will have vanished, before the entire proletariat is politically mature and economically organised. These are prerequisites which will never be fully met in capitalist society. In fact, one of the main tasks of the victorious proletariat will be to raise up the backward layers of the population and provide them with the means for a higher mode of production and a higher culture. Measures to elevate the peasantry by suggesting, and facilitating as much as is possible, the transition to socialist production will certainly play a major role in this. Social Democracy will certainly need this type of agrarian programme.

The question is simply whether the time for such a programme has arrived: whether a Social Democratic agrarian programme which promotes the development of agriculture in a socialist sense is possible on the foundations of *present-day* society.

The main driving force of economic development in capitalist society is the interests of the capitalists, *profit*. The encouragement of economic development initially implies the encouragement of *profit*.

However, there are specific capitalist means which correspond to this specific capitalist goal. What position should Social Democracy take towards economic development under these circumstances?

We cannot, and ought not, to impede capitalist development; but this does not mean that a proletarian socialist party has any reason to support it.

We cannot prevent the introduction of labour-saving machinery, or the replacement of men by women as wage-labourers. But it is not our place to egg the capitalists on, or to support them at the state's expense. The same applies to the expropriation of peasants and handicraft workers.

Social Democracy is sometimes accused of rejoicing in the proletarianisation of these classes. Nothing could be further from the truth. It does indeed regret that this happens: and if it took over the helm, it would immediately put an end to such methods of economic progress. Its position is simply that it is hopeless to try and hinder this process within the context of present-day society. Social Democracy's own historic role is not the expropriation of independent producers but the expropriation of the expropriators.

The same situation, if not quite as clear, is evident in economic development via the extension of the world market and colonialism. This method is also fundamentally a method of expropriation: it rests on the expropriation of the original inhabitants and owners of the colonial territory, and the ruin of their indigenous industries. If Chinese coolies ever come to Europe and compete with European workers, the latter ought not to forget that the former had previously been expropriated by European capital.

This process also cannot be stopped; it is also a precondition of socialist society, although Social Democracy ought not, on these grounds, to lend a helping hand. As with the case of maintaining the handicrafts and the peasantry, it is a reactionary utopia to call upon Social Democracy to support the resistance of the indigenous peoples of the colonised countries against their expropriation. But it would be flying in the face of the interests of the proletariat if one wanted to call upon it to support capitalists by granting them the assistance of the power of the state. Such work is too dirty for the proletariat to become an accessory. The whole rotten business is one of the historic tasks of the bourgeoisie; and the proletariat should be glad not to have to soil its hands with it. There need be no worries that the bourgeoisie will neglect its duty and allow economic development to come to a standstill. As long as it continues to have social and political power, it will not shirk this historical task, since it is, by its nature, a task which commands the bourgeoisie to increase profit.

The interventions of the proletariat in this process of capitalist development ought not to consist in its promotion, in the lending of voluntary support – either directly or, through the state, indirectly. But it ought not to impede it. Its task is to mitigate the ruinous and degrading consequences for those sections of the population affected – as much as it can – without impairing the development itself. Not a ban on machines and female labour, therefore, but protective legislation. Not the prevention of exports, but the refusal of various types of state support for them (protective tariffs, premiums, colonial acquisitions and so on). And where this remains in practice ineffective, at least the maximum protection of those affected by this policy, such as the indigenous peoples of the colonies.

We shall come later to how this principle should be applied to some of the methods used to expropriate the peasantry.

The task of a socialist agrarian programme is clearly not to promote the capitalist economic development of agriculture. And no one is proposing this. What are being considered are methods which can begin to prepare the ground for *socialist* production in agriculture, and which accelerate agriculture's transition to such a form of production as painlessly as possible.

Such an approach is only rendered possible by the contradiction between landed property and the agricultural enterprise. The agricultural enterprise is far more backward than the industrial, and much further removed from socialism. It seems to be an absurdity to pass over to a socialist organisation of agriculture as long as capitalism still rules in industry, and hence in society.

But what applies to production does not apply to property. Private property in land has entered into a contradiction with the conditions of production in agriculture much more rapidly and much more acutely than in industry, and has become much more of a fetter on it. Property in land has already become completely detached from the practice of farming. Whereas the tendency towards centralisation is scarcely perceptible for farms – in fact there is often a visible tendency towards fragmentation – landed property displays a marked tendency towards centralisation, particularly evident in mortgaged land, which is now overwhelmingly non-personal property.

The nationalisation of landed property is therefore already possible within capitalist society: it can be accomplished whilst retaining commodity production. Bourgeois parties, and often farmers themselves, already call for it in one form or another – often quite urgently. At the same time, socialist agrarian programmes of the type under discussion do not amount to any more than one method or another for the nationalisation of land.

Our attitude to land nationalisation in present-day society will also reveal our attitude to Social Democratic agrarian programmes of the progressive variety.

Alongside true *land nationalisation*, which has become very popular, in particular in countries with a tenant system of farming, we also have to consider the *nationalisation of mortgages* and the *nationalisation of the grain trade*.

Whoever holds the mortgage is the true lord of the land: the mortgage debtor stands in a similar relation to the mortgage holder as the tenant does to the landlord.

But the monopoly of the grain trade makes those farmers who grow grain for sale – or the vast majority – completely dependent on the holder of this monopoly. If not *de jure*, then *de facto*, this monopolist controls the entire land area planted with grain.

The socialists were the first to raise these demands. The eight demands made by the Communist Party in Germany, set out by the Committee of the Communist League in March 1848 (including Marx and Engels) read: 'Mortgages on peasant lands shall be declared the property of the state. Interest on such mortgages should be paid by the peasants to the state.'

And the preceding demand called for the conversion of large estates into state property.

Thirty years later, the workers' associations of the canton of Zurich began a movement for the introduction of state trade in grain.

Today, Social Democratic parties often look on these same demands with suspicion when they are raised by farmers, if not rejecting them outright. What has changed since then?

Both the general judgement and the social situation.

'When the February revolution broke out', wrote Engels in his memorable introduction to Marx's *Class Struggles in France 1848-1850*,

> all of us, as far as our conceptions of the conditions and the course of revolutionary movements were concerned, were under the spell of previous historical experience, particularly that of France ... there

could be no doubt for us, under the circumstances then obtaining, that the great decisive combat had commenced, that it would have to be fought out in a single, long and vicissitudinous period of revolution, but that it could only end in the final victory of the proletariat. (Engels, ibid., p. 644)

However, the Swiss workers' movement of the 1870s was still under the sway of the democratic superstition which disregards class antagonisms and believes that the required democratic forms and enlightenment are all that is needed to clear the path towards socialism.

The current view is very different: and the present situation is very different too. Now it is propertied farmers, not proletarians, who are clamouring the most for the nationalisation of the grain trade and mortgages – a demand intended to foist the *disadvantages*, not confer the *advantages*, of private landed property on society in general, at the same time allowing the advantages of private landed property to persist untouched, in fact securing and enlarging them. It is not proletarians, but landowners and capitalists who control the state, and would implement a policy of nationalisation. And the position of both farmers and proletarians in 1898 is very different to that of 1848, or 1878.

Up until 1878 grain prices were steadily rising; farmers prospered but consumers suffered. State intervention would have meant coming to the aid of the consumer, and combatting price rises.

Today grain prices are falling. It is not consumers, but producers who are moaning about the price of corn. No one remotely imagines that the state would bring about a further fall in prices – state intervention in the fixing of grain prices only takes place to raise them. Hardly surprising that the state grain trade now shows a very different sort of face.

The same applies to the nationalisation of mortgages. Ground-rents were steadily rising between 1848 and 1878. As long as this continued, the nationalisation of mortgages would have held no benefits for land-ownership. Its sole purpose would have been to serve as a transitional measure of the revolutionary proletariat towards a socialist society, a means of making land-ownership dependent on the state and removing a sphere of exploitation from the capitalists.

Matters have changed since 1878, when ground-rents started to fall. At the same time, the mass of mortgage interest and indebtedness is rising. Landowners are increasingly unable to meet their obligations: unless something unexpected happens, the mortgage lending banks are heading for heavy losses.

Nationalising mortgages would now be a means of guaranteeing that capitalists received their interest since their debtors would become the state, rather than individual owners. Their interest payments would be safe. In return, the state would be permitted to burden itself with the entire risk previously borne by the capitalists. The latter would gain – and landowners too, at least temporarily, should nationalisation lower the interest rate on their mortgages. The bill would be met by the taxpayer.

The situation would not be much different were land to be nationalised with compensation and no change in the capitalist mode of production, as demanded by bourgeois land reformers like Henry George. No one would have benefitted more than the bought-out landlords had such reformers succeeded in pushing through land nationalisation in England in the late 1870s. The state would have taken the entire loss on ground-rents – up to 30 per cent or more, now borne by the landlords – leaving the ex-owner free to enjoy the interest on the capital supplied to them by the state at their leisure.

Unlike the nationalisation of mortgages, nationalisation of land does admittedly have the advantage that the state can introduce improved farming methods to offset the consequences of the drop in ground-rents: nationalising mortgages confers no such influence over actual cultivation.

However, not too much trust should be placed in the state as farmer. The state is principally an *institution of domination, of rule*. And it will not abdicate this character when asked to exercise economic functions. The dominant outlook will be that of lawyers, policemen and soldiers, not technicians or the business-minded. This will only change when the proletariat succeeds in overcoming class differences and depriving the state of its character as an institution of domination. Under present conditions, the state is more expensive and less competent in its economic activities than the private capitalist – an argument gladly employed by the bourgeoisie against socialism, but in fact merely an argument against the modern state. Nevertheless, the nationalisation of an enterprise can economically benefit society as a whole where such establishments are either natural monopolies – such as railways, and some mines – or social monopolies such as cartels and trusts. The exploitation of the public by private monopolies can reach such levels that running them under state administration will appear as a deliverance, especially if the state is dependent on the people, preventing the Exchequer from merely perpetuating the exploitation of the private monopoly.

But where there is no such situation, there is no *economic* reason why a business undertaking should pass into state administration under the *present-day* state. On the contrary. The economic reasons militating against state administration are joined by *political* reasons which originate in the state's character as an institution of domination. Multiplying the economic powers of the present-day state means multiplying its means for oppressing the ruled classes. This becomes less and less applicable, as do the economic arguments, the more the state comes under the influence of the proletariat. But democratic forms alone offer no guarantee against the use of state power to suppress the proletariat. Where peasants and petty bourgeois are in the majority, they may well be perfectly happy to restrict the exploitation of workers by *big capitalists*, but are extremely jealous of the 'economic freedom' of the small exploiters. The Swiss peasants and petty bourgeois give workers full scope in all *political* matters, but can barely control themselves should these workers strike against their handicraft masters: with the state behind them, they often behave more brutally than their comrades in unfree countries. And should government workers and civil servants seek to improve their working conditions, democratic freedoms, in particular the referendum, are set to work to force them to tighten their belts even more.

Social Democracy has no reason to enthuse over the extension of state economic activity and state property where the proletariat does not play a major role – except possibly where a particularly grave situation exists. Is there such a grave situation in agriculture?

Up until the 1870s, the ownership of land constituted a monopoly, which led to the increasing exploitation of the population. This monopoly was broken in agriculture by the development of transport and trade, at least where the state refrained from imposing artificial restrictions. On the other hand the organisational form of the enterprise in agriculture is not yet suitable for state administration. The agricultural industries – sugar-refining, distilling, brewing and so forth – will be ripe for nationalisation long before agriculture proper. The state itself currently prefers to lease out its estates to capitalist farmers rather than farm them itself. Social Democracy has no reason to multiply the number of capitalist state tenants, and thus render the government even less dependent on revenues voted for by the representatives of the people.

The Nationalisation of Forests and Water

One significant branch of rural economic life, albeit not a part of agriculture proper, represents an exception to this: *forestry*. Rational husbandry of woodlands is incompatible with the exigencies of capitalist profit-grubbing. In fact, the subjection of woodlands to capital, and capitalist valorisation, leads to their ruin. Valorisation requires the fastest turnover of capital which can be achieved: however, the turnover of capital in forestry is unusually slow.

> The long production time (which includes a relatively slight amount of working time), and the consequent length of the turnover period, makes forest culture a line of business unsuited to private and hence to capitalist production, the latter being fundamentally a private operation, even when the associated capitalist takes the place of the individual. The development of civilisation and industry in general has always shown itself so active in the destruction of forests that everything that has been done for their conservation and production is completely insignificant in comparison. (Marx, *Capital*, II, p. 322)

Marx cites Kirchhof's textbook of farm management:

> The production process is also tied to such a long period of time that it extends beyond the plans of a private undertaking, and sometimes beyond a single human life. Capital invested in the acquisition of forest land [in communal production this capital disappears and the question is simply how much land the community can withdraw from arable and grazing land for timber production] only bears fruit after a comparatively long period of time, and turns over only partially, taking up to 150 years in the case of many types of wood. Moreover, effective timber production actually requires a reserve stock of growing timber amounting to between 10 and 40 times the annual yield. Thus someone who does not have other income or possess substantial areas of forest cannot pursue regular forestry. (Marx, ibid., p. 321 quoting Kirchhof, 1852, p. 58)

Where capitalist considerations alone decide, merciless felling can all too easily spell the total extinction of the forests. And the plight of the peasantry is no less ruinous in its effects. However, the forests are of such significance for the habitability and fertility of a country, its climate, the regularity of water levels, the mitigation of floods and the silting of rivers, the protection of cultivable soil in mountainous and coastal areas that their uncontrolled devastation will cause the most serious damage to the cultivation of the land. As with the labour-power of workers, states have often found themselves obliged to protect forests from being squandered by capital, whose blind greed drive it on to kill

Social Democratic Agrarian Policy 337

the goose who lays the golden egg. Forestry protection laws have been introduced, but unfortunately only inadequately and not everywhere. In the German Reich only 30 per cent of the forested area in private hands is subject to such legislative control. In Prussia, Saxony and several smaller states there are no such provisions at all.

States also attempt – at great expense – to make good the damage so blithely inflicted by capital's mania for profit, either by extending state forests or afforesting barren mountain sides or dunes.

This general development is only partly offset by another process which arises from the growth in capitalist revenues, a process already touched on above in a different connection. Whereas *capitalist exploitation* is constantly encroaching on the forests, *capitalist luxury* allows them to creep outwards again. However, the extension of forestry through the indulgence of such profligate whims, for luxury, means that it is neither rational nor planned. In the Austrian Alps, for example, forest can be seen to be creeping forwards at the expense of pasturage, or even arable land in some areas, whilst retreating in another where its presence is vital to protect against avalanches and torrential flooding: the outcome – the ruin of cultivable land by avalanches, floods and mud-slides. Cultivable land is either restricted and agriculture rendered impossible by an excess of forest, or is forced to suffer through the lack of it. This is the forestry of the capitalist epoch.

The one is as pernicious as the other. Both have to be stemmed in the interests of society as a whole. The most efficient way of doing this, and the only measure able to ensure rational forestry, is the nationalisation of the forests – at least where the state is not financially bankrupt and where the government is not under the sway of the very same noblest and best who regard the ruination of agriculture by their sport as one of their most precious privileges. In a financially healthy and democratic state, Social Democracy can certainly press for the *nationalisation of forests*, even if the proletariat still has only meagre influence.

Closely related to the nationalisation of forests is the *nationalisation of water*. This is not a demand related solely to the interests of agriculture, such as irrigation and drainage; many other very important interests also enter the picture. In particular, these include *transportation* (river, lake and canal navigation), *industry* (which uses a great deal of hydro-power, and will use even more, the greater the development of the electrical engineering industry), *hygiene* (the draining of swamps, the provision of drinking water, removal of sewage and other wastes) and finally, *public safety* (in particular, protection against floods).

The need for the rational management of water increases, the more the capitalist mode of production develops. Of all modes of production, the capitalist intervenes the most in the naturally-given pattern of water through deforestation, draining, lowering the water level of lakes, pipelines, canal construction, flood control and dams. And it has created more means than any other mode of production for forcing water to conform to its requirements. The more artificial the system of water-courses becomes, the more ruinous the effects which improper development can wreak. The divergence of the interests of the individual from those of society in general is especially acute in this sphere. Although a river can be juridically divided into separate parts, and a title of ownership allotted to each, it nevertheless remains a river, in fact a complete river basin, one single entity from source to mouth: and what might be beneficial to the lord of the river in one stretch, can mean devastation for those living downstream. Rational management of water has to be a system of management which regulates the entire basin in a planned fashion according to uniform criteria: this necessarily involves linking it with forestry. The lord of the river has to be lord of the forest too.

The demand for the nationalisation of water is currently especially legitimate, since the ground-rents yielded by flowing water are rising, not falling, as a consequence of the increasing capitalist exploitation of water for industrial purposes. Such nationalisation would not impose a financial burden on the population at large; in fact, it would enrich the state, at least where it was carried out skillfully. It is therefore quite permissible to demand the nationalisation of water wherever the state is not so corrupt that any act of nationalisation simply leads to the plundering of the state's coffers, or so bureacratically fossilised that it is incapable of undertaking any technical task; and as long as it is passably honest and subject to the control of a democratically elected assembly.

Although doubts may be raised as to administration by the bourgeois state, and even more to administration by the police state, as far as forests and water are concerned, both are superior to private management.

The nationalisation of forests and water should not be equated with the common ownership of forests and water practised in the *Mark* community. Such communal ownership was the product of the communal exploitation of forests and water, of common fishing, common hunting, common pasturage. Forest grazing has now virtually ceased; the hunt has become the private pleasure of the aristocracy, and fishing from rivers is no longer an important element in the popular diet. Considerations of fishing, hunting and grazing are not relevant to the present need to nationalise forests and water. They have been replaced by factors which played no part in the *Mark* community, since none of the preconditions for them were then in existence.

Village Communism

So much on the subject of state administration of the land. But in addition to state administration – 'state socialism' – there is also administration at commune level, 'municipal socialism'. Should this be the preferred lever for accelerating stagnating development in agriculture and pushing it towards socialism? Isn't village communism a venerable institution, closer to the heart of the conservative peasant than that of the town-dweller, with numerous vestiges still in existence?

According to the 1895 Census there were in Germany:

	Parishes	Farms	Cultivated area (hectares)
With undivided pasturage	12,492	429,468	441,635
With undivided woodland	12,386	570,846	1,340,100
With divided land, but in communal ownership	8,560	382,833	264,309

Couldn't these vestiges of village communism simply be extended in such a way that the growth of peasant agriculture within them would propel it into socialism?

This sounds very tempting. In Russia, where village communism was still very strong until recently, a very powerful tendency within the socialist movement did in fact live in the conviction that such communism placed Russia closer to socialist society than Western Europe. In the West it was bourgeois social reformers, such as Lavaleye, who first became interested in, and enthusiastic about, the original village communism of the soil, and regarded its revival as a means of solving the social question in the country, and hence in the town, which would be cut off from the steady supply of new proletarians from the land. Some Social Democrats have also recently come out in favour of strengthening and extending this primitive communism in their search for an agrarian programme, at the same moment as Russian Social

Democracy, learning from experience, has completely broken with the view that the village communism handed down from the Middle Ages could become an element in modern socialism.

Communism and communism are clearly two different things! The revolution sought by Social Democracy is not, in the final analysis, a *juridical*, but an *economic* revolution: its aim is not a transformation of *property relations*, but of the *capitalist mode of production*. Its only motive in abolishing the former is to effect the abolition of the latter. Socialism's main problems are not juridical, but economic.

The mere extension of communal property in land as preparation for the socialist mode of production is pointless if it is not intended to facilitate the extension of communal production, or if the preconditions for communal production, understood as modern socialism, are lacking.

Communal property in the *Mark* community arose out of the requirements of a type of agriculture which is now completely obsolete. The demise of this type of agriculture would have been impossible without the suppression of the type of common property corresponding to it. Where common pastureland (*Allmend*) or its remnants can be found, they still generally represent an obstacle to agricultural progress. The only economic justification for it is under exceptional circumstances, such as the alps in Switzerland, which can only be used as pasture. Its revival and extension would be meaningless without a simultaneous return to the old method of farming – the three-field system with pasture on the common land and grazing in the common forest.

Those agronomists now calling for the creation of new common pastures are definitely not socialists. Their demand is in the interests of large landowners, and their purpose is to bind agricultural labourers to the land permanently by tempting them with the possibility of acquiring a small holding (either on lease or as free property). Common grazing is an essential complement to this, since it would be impossible for them to keep cattle or obtain manure on such small holdings without it – that is, to sustain themselves for any length of time. The fresh creation of feudal common pasture (*Allmend*) is intended to round off and secure the work of the fresh creation of a class of feudal dependents (cf. Goltz, Die ländliche Arbeiterklasse, p. 262ff.; Sering, in *Thiels landwirtschaftliches Jahrbuch*, 1897 Supplement, pp. 131, 271ff.).

But, if common land has become a means for impeding agricultural progress and perpetuating feudal conditions, the right to use this common land has become a feudal privilege. The hereditary peasant inhabitants of the *Mark* have become an aristocracy, a commune of burghers which isolates itself from that of the general populace, the mass of incomers, and sets itself above it. Miaskowski, a warm admirer of the *Allmend*, says:

Inasmuch as this usage increasingly no longer occurs without payment, and nowadays frequently only benefits a part of the resident population, the *Allmenden* have become transformed from free goods for all those resident in a locality into a kind of collective fee-tail, the usage of which is now only accesible to members of a private corporation and not always free of charge. (Miaskowski, *Die schweizerische Allmend*, p. 3)

Where original communal property is still plentiful, and is used by a plentiful peasantry, it has become – as Miaskowski tellingly puts it – a fee-tail, only distinguished from other aristocratic fee-tails by the fact that it belongs not to a single family but is owned collectively by a number of families. Social Democracy must oppose it, as it would any other feudal fee-tail.

However, where original communal property only exists as meagre remnants, as small pieces of common pastureland, the collection of leaves for animal litter in the woodland and so on, and is only used by poor people, it has become a prop for entailment and the exploitation of the agricultural working population in general by helping to bind them to the soil. It has exactly the same effect as some of the charitable works of manufacturers, such as dwellings, which are built and let out to their workers. There is no reason why Social Democracy should interest itself in the extension and expansion of this type of communal property.

On the other hand, it would of course be going too far simply to demand the *abolition* of common forest or grazing rights where a poor population has managed to retain them. The abolition of such rights is a part of the larger process of the expropriation of the mass of the population to the benefit of a small number of owners. This process is immutable and the necessary prerequisite for the development of modern socialist production. But as we noted above, its furtherance does not figure amongst the historical tasks of the proletariat. Inasmuch as it intervenes in the process at all, its task should simply be to render what support it can to those displaced, to mitigate the consequences of this necessary and inevitable development as much as possible without obstructing it as far as the constraints set by prevailing power relations and economic conditions allow.

Social Democracy does not, therefore, have to work for the abolition of the grazing and forest rights retained by small peasants and day-labourers. We have compared their effects with those of the dwellings put up by manufacturers for workers. But as much as one may regret the binding and subjugation of workers fostered by such dwellings, it would be perverse to advocate the eviction of their inhabitants.

Social Democracy can quite safely leave the abolition of all forest and grazing rights to the ruling classes, wherever these block the path of rational agriculture or forestry. Social Democracy's task is to ensure that where such abolition takes place, those whose rights are at stake suffer as little as possible, and are not – as usually happens – cheated of their meagre entitlements.

At the same time, Social Democracy must never mistake the way backwards for the way forward: it should not regard the revival of medieval communal property in land, the extension and new creation of common pasture land, common woodland, and the extension of woodland use for agricultural purposes as the creation of a transitional stage to socialism.

But if the basis of medieval agrarian communism, and hence that system itself, is now irrecoverable, the conditions for a type of modern communal socialism are now developing within contemporary society – not in the *countryside*, but in the *towns*. The concentration of population in the towns is creating new tasks for communal administration, necessitating the replacement of private property by communal property in a large number of spheres.

On the one hand the accumulation of large masses of people within a small area means that economic functions exercised by individuals on their own behalf in villages – such as lighting, obtaining water, and transport – are assigned to large centralised bodies which would become intolerable monopolies in the hands of capital, such as gas works, power stations, water supplies, trams and so on: sooner or later these have to pass into communal hands. On the other hand, the concentration of population creates new tasks for communal administration and new means for solving tasks which would prove insoluble for rural parishes. The crowding together of large masses of people in a small area, the increase in ground-rents which drives landowners to cover every square metre of land with as many buildings as possible and deprive the population of light and air, the masses of foodstuffs which are constantly shipped into the towns, the masses of waste and refuse which have to be shipped out – all create a profusion of very difficult tasks unknown to the rural parish, the solution of which requires a number of major communal utilities – the creation of a sewage system, public squares and gardens, markets and so on. The accumulation of population in towns not only creates new needs, unknown to the country, but also provides the conditions for meeting needs existing both on the land and in the town, but which the former is unable to satisfy. This concentration also allows the creation of institutions unknown in the countryside. Secondary schools, hospitals, and almshouses are just as necessary in the open country as in the town, but the 'raw material' for them is not available in sufficient volume, and there is an even greater shortage of the necessary physical and intellectual resources. The countryside gets poorer whilst wealth piles up in the towns; the land also withers intellectually whilst intellectual life blossoms in the town.

The consequence is that communal administration increases in scale in the towns, and grows much more quickly than the municipalities themselves.

However, the commune is still primarily not an institution of *domination* but of *administration*, at least where it does not coincide with the state, which is usually the case in the modern system of government. The more independent it remains from the state, the less subservient it has to be to state authority, the less it will be an institution of domination. The industrial towns are also the site at which the proletariat first asserts itself, where it collects in masses, attains class consciousness, organises itself, achieves political maturity and sets about defending its interests against the capitalist class. If it obtains universal suffrage for municipal elections, it can, with sufficient communal independence, go as far as to organise communal administration in line with its own interests – hence the interests of society in general – and practise municipal socialism. Although this may be within the very narrow limits set by the general capitalist character of the state and society, much of significance can still be achieved given the knowledge and skill.

Communal administration will be more planned and rational, the more the commune is mistress of its own territory, the more of it is municipal property. Ground-rents are rising in the towns; the results of this increase accrue to the municipality wherever it owns the land. Given communal independence, universal suffrage and a given level of proletarian development, this increase can be used not to augment the powers of the ruling classes, but to promote the welfare and educational policies of the commune. The municipalisation of land also allows a fundamental reform of the living conditions of the population via the positive act of building municipal housing: mere building regulations, bans and building and housing inspections only remove the most glaring abuses, but do not get at their roots – rack-renting by the monopolists in land.

The maximum possible extension of the municipal ownership of land is therefore one of the most important tasks of a modern, independent, democratic town council. Modern urban administration should not only refrain from selling any municipal property, but should buy land wherever it can be had on favourable terms. At the level of the state, the proletarian parties should work towards as wide as possible an extension of the powers of municipal administrations over rack-renters, with as extensive a right of expropriation as can be obtained.

The position is different in the countryside. The proletarian has no say in the commune, even where universal suffrage prevails. It is too isolated, backward and economically over-dependent on a few employers, who can control it very tightly. It is inconceivable that a rural parish could pursue any other policy than that consonant with the interests of land-ownership. The economic, as well as the political, foundation for 'municipal socialism' is lacking. It is impossible for the economic functions of the modern urban municipal council to be transferred to the village. The old feudal agriculture, the object of so much communal administration, has gone. And it is not yet possible to conceive of a modern type of agriculture which could be practised by the commune, of a large-scale cooperative agriculture run by the village commune. Production cooperatives seldom have success even in the towns; large-scale producer cooperatives in the hands of peasants would lack all the elements needed for success – the necessary intellectual capacity, discipline and money. Not *one* village commune would, in our view, be prepared and able to assume the cultivation of a modern large-scale farm. But if this is so, if the basis of the communism of the soil is gone, and municipal socialism as practised in the large towns is impossible, what is the point of demanding that rural parishes should buy land or extend their holdings? The point is not for them to buy land simply to *own* it, but to put it to use. And where no use can be found, the purchase is more than superfluous. At most they could lease off their land, but this would not cover their long-run costs because of falling ground-rents.

The creation and enlargement of communal property in land might perhaps constitute one of the methods for the socialisation of the means of production in the countryside, just as it does in the town. However, under present circumstances it should only be raised as a *general demand* for the towns – and general demands are what we are talking about here. Our concern is not with what might become necessary under specific local circumstances since the object of our discussion is Social Democratic agrarian policy in general.

13
The Protection of the Rural Proletariat

Industrial and Agricultural Social Policy

Our discussions of Social Democratic agrarian policy have so far come to an overwhelmingly negative conclusion: this is not very encouraging for those who are looking for a Social Democratic 'agrarian programme' – that is, for demands which should be raised by the proletariat in order to save the peasant mode of agriculture or to offer a painless route to socialist farming, avoiding the capitalist transitional state, but yet still within capitalist society.

Such a negative judgement does not mean, however, that our position implies that no positive Social Democratic agrarian policy is possible and that we are condemned to agrarian nihilism. If Social Democracy's perspective can have – in fact must have – a positive effect in the sphere of industry in present-day society, the same must also apply to agriculture, by virtue of the fact that, as we have already repeatedly stressed, society as a whole constitutes one unitary organism. The policy of Social Democracy in agriculture cannot differ fundamentally from its policy in industry. One the other hand, the proletariat cannot simply transfer its previous social policy, created out of conditions in industry, into agriculture. It must adapt them to the conditions peculiar to agriculture. *This is the first task Social Democracy has to accomplish if it wishes to carry out rural agitation.* It does not need to search for new axioms or new programmes for its activity in the countryside; rather it has to investigate the consequences of its previous overall programme when applied to agriculture, and the modifications which its demands will undergo in the course of such an application.

Such a study would represent a major exercise in itself. And given the enormous diversity in rural conditions, it would produce a different result for each country, in fact for each district. Furthermore, it could not be undertaken solely by theoreticians: it would require the collaboration of one, or more, 'practitioners' – that is, people well-acquainted with the agricultural practice of the various types of farming and with the areas under consideration. It could never be brought to a conclusion and, like the Social Democratic programme for industry, would always be merely provisional in character, since conditions are constantly changing.

If, despite all this, we insist on carrying out such a study here, our only aim is to adduce a few concrete *examples:* and these show, quite unmistakeably, that a positive agrarian policy is possible for Social Democracy from our standpoint too. We have no desire here to provide the definitive and exhaustive declaration of Social Democratic agrarian policy.

Social Democracy's historic task consists in advancing the development of society beyond the capitalist stage: this requires measures both in the interests of society as a whole and in the interests of the proletariat, the sole driving force capable of lifting society beyond this stage. Social Democracy's social policy also displays these two aspects. Its agrarian policy can accordingly be divided into measures:

1) which benefit the rural proletariat;
2) which benefit
   a) agriculture
   b) the rural population as a whole.

There is no place here for measures to 'protect the peasantry'.
Measures subsumed under (1) can be further subdivided into:

i) those which remove obstacles to the free activity and organisation of the proletariat;
ii) measures by which state power intervenes to protect the physical, intellectual and moral capacities of the proletariat against the oppressive effects of more powerful economic factors, wherever the activity of individuals or the organised mass of the proletariat is unable to do so.

Freedom of Combination, the Servants Ordinance

The first group of measures consists primarily of those aimed at the abolition of the remnants of feudal dependence still in existence in Germany. Of these, the best known is the *Servants Ordinance,* in which the ruling classes saved what they could of serfdom when the feudal-absolutist state collapsed. 'No phenomenon in modern civil society', writes Anton Menger, 'more closely approaches slavery and serfdom than that of the relation of the domestic servant to master' (Menger, 'Das bürgerliche Recht und die besitzlosen Volksklassen', p. 403). The feudal character of this relation is still being reinforced where special laws directed at domestic servants give it statutory confirmation. It hardly does credit to the honour of the drafters of the Reich Civil Code that this feudal remnant – along with a number of others – still remains completely untouched 100 years after the great bourgeois revolutions. Only Alsace-Lorraine is free from the Ordinance, thanks to French law (see on this the very instructive article in Wurm's 'Volkslexikon', 1895, Vol. II, p. 926 ff., and the book by W. Kähler, *Gesindewesen und Gesinderecht in Deutschland*.)

But in addition to special laws directed against domestic servants, there are also laws directed against the entire rural working class. They still have not yet obtained the right to organise in trade unions in Germany: this right only applies to industrial workers. For the mass of rural workers, domestic servants, day labourers, *Instleute, Einlieger*, etc., just as with ships' hands in Prussia, for example, the law of 24 April 1854 forbids any agreement to stop work on penalty of up to *one year in jail* – and this law is *still* in force. For the modern proletarian, the right to combine is, alongside universal suffrage and freedom of movement, the most important of all basic rights. The proletariat cannot develop without this right; it has become a condition of its life. If Social Democracy wishes to rouse the rural proletariat, organise it and incorporate it into the proletarian army in struggle, it has to win this right for it. However, the right to form trade unions remains more important for the urban worker than for the rural worker, since possession of the right cannot, on its own, overcome isolation and economic dependency.

In England attempts to organise agricultural workers go back to the 1830s. And today? 'Of the nearly three-quarters of a million agricultural workers in Great Britain, not more than 40,000 are organised' (Sidney and Beatrice Webb, *History of Trade Unionism*, p. 429).

If the right to organise in trade unions is an indispensable right, the importance of which should not be minimised, the *right of free movement* is of much more practical importance. Any improvement in the position of agricultural workers over the last ten years is due to their freedom of movement, which allows them to migrate from the land and travel to the towns and other industrial districts. This is why freedom of movement is the most hated institution of the modern state from the point of view of the Agrarians. And although they are, as yet, powerless to impinge on it directly, they resort to every conceivable devious method to get around it: binding the worker to the soil by rent-fee farms, reviving the common pastureland (*Allmend*), either as common meadow or arable and garden land which is rented to the day labourer, and similar devices, using the authorities to impede emigration (a favoured method of controlling the flight from the land of dwarf-holders in Galicia), increasing rail fares, charging for entry permits to the towns and similar reactionary rubbish.

Social Democracy has to oppose such moves with as much determination as it can muster. The Agrarians may try and establish a gulf between industrial and agricultural workers by claiming that the flooding of industrial districts with workers from the countryside worsens the working conditions of the industrial work force and reduces their power to resist the capitalist. On these grounds, industrial workers are supposed to have an interest in seeing that movement off the land should cease.

And such arguments can be heard amongst industrial workers. It was even claimed during the discussions preceding the creation of the Agrarian Programme, which was rejected at Breslau in 1895, that such movement off the land was the reason why it was necessary to preserve the peasantry and improve the agricultural worker's lot – to keep them in the countryside. Trade union agitation in the industrial districts was regarded as a hopeless task as long as new hordes of proletarian elements kept flooding in from the countryside – low in expectations and intellect, and economically weak – paralysing the efforts of organised workers by acting as strikebreakers.

This argument is correct from the standpoint of the passing interests of particular strata of workers, from the standpoint of the narrow-minded guild mentality of the 'we-are-only-trade-unionist' types, but not from the standpoint of the proletariat as a whole, considered as the driving force in the development of a new social order. Were this argument correct, it would be in the interests of the industrial proletariat to resist any increase in its ranks – that is, destroy the precondition of its victory. The migration of country dwellers into the towns may make it more difficult for organised workers to obtain a privileged position within the proletariat as a whole, but such migration holds out the prospect of organising very many strata of the working population and incorporating them into the proletariat in struggle, people who would otherwise have remained outside its ranks, and may have let themselves be used as weapons against it. Obviously, it is more difficult to lead recruits to victory than to march at the head of veterans. But the recruit armies of the great French Revolution, with their enthusiasm and great numbers, defeated the veterans of monarchist Europe, who had no way of filling the gaps in their ranks. The guarantee of the proletarian army's victory lies less in the training of its veterans than in the rapid growth in the number of its recruits rushing to march behind its colours.

And it should also be remembered that the proletariat's certainty of victory has much less to do with the absorption of the small farm by the large – a very slow, and in some areas non-existent process – than with the growing dominance of industry in society, the product of the supplanting of agriculture by industry on the one hand, and agriculture's growing dependence on industry on the other.

It would be suicidal for Social Democracy to place deliberate obstructions in the way of this process; to seek to block the growth of industry and the increase in the industrial proletariat by clamping down on the inward movement of fresh labour-power from the land. Fortunately, it cannot.

It is impossible both to put an end to the low expectations and apathy of the rural population and keep them on the land. In present-day society the rural workforce will always live under less favourable conditions than the industrial proletariat: since the development of the former will always trail behind that of the latter, industry will continue to exercise a powerful attraction for the agricultural population. In fact, this attraction will continue to grow the more the rural population is stirred up, woken from its torpor and put into closer contact with the industrial population.

The rights of combination and freedom of movement are the two most important means for the free activity and organisation of both the agricultural and the industrial proletariat. Social Democracy's task is to win these weapons of class struggle and fight for their retention wherever they have already been won, and then to instruct and support all the various strata of the working population in their use. This covers the first set of measures in the interests of the proletariat.

Protection of Children

The second type of measure encompasses laws for the protection of all workers, but especially of working women and children.

Are such laws needed to protect the rural population? One might be incredulous that such a question should even be asked. But incredulity has to give way to astonishment that there are German *Sozialpolitiker* who would answer no. Their evidence rests on the Enquiry conducted by the *Verein für Socialpolitik* on the situation of the rural worker, which we have already cited many times above.

This Enquiry did admittedly come about under very singular circumstances. Only agricultural employers were sent questionnaires. For the *Sozialpolitiker* these were the only source which could be relied on to tell the unvarnished truth about the situation of agricultural workers.

When the attention of Oberregierungsrath Thiel, one of the directors of the study, was drawn to the absurdity of this, his reply in the Foreword to the publication of the results read as follows:

> If there is somewhere where confidence can be placed in information provided by employers, without correction from workers, this might be expected to be in agriculture, as circumstances are more straightforward there: the patriarchal relationship between employer and employee has been poisoned neither by many years of *struggles over wages, by strikes and the conduct of class-struggle, nor by deeply antagonistic interests and struggles* ... Subjective judgements may have crept in, and may often have been coloured by the standpoint of the employer; but these were easily identifiable and would not mislead anyone. (Verein für Socialpolitik, *Verhältnisse der Landarbeiter in Nordwestdeutschland*, I, p. xii).

In other words, those carrying out the study regarded what was to be investigated and what they wanted to see proven as already proven. And it seemed self-evident to them that no one would be more fitted than the employers to answer such questions as: 'Is excessively long working time leading to overwork, particularly for women and children? Does female labour lead to a neglect of the household? How does work affect the intellectual development of the child? Does the existing Servants Ordinance appear to be in need of reform?' etc.

Naturally, a 'subjectively coloured' answer to one of these questions would be 'easily identifiable'!

One can scarcely imagine a more astonishing claim from people who hope to be taken seriously as scientists.

No doubt there were very honest and knowledgeable people amongst the farmers asked, and much could be learnt from them. We have a lot to thank the Enquiry for in this respect. But it was utterly unfitted to provide any elucidation on the issue of the need for reform in the position of agricultural workers – in fact, it was worse than unfitted, it was quite misleading. No reasonable person would seek for enlightenment on the need for reform from people with good cause to frustrate it.

The *Sozialpolitiker* did have other reasons for only asking the Junkers, apart from their curious confidence in the patriarchal benevolence of these gentlemen. In the first place there was a shortage of resources and workers – a deplorable testimony to the scientific interest of our ruling and favoured classes. They should have come to

Social Democracy: proletarians would certainly have supplied the means and the people to ask the agricultural workers as well as the agricultural employers. And Social Democracy could also have helped to surmount the second obstacle which, according to Herr Thiel, prevented the consultation of farm workers – their intellectual backwardness. This backwardness certainly exists thanks to that patriotism which thinks more of Kiao-chau than of Prussian elementary schools; but our comrades would have been able to find at least a few agricultural workers who could have given the plain truth to our gentlemen *Sozialpolitiker*.

Of course, one should not expect *German Sozialpolitiker* to make links with *workers' organisations* when they are studying *workers' conditions*. Those who have done so, such as Sax in Thuringia and Herkner in Alsace, have made rich scientific pickings, but they have had to so in secret. And these were young men without posts or prestige. In contrast, no reasonable person should expect the gentlemen Privy Councillors who direct academic social policy in Germany to investigate the circumstances of workers in anything but the best circles.

But even if they did not want to lower themselves to actually asking workers about workers' conditions, there were other people they could have asked without compromising their sense of rank, people not directly in a situation of a conflict of interest with workers. For example, one might think that the question as to whether child labour led to a neglect of school could be better answered by teachers than by the children's exploiters; or that doctors might have been a more appropriate source of information about the adequacy of diet and housing, or whether work was excessively strenuous, than the farmers. There are also country *clerics* who take their calling seriously and could be expected to provide more unprejudiced answers than employers.

The procedure adopted by the *Verein für Socialpolitik* would have been reasonable had it been intended to deal with *employers*, not workers, from the start; if the Enquiry had not set out to document the distress of workers, but to provide material for a programme of aid to alleviate the distress of employers.

Of all the experts engaged in the study, this point was best understood by Dr K. Kärger; and he came to the conclusion:

> In my opinion the rural labour issue culminates in the following question: how can the rural worker, especially in East Prussia, be prevailed upon to take up service in their home area with the local landowners? In putting the question in this way I want to show that in essence there is only a *rural labour question from the standpoint of the*

employer, not from the workers themselves. Apart from a few exceptions, the material situation of agricultural workers, irrespective of which category they belong to, is *a good one throughout Germany*, and has showed a steady tendency to improve over the last two or three decades. *The rural labour question cannot therefore consist in the question as to what means should be employed to improve the economic situation of the worker.* (Kärger, *Die Verhältnisse der Landarbeiter in Nordwestdeutschland*, I, p. 217)

The only legal reform which Kärger therefore suggests is severe punishment for breach of contract. These are the results offered by German *scientific* investigation into the situation of workers.

Nevertheless, if the will to see is there, despite the fact that the Enquiry paints as much as it can in the brightest colours, and glosses over the things which cannot be given this treatment, there are ample facts available which show the necessity for far-reaching measures for the protection of workers from the standpoint of hygiene alone. And even more naturally from the standpoint of socialism, which not only wants to avoid a degeneration of the workforce, but also to elevate it intellectually and morally, and enable it to assume control of the economic mechanism. A social policy based on the belief that rural workers are so depressed as to be unable to answer questions about their own position, yet which arrives at the result that the position of this same class is a good one and that measures for its improvement are superfluous, has to be condemned from the outset from a socialist point of view.

The most important items of labour legislation are those which aim at the protection of the rising generation. In fact the entire socialist movement is more a movement for our children than it is for ourselves.

The productive employment of children is not something peculiar to capitalism. It is as old as humanity, and in a certain sense older, since animals begin to search for food long before they are fully grown. However, like labour in general, the capitalist mode of production has structured child labour in a unique and distinctly non-beneficial way. It replaces labour within the family by wage-labour for an employer; the one-time helpers of working parents become their competitors; an intellectually and physically crippling monotony takes the place of an eventful alternation between a wide variety of activities which developed both mind and body; what was almost a game becomes an exhausting drudgery. This is characteristic of all wage-labour in capitalist society; but has especially striking effects in the field of child-labour as children are far more defenceless than adults, and at the same time much more sensitive to any physical or intellectual damage, which they will have to live with for the rest of their lives.

The devastating effects of the capitalist exploitation of children first revealed themselves in large-scale industry. This was soon followed by the handicrafts and *agriculture*. As in industry, it is the *large-scale* agricultural enterprise with its division of labour, which creates a large number of simple and light tasks supposedly easily undertaken by children, and allocates them exclusively to these cheap and compliant workers.

But also as in industry, children's wage-labour is not confined to the large establishment; in fact by supplanting cheap labour it is a means of sustaining the small farm. And the more the flight from the land increases, the more scarce that adult workers become in the countryside, the greater the need to draw children into wage-labour.

Wage-labour by children in agriculture is not accompanied by any harmful effects: at least, this is what the employers questioned by the *Verein für Socialpolitik* assure us. Other people have different opinions. Although agricultural work takes place in the open air, and the work carried out by children is light – collecting stones, picking hops and the like – the system of wage-labour is always pushing towards the maximum possible extraction of effort from labour-power, the maximum intensity and duration of labour, and at the same time maximum monotony, since transfers between jobs mean a loss of time and more difficult supervision. The lightest and, within certain limits, the healthiest work will become hazardous once it is performed uninterruptedly beyond a certain limit.

The type of nightwork seen in industry does not have to be feared in agriculture. However, encroachments into children's night rest are very frequent in agriculture, where work begins very early in summer (and cattle tending in winter too) and ends late. For example, Konrad Agahd reports cases of children (in the Lissa district of Posen) 'who work in the fields from 4 am until school begins; then go to school and work afterwards until dark' (Agahd, 'Die Erwerbstätigkeit schulpflichtiger Kinder im Deutschen Reich', p. 413).

Dr E. Lauer, an agricultural teacher in Brugg, comments:

Agricultural work can be dangerous for children, especially where their necessary night's rest is shortened. Employers and many parents do not bother about how essential a child's sleep is. To wake children of between 10 and 15 years at 4 or 5 in the morning and not let them go to bed until 9, or later, in the evening is an act of callousness which can seriously impair their development. Child protection must intervene here and prohibit children under 15 from working before 7 in the morning and after 7 at night. An afternoon break of at least two hours should be guaranteed. If such a provision is to fulfil its aim, it must also be extended to school and domestic industry. School lessons should also be held within these hours. (Lauer, 'Die Beschlüsse des internationalen Kongresses für Arbeiterschutz in Bezug auf die Landwirtschaft', *Schweizer Blätter für Wirtschafts– und Sozialpolitik'*, vol IV, p. 269)

The child's physical well-being can also be damaged by being set to regular work in general at too early an age. No intelligent farmer would harness a colt to a cart. But children of only six are sent to do agricultural wage-labour. Aghad describes a school in Posen in which only 2 children out of a class of 55 children did no agricultural work. 'Twenty are employed by outsiders and have left the parental home, 2 at the age of 6 (!), 1 at the age of 7, 2 at the age of 8, 3 at the age of 9, the others at 10 or over.' Such 6-year-old children are expected to perform a working day of 12 or more hours, excluding the journey to and from work to home, which is often considerable on the land.

How such appalling conditions can develop in the exploitation of children is illustrated by the following order issued for the protection of children by the government of Anhalt – and what they permit is scandalous enough:

Children required for an *entire day's labour* must be at least *8 years old:* younger children should only be employed for *half* or *two-thirds* of the day. Working hours are fixed at 6 in the morning until 6 in the evening, with a two-hour midday break. If a *journey by foot* is necessary after this, working time should end so that the return home can be accomplished by 8 in the evening at the latest. If transport is by cart, care must be taken not to overload carts or let children fall out. No employment is permitted before the early school session. On hot days the employer must provide sufficient to drink. (Agahd, in *Brauns Archiv für soziale Gesetzgebung und Statistik*, Vol XII, p. 423)

In fact it was conditions on the beet plantations of our sugar refineries which moved the government of Anhalt to take these steps. Schippel writes:

Some tasks were exclusively reserved for children, such as 'beet-plucking', pulling up the unwanted small beets. Imagine children of 6 to 14 daily working 12 to 18(!) hours, crouching on the ground, bent over so that the blood rushes to their heads. An adult could not maintain this posture for ten minutes: it is hardly surprising that children return mentally abnormal after a week's work, apart from the illnesses which they contract because of the dampness of the soil to which they are directly exposed. And schools allow holidays for such work, so-called 'beet-holidays'. One correspondent writing to the *Preussische Schulzeitung* about conditions in the Merseburg area notes: 'These holidays are a pestilential nuisance to the schools. When children have been crawling around in virtually *sans-culotte* dress for weeks or days – depending on the size of the local fields – with all shame and virtue going to the wind with such massive and close proximity of the two sexes, and then return to school, they are so exhausted, so stupified and mentally weakened that all efforts at intellectual stimulation are in vain. Their faces are swollen, their countenance grim, their skin is blistered by the heat of the sun, their hands cracked and roughened by the constant grubbing in the soil, and the dirt has ingrained itself in their cuts and pores to such an extent that repeated washing with the strongest soap is not enough to get their hands clean. The constant animal-like crawling on all fours means that it is difficult to move the spinal column into a straight and erect position when sitting and standing.' If the village children are not sufficient in number, the estate-owners employ agents to go on a child-hunt in the neighbouring villages, paying them 5 to 10 Pfennigs for every child thus obtained on top of their regular daily wage. This hunt is conducted with every conceivable form of enticement and trickery. The children are promised lemonade, cakes and beer: they are then loaded on to carts, preceded by a musical band, and carried off to the village concerned. A child's daily earnings amount to 50 to 80 Pfennigs: for this they have an inhumanly long working day: from 5 in the morning until 9 in the evening. They even have to work on holidays! If children are enticed from surrounding villages it is often 11 o'clock at night before they get home – in a state all too easy to imagine. (Schippel, *Die deutsche Zuckerindustrie und ihre Subventionirten*, pp. 22, 23)

What has Kärger got to say for himself? 'A rural labour question exists only from the standpoint of the employer.' Perhaps the resources of the *Verein für Socialpolitik* might at least have been sufficient to send a questionnaire to the government of Anhalt. The Privy Councillors would have been well-counselled had they bothered to do so.

But we are being unjust to the Enquiry. Now and then we find a few strong utterances against child labour. For example, Weber tells us that, 'in a report on the Johannesburg district it was confirmed that the child labour of *shepherd boys* was "very long" and "contributed a good deal to the corruption of their morals"'(Weber, *Die Verhältnisse der Landarbeiter im ostelbischen Deutschland*). A general report from the Labiau-Wehlau area identified 'the system of child shepherds as a clearly visible abuse, but one difficult for farmers to avoid, leading to the brutalisation of children' (ibid., p. 125).

This is in full accord with Agahd's arguments:

> The greatest damage is caused by the shepherding system. This has been quantitatively exposed, in particular by the teachers in Pomerania, where 58 informants on the theme 'Child labour in agriculture' noted that out of 3,275 children, 2,310 were exposed to moral danger, with 312 doubtful cases and a further 653 denied. In addition, 1,382 were exposed to danger to their health. (ibid., p. 414)

Von der Goltz also refers to the 'morally and economically pernicious system of child shepherds' (Goltz, *Handbuch der gesamten Landwirtschaft*, p. 265).

Our poets have lyricised the life of the shepherd boy. And formerly, when it involved driving large numbers of animals into woodlands and inhospitable places, keeping them together and protecting them from dangers, the shepherd's life certainly had its attractions and excitements. It developed strength, suppleness, courage, stamina and keen senses. But the young shepherd's day now merely consists of tending a couple of animals on a speck of grass, and making sure they do not stray outside their prescribed limits. No more is expected of his intellect than to exercise the function of a fence. That such enforced inactivity and lack of movement calls forth all manner of wicked and stupid thoughts and instincts is entirely understandable. The system of child shepherds must be opposed on educational, if not hygienic, grounds.

But why do the *Sozialpolitiker* farmers oppose the system of child shepherding? What is the source of this philanthropy? Very simple: 'Shepherd boys are predominantly employed by peasants, since the large landowner has his own shepherds' (Weber, *Die Verhältnisse der Landarbeiter im ostelbischen Deutschland*, p. 127). It is not the lot of the children which upsets the large landowner, but the waste of this cheap labour by the small farm in the face of labour shortages: 'Consider how much more usefully the energy of these children could be used if they were employed in field work; this would not only benefit the children and their parents, but also the agricultural employers' (Goltz, *Handbuch der gesamten Landwirtschaft*, p. 265).

This is a form of beneficence towards children which is at the same level as that of a reporter from Westphalia who denounces the local mine-owners for violating the provisions against the employment of young workers, and would prefer to ban such workers from industry completely:

> If a strict ban was placed on employing children before the age of 16, and preferably before the age of 18, they would be forced to take up service with farmers or craft-masters, to the considerable benefit of both agriculture and industry. (Kärger, *Die Verhältnisse der Landarbeiter in Nordwestdeutschland*, p. 140)

Thus, the hearts of the farmers questioned by our *Sozialpolitiker* are not completely hardened on the issue of the protection of children. As long as protecting them in one sphere helps round them up for the other, it is welcome.

The position of children in wage-labour is especially wretched where they are away from home, and have no one to offer them protection and support, where they are completely at the mercy of their exploiters. And this is not an infrequent situation. Migrant labour without the accompaniment of parents is often seen, especially in South Germany, Baden and Württemberg. In Tyrol there is a specific corporation – the 'Child Shepherd Corporation' – which concerns itself with the trade in children. In the Vorarlberg the 'Swabians' are a group on their own amongst the other schoolchildren; these are children who from the age of 10 enjoy the 'concession' of being freed from the obligation to attend school from 15 March to the middle of November in order to hire themselves as farm workers in the neighbouring states. The principal market is Ravensburg to which hundreds of children are driven from the Tyrol and Vorarlberg to be sold to the highest bidder for the summer. The carriage of this delicate human cargo is entrusted to the village priests.

One can imagine the type of treatment which these poor, completely friendless, children receive. The peasant journal *Bernische Blätter für Landwirtschaft* observed in an article (1 September 1896) on the 'Labour Question in Agriculture', that the bulk of the responsibility for the shortage of labour on the land lies with the poor treatment of house-servants, especially 'farm boys'.

Supplying peasants with children who have fallen on poor relief can be placed at about the same level of humanity as the temporary sale of children abroad. A specialist working on *Neue Zeit* (XVII, 1, p. 197ff.) prepared a report in Switzerland under the pseudonym of Rusticus – but the system is not unknown in Germany too. Rusticus's article illustrates how the maltreatment of children under the influence of the peasant milieu even continues in reformatories.

One incidental result of the investigation into the Jordi case (sexual and disciplinary abuse of foster children, January 1898) showed the lively methods used to train girls in Bernese reformatories for higher agriculture. Girls at the Kehrsatz reformatory had to get up in summer at 4 or 4.30 to load feed. They also had to muck out the stalls, load manure, pump liquid manure, turn the soil in places too steep for the heavy plough, and clear and plough marshes in the valley floor. All of these duties are far beyond such young capacities, and for the most part not appropriate for women at all, according to common opinion in Bern. They are a brutal imposition in the eyes of all right-thinking people, a brutality irrespective of how often the 'blessings of work' are reiterated – blessings which combined with biblical texts and prayers are intended to extirpate the 'roots of evil'.

However, those children who leave their homes to toil as slaves under the iron hand of a gang master, an agent, are in an even worse position. We shall come back to the gang system and migrant labour in general in another connection: 'Those of very youthful years must be protected from the dangers posed by the *Sachsengängerei* not only to morality, but also to the health of a still weak body as a result of the excessively hard work on the beet estates' (Kärger, *Die Sachsengängerei*, p. 207).

In view of all this, it should not be surprising to find that not only theoreticians, but also 'practicians', well-acquainted with agricultural circumstances, energetically speak out in favour of legislative protection of children. Thus, Dr R. Meyer stated at the Conference for Labour Protection at Zurich:

> The informant appears to believe that agricultural work is very healthy for children. I believe that this gentleman has never seen North Germany, Bohemia and Hungary, the large sugar-beet fields and extensive potato acreages. He has never seen how children have to crawl around on the ground in autumn in the cold and wet from dawn to dusk to cut beet or dig up potatoes. And there are many more such children than there are factory children, the sole focus of your interest.

In fact, there were 460,474 children in employment below the age of 15 in the German Reich in 1882; of these 143,262 were in industry, mining and construction, and 291,289 – more than double – in agriculture. 1895 was the first year in which separate records were kept of employed children below the ages of 14 and 12. In all, 214,954 children below the age of 14 were in employment – 135,125 in agriculture. Of the 32,398 children below the age of 12 in employment, no less than 30,604 were in agriculture. All these figures should be treated as minima. The number of children really in employment has been estimated as much more, a million and over. Von der Goltz estimates the number of child shepherds in East Elbia as ranging between 50,000 to 'far over 100,000' (Goltz, *Die ländliche Arbeiterklasse*, p. 265). Nevertheless the official occupational statistics do give some idea of the proportions of industrial and agricultural child labour.

The exploitation of children in agriculture is therefore widespread, and the protection of children an urgent necessity.

However, the question of child labour is by no means an entirely straightforward one, as Bernstein has already observed in a very commendable article on 'Socialism and the Industrial Employment of Youth' published immediately after the Zurich Congress.

The productive physical labour of children contains a number of important educational elements. Nothing is more damaging than one-sided mental labour during the years of development. Plentiful physical activity is vital, and anyone who does not learn how to do physical work at this age will later have to live in the knowledge that they will never attain that confidence and ability in work achieved by those who have performed it from childhood. But there is also a strong ethical element in productive work; one should not be indifferent to whether children grow up as parasites on society or as useful members of it. The bourgeois son who lives from the labour of others during his formative years will all too easily emerge as nothing more than a characterless weakling, a grovelling and apron-string tugging creature seeking to live from the favour of others and not from his own powers, when eventually forced to stand on his own two feet. In contrast, the proletarian comes to an early awareness of the need to work productively both for themselves and possibly even to care for others – a feeling of responsibility, but also an awareness of the individual's own capacities.

The great Utopians of socialism, who were at the same time great teachers, also wanted to introduce young people to work early on in their lives. John Bellers, like Fourier, allowed children to start carrying out useful work between the age of four and five. Robert Owen started them at eight.

In this they shared common ground with the industrial capitalists. But what can be seen as one of the most effective means of elevating and ennobling humanity in the social plans of the utopians, becomes one of the most effective means for inflicting the most appalling degradation on the working proletariat in capitalist reality. There is no need to prove this here – since Owen's work, proof has been supplied countless times.

Capitalist society is therefore confronted with the dilemma of either abandoning youth to capital and hence leading the workers of the future – including the future of the working class – to ruin, or excluding youth from productive work, and thereby seriously jeopardising the formation of their character and capacity for work.

No complete solution to this contradiction – and hence no completely satisfactory way of educating the mass of the population – is possible within the capitalist mode of production.

Inasmuch as the more perceptive and unprejudiced of its representatives win out over the short-term interests of the manufacturers, capitalist society has to make do with a compromise. Productive labour is completely expunged from education up until a certain age (12 to 14 years). At that point it declares the education of the growing proletariat completed and gives it over exclusively to productive work – that is, under current circumstances, capitalist exploitation.

Thus far, Social Democracy's practical interventions into this field have been based almost totally on this compromise. It has only distinguished itself from those friends of the workers amongst the bourgeoisie by seeking – in a completely mechanical fashion – to raise the age limit for the total ban on children labour as high as possible. But the further one goes along this path, the more one approaches the aim of only allowing productive labour for young people to begin at maturity, the more remote one becomes from any opportunity of allowing productive work to influence the formation of character and the capacity to work of the rising generation: one avoids Scylla, only to be driven to Charybdis.

It is scarcely in the interests of the working class to extend the age limit up to which child labour is absolutely forbidden beyond the current level of 14 years.

However, the lower one makes this age limit, the more strict provisions for the protection of children at work must be – and we take the notion of 'children' here in its broadest sense, up to 18 years of age. In a period in which the intensity of work on the one hand, and on the other, the need of the worker to be active as a human being outside work, in particular to educate themselves, have grown so markedly that there is a universal call for an eight hour day for *adults*, the same working time seems to us to be too long for young workers. We would have preferred it had the Zurich Congress demanded the four-hour working day for young workers, instead of increasing the age at which all work is prohibited up to 15. The system presently operating for children up to 14 working in English textile factories, who are only permitted to work half a shift – four and a half hours a day – should be put into effect for young workers up to 18 years of age.

A lower age limit for the employment of children requires stricter legislation on the exclusion of those branches and types of work in which the use of children and young workers is totally forbidden, stricter hygienic provisions at work, and more thorough factory inspection – requiring more numerous and independent inspectors: and the more important it becomes for doctors, teachers and practical workers to also have a say in the inspection of premises, as well as technicians.

Naturally, this must not only apply to factories, but also to handicrafts and domestic industry where child labour has given rise to the most appalling conditions.

The School

However, the desire to organise child labour as rationally as present-day society will allow cannot really fulfil its purpose if it restricts itself to *workplaces:* it must also take in the *school*, and adapt education and work to each other's requirements. The gulf between Social Democracy and reactionary, petty bourgeois, Christian 'socialism' is revealed very starkly here. Both parties want to limit capitalist exploitation: but whilst the latter seek to accomplish this by bringing the development of society to a halt, the former want to accelerate this development. 'Christian' socialism wants to lead the proletariat back, if not to petty bourgeois conditions of existence, then at least to a petty bourgeois, medieval, mentality. Social Democracy seeks to raise the proletarian mentality to a higher level, to empower the proletariat to advance beyond capitalist society. Both Social Democracy and Christian socialism have an energetic interest in the modern school: but whereas Social Democracy needs it to achieve its purpose, Christian Socialism, of necessity, presents a face of hostile opposition.

The importance of schooling should not be overestimated. Nothing could be more erroneous than to believe, as some do, that those who own the schools will own youth – the future. Education is not obtained solely in school but in life in general, of which school is only a small part. Conflicts between the lessons of school and those of life are inevitably resolved to the benefit of the latter. Schools may be as pious and sycophantic as one likes: if life teaches materialism and democracy, then it will produce neither grovellers nor bigots. Where the lessons of school conflict with those of life, school's only effect is to damage children by wasting their time: any educational effect on the child soon turns into its opposite. But at least it is of precious little use to the rulers, whose power it is meant to cement.

And even the best school cannot contribute much to the intellectual and moral elevation of humanity if the overall milieu does not support it. The reform of society cannot begin in the schools.

However, every form of society, every class, needs a particular type of education and upbringing; without this it would be unable to thrive and carry out its task to the full. In this respect the structure of the school system is by no means irrelevant.

There is no reason to believe that the possession of academic knowledge raises the modern average human being to a higher intellectual and moral level than those who peopled primitive society. In fact, both the singers and the public of Homeric poetry and of the Edda not only appear superior to the singers and audience of modern folk poetry in terms of aesthetic sensibility: their moral insight, intelligence, and understanding of nature and humanity also seem higher. They did not require a school to sharpen and ennoble their senses and spirit, to obtain knowledge. The public life of their communes, tracing the same course over millennia, was all they needed; oral communication and personal observation were fully sufficient to convey all the stimulus and knowledge of society to the average individual.

The life of society in the current age of world communication, the age of constant revolution – not just political, but above all technical and commercial – is acted out on such a scale, and in such giant leaps that any individual reliant solely on oral communication and personal observation would be rendered helpless. Reading, writing, mathematics, the elements of natural science, geography and statistics, political history are an absolute necessity for anyone wishing to find their way through the mechanism of society. However, in itself this school knowledge, especially in the form in which it is taught today, offers much less stimulation or reliable insight than the knowledge once disseminated through the oral tradition and personal observation in the public market place; academic knowledge is a poor substitute for actual observation, and customary popular reading – cheap sensational papers and trashy novels – tends to stupefy rather than elevate. Contrast it with our forbears' observation of nature, against which they constantly had to struggle, and with the tales related by travellers from afar which provided them with continuous intellectual refreshment and knowledge. Although the replacement of observation by academic knowledge does not in itself mean that the civilised individual is morally and intellectually superior to the primitive, such knowledge is still an indispensable prerequisite for the former to fulfil his or her tasks. The life of civilised humanity has become so enormously extended, both temporally and spatially, that no individual, no matter how gifted or industrious, can comprehend it all through the medium of personal observation. Important as this might be, it can never do more than encompass a small segment of life: the rest has to be learnt in school.

Neither individuals nor nations can maintain their position in the competitive struggle, and meet the demands of modern civilisation, without a certain level of school education. And the more that society develops, the more inadequate the education offered by the present-day elementary school; the improvement and extension of elementary schools, and the addition of general further education for some years beyond 14 is now indispensable.

When assessing the amount of child labour which should be permitted, this educational aspect has to be considered in addition to the considerations of hygiene. Child labour over the age of 14 must also be kept within limits which allow a regular, ample and productive attendance at school.

However, school is not meant merely for the *instruction* of children, but also their *upbringing*.

As long as social life remained public, it offered all the elements of education and upbringing necessary to meet the aims of society. The company of their peers, their contemporaries, in play and at easy tasks, the model of the adults and helping in their daily round, and the lessons of the elderly all sufficed to develop the social virtues. Today public life has been replaced by family life, especially for children and in particular in the towns. It is now supposedly parents, not society, who bring up children. But parents are generally lacking in all those educational elements offered by life in society, life amongst one's peers: at best the child may learn obedience from its parents, but not comradeship, common feelings, self-sufficiency. And how many parents have either the ability or opportunity to bring up and educate their children? They are totally trapped in the need to work for a living. In addition, the urban family not only denies the child the company of its peers, but also useful activity, especially for boys. The separation of the family from society also means its separation from work. And if children do not accompany their parents to work, they lose all the educational and social influences which the example of work and lending a hand in it can provide.

This is where school comes in: it reunites the isolated children and thus offers them the powerful device of education by one's peers, at the same time providing planned and thought-out employment under a set of supervisors. To have its full educational effect this must be an all-round type of activity: it must not simply fill the children with book learning but with a living humanity. The teacher must get to know the children, not simply during instruction, but also at play and at work – that is, an activity which, in contrast to play and instruction, yields up an immediate, tangible result, is an immediately recognisable end in itself for the child and awakens self-confidence and the joy of creating through the joy of accomplishment. This coordination of productive labour and schooling should not be confined to older children: it should also characterise the first years of school attendance – not simply on economic but also on educational grounds.

The linking of instruction with productive work, the linking of school with training workshops and gardens, where the simplest elements of the various crafts and agriculture can be taught and practised, is indispensable at any age where wage-labour is completely banned – and is all the more indispensable, the higher this age limit is set.

The issue of child labour clearly conceals a host of other problems; and very little is achieved by merely mechanically raising the age limit at which wage-labour may commence.

The question of child labour also takes on particular forms when we turn from industry to agriculture. The early acquisition of skills, and familiarity with work, is even more vital in agriculture than in industry. In industry, the division of labour and the machine generally reduce the individual's activity to a few tasks, which demand neither extraordinary physical strength nor dexterity, but whose acquisition is still quite difficult for the completely unpractised. Agriculture has a great variety of tasks demanding care, dexterity and frequently physical strength and indifference to the weather – tasks which need to be practised from an early age. Present-day urban workers are unfit for agricultural work.

In contrast, the countryside is free of the dilemma encountered in the towns – that banning wage-labour for children nowadays almost universally also means banning them from any type of productive work, and that the ban on their exploitation by capital also constitutes a ban on developing their ability to work and a denial of access to the educational influence of useful activity for society.

All households on the land are linked to an agricultural establishment. Even wage-labourers practise cultivation for themselves if they have a family. Children do not have to turn to wage-labour outside the home to occupy themselves usefully. Under such circumstances, banning wage-labour for children does in fact only mean a ban on their exploitation by capital. If the minimum age of wage-labour in industry has been set at 14 years, this could be made earlier in agriculture. However, the ban on migrant labour by children should be extended up to a greater age. As found in the form of the gang system it represents the most appalling and depraving form of wage-labour.

Such a ban does not solve the problem of child labour in agriculture, however. We already noted that labour on the parental farm already provides sufficient opportunity for activity for children in the country. However, this opportunity is often used by the parents to sweat and overwork their children. Maximising the labour of one's own children is one of the methods employed to keep the small establishment going in both agriculture and domestic industry. The importance which this has acquired for the peasantry is revealed in the massive efforts made to reduce school hours for country children.

These pressures must not be submitted to. The land in particular needs an improvement and extension of the school system, and this is in the interest of agriculture itself. The modern mode of production has simplified the work of the manual worker in industry to the extreme. This is not so in agriculture, which is becoming increasingly more complex, its implements increasingly sensitive and its methods ever more demanding of knowledge and intelligence. Agriculture requires more and and more intelligent workers, precisely the ones least attracted to it. We already noted the intellectual desolation of the land in Part I: the most gifted workers flee to the town. And whereas the town can offer innumerable stimulations and aids to education once school is finished – newspapers, associations, meetings and museums – scarcely anything exists in the countryside to counteract the atrophy of what scanty academic knowledge the adult country-dweller still possesses. A rich school education, not only up to 14 years of age, but beyond this, is even more important in the country than in the towns – a form of instruction which carries within itself the impulse to further education.

The country-dweller is demanding more child labour. And the demand will become more vociferous, the more of a rarity wage-labourers become. But they also need further education. This could be achieved without any lengthening of school hours – in fact possibly with some shortening of them, were the morally, educationally and scientifically utterly useless – in fact damaging – teaching of religion to be replaced by instruction in the basics of those disciplines required for rational cultivation (chemistry, mechanics, botany, zoology, geography); knowledge of these would also enable the farmer to enjoy subsequent further education.

But it is precisely those parties which have made the salvation of agriculture into their hereditary property, who advocate a restriction of compulsory school attendance whenever the opportunity is favourable, and continually urge replacing what meagre factual instruction there is by yet more religious instruction, who already dominate the elementary schools. If any parties sacrifice the prosperity of agriculture to their philistinic transient interests, it is these 'loyal' 'Christian' parties.

The worst of these are the *Ultramontanes* of Austria. But one can note similar movements in Germany, even amongst Protestant clerics. One rural priest from Thuringia, for example, has written a book on peasant morals and beliefs, in which a highly unfavourable view is taken of the effects of the new schools on the peasantry.

> This obsession with reading is leading straight to the madhouse: though rarely for the peasant – they are already accustomed to it in school. But this does seem to present one, all-too neglected, danger: namely that the amount of reading undertaken in instruction, as in present-day school education in general, will rob the country dweller, while still in youth or childhood, of practise in manual work and what is more important, of joy and satisfaction in their lot. Any unprejudiced observer can see how boys and girls who, disregarding infant and secondary schools, are kept at their 'books' and away from agricultural work between the ages of seven and fourteen, stuffed full with 'every type' of knowledge and trained to be virtual scholars [K.K.!], subsequently lack the taste for employment in the fields, with animals and other agricultural work: as I have encountered, in particular, with the keenest and most diligent schoolgirls, such children are very loath to leave school and only take up their destiny of helping their fathers and mothers with a great deal of hidden resentment. It is also quite understandable that 'education' in school not only prevents punctual – i.e. early – training in agricultural work, but also awakens and feeds a yearning for the richer and more pleasurable life, free of sweat and toil, of the 'better off' depicted in the 'pleasant tales' of young people's and popular books, particularly amongst the more intellectually able children. *The educational*

fanatics will one day realise, perhaps in a very hair-raising fashion, that 'intelligence' in the populace also has its shadowy side. Since nowadays everything moves at full-steam – including the drawing of conclusions, and if the disgruntled country dweller begins to incline towards 'freethinking' or 'progress' as a result of dissatisfaction with their station, it is logical that this will bring the poor country dweller much nearer to Social Democracy: 'Something's afoot,' said an experienced old parish chairman; he added 'people never used to think about such things, they accepted everything that they had; now they compare their circumstances with those of other people and ask, "Why should they be better off than we are?"'

One could not put it more cynically; the people should be kept in ignorance, because education turns them into Social Democrats. Who cares if ignorant peasants are much less able to practise rational agriculture than knowledgeable ones! We want subservient not prosperous peasants, so bring on the hymn book and catechism, and out with the little bit of education about nature and society which trickles down through the village school into the heads of the village children.

Hardly surprising that our peasants' friend notes the diminishing interest of the peasant in education with such satisfaction (*Zur bäuerlichen Glaubens – und Sittenlehre. Von einem Landpfarrer*, p. 24–6).

A correspondent from the Wiesbaden district writing for the Enquiry carried out by the *Verein für Socialpolitik* has similar views: although educational standards amongst the peasantry had improved as a result of better schools, their coarseness had increased too – other correspondents claim the opposite. The cause of this coarseness is supposed to be the excessive reading of newspapers.

A report from the same, mainly small peasant, district also reports that attendance in agricultural secondary schools which were still heavily frequented in the 1870s, has dropped off considerably (Auhagen, *Die ländliche Arbeiterverhältnisse in der Rheinprovinz*, pp. 54, 61, 63).

As the following table shows, there is still an enormous amount to be done in the sphere of further education in the countryside:

	No. of agricultural secondary schools in winter 1896/97	Upkeep Marks	No. of pupils	No. of young boys on the on the land 14-18 years
East Prussia	-	-	-	64,000
West Prussia	8	1,265	91	47,000
Brandenburg	1	50	26	65,000
Pomerania	3	150	25	45,000
Posen	21	1,441	213	57,000
Silesia	33	5,297	910	131,000
Saxony	41	4,932	735	65,000
Schleswig	50	5,027	394	36,000
Hanover	133	14,753	1,982	70,000
Westphalia	8	1,430	138	77,000
Hesse-Nassau	320	27,812	4,518	48,000
Rhine Province	206	26,132	3,791	121,000
Hohenzollern	51	3,519	504	2,600
Total	875	91,808	13,317	828,600

The total costs for these schools amounted to 91,808 Marks, of which 33,174 were paid by the state! About the same as a couple of rounds from a big cannon.

At the same time huge sums are expended to 'save agriculture'. Of course, further education does not contribute to raising ground-rents.

The peasant is in a serious dilemma as far further education is concerned: the more ignorant they remain, the more irrational their cultivation, and the less able they are to make use of even that little bit of technology which can be used on a small farm. But the greater their education, the more they will suffer under the struggle for existence which forces them into overwork and a reduced standard of living, and the more they will begin to turn their back on the job at hand.

This is very unpleasant for those who want to preserve the present peasant mode of cultivation as the firmest foundation of present-day society, although not for the representatives of social progress. If the peasant economy is incompatible with the demands of a higher civilisation, of the type created through a rich and useful school education, this constitutes an argument against the former, not the latter. The improvement of school instruction must result in a more rational organisation of the peasant farm in areas where it is still capable of improvement. Where circumstances do not allow for this, higher school education will inevitably lead the population increasingly to turn away from peasant life: it will be a factor for economic progress in both instances.

School education also has a further good side. It steps in where child legislation fails: it has already proved to be an excellent means of combatting the excessive sweating of children by *their own families* in both agriculture and domestic industry – something to be valued, the more that legislation refrains from intervening in the inner life of the family. Compulsory school attendance would be necessary to stem wage-labour by children in the countryside even if child labour were to be banned completely, since the great distances, and the dispersion of the children over large areas, make the enforcement of child legislation much more difficult than in big industry. A ruthless implementation of compulsory school attendance would reduce wage-labour by children to such dimensions that it would no longer be worthwhile.

It is indicative that the only labour legislation in agriculture, the English 'Agricultural Children(s) Act' 1874, has only suppressed child labour indirectly through compulsory school attendance. According to this law, children under 8 may not be employed in field work at all. Between the ages of 8 and 10 they can only be employed if it is shown that they have attended school 250 times in the year: and between the ages of 10 and 12, 150 attendances per year are required. Migrant labour is prohibited. As meagre as these provisions are, and they do have a number of loopholes, they have nevertheless reduced child labour before the age of 12 to a minimum.

School, both elementary and secondary, has a more significant mission in the countryside than in the town. Attempts to protect working children must address themselves to extending it.

A ban on the wage labour of children up to 14 years; a ban on work between 7 in the evening and 7 in the morning for all children *and youths* without exception; a ban on *migratory labour by youths;* a ban on exemptions from compulsory school attendance on commercial grounds; adequate obligatory secondary schools for young persons – these are the demands of Social Democratic social policy towards child labour in the countryside.

Women's Labour

We can be a little briefer on the question of women's labour.

The development of women's labour in agriculture does not run at all parallel to that in industry. It provides a clear example of how variable the division of labour is between the sexes, how the lines of demarcation between women's work and men's work are constantly shifting, and why it is therefore inappropriate to regard such lines as natural – that is 'eternal' as far as social institutions are concerned.

When cultivation first began, it was exclusively carried out by women, with men attending to hunting and tending the stock. The more importance that arable farming had for society, the higher the status of the woman in the family and society, for which she was, literally, the main breadwinner. (Cf. von Cunow, 'Die ökonomischen Grundlagen der Mutterherrschaft', *Neue Zeit*, XV, pp. 106ff.).

However, as cultivation began to push hunting and stock-tending into the background, the men had to become involved too. But the more that arable farming developed, the more the population began to settle in one place: the cramped tent became the permanent spacious house, with a substantial household. The woman's labour in the household grew and soon occupied her fully; the once purely female art of cultivation, whose invention the Greeks and Romans quite properly ascribed to the female deities, became a male affair.

Lippert asks how it came about that in Jewish mythology cultivation was practised by men from the outset – Adam, Cain, Noah: his answer is that the Jews did not pass through the stage of *inventing* cultivation, but learnt it at a higher level when they conquered Canaan whilst themselves still living a Bedouin-like nomadic existence (Lippert, *Kulturgeschichte der Menschheit*, p. 447).

In contrast, the more that the predators from whom the flocks had to be protected disappeared, the more stock-tending became a matter for the women. More stock was kept in stalls, and constituted part of the household – apart from periods of migration to other pastures [*Weidegang*].

The capitalist mode of production drives women back into the fields, partly by creating a mass rural proletariat whose wages are so low that the male income is not sufficient to keep the family, which means the use of women and children to supplement the wage – naturally with the result that the man's wages fall even lower – and partly because of the worsening of the position of the peasantry which is forced to flog every last drop of sweat out of anyone able to work, including women and children, in order to eke out some kind of existence.

Where the peasant is well off, the woman will confine herself to the household where she has more than enough to do. The same applies to the wife of the rural day-labourer. In America she does not even participate in the harvest, despite the shortage of wage-labourers. Sering notes:

> Nothing is more indicative of the attitudes and expectations of the American farming population than the position of women there. Female members of the farmer's family concern themselves solely with the household, in the narrow sense of the term, and leave heavy work to the men. One rarely sees women working in the fields in America, and those that are are certain to belong to the family of an immigrant farmer. (Sering, *Die landwirtschafliche Konkurrenz Nordamerikas,* p. 180)

This fact is difficult to record statistically, since occupational statistics only establish the *fact* of employment in a particular occupation, and not its *nature*. Nevertheless, it is indicative that in 1895 there were 2,380,148 female wage-labourers in agriculture to 3,239,646 men, whilst in the United States there were 2,556,957 male, and 447,104 female 'agricultural labourers' and 1,858,558 male and 54,815 female 'labourers' (often agricultural too).

However, this tendency is not confined to America. In England, the postion of rural workers has by and large changed for the better over the last few decades, thanks to migration off the land. This is partly due to increases in wages and partly to the fall in the price of foodstuffs. The reduction in female wage-labour has gone hand in hand with this development. 'The widespread withdrawal of women from fieldwork is proof of the improvement in the position of the workforce', observed the Royal Commission (p. 37). The number of agricultural workers in Great Britain (excluding Ireland) changed as follows:

	Men	Women
1871	1,060,836	100,902
1891	878,480	46,205

The number of men fell by 18 per cent, and that of women by 54 per cent.

In Germany such a change is less apparent: but here too the number of women engaged in fieldwork as day-labourers is falling. Weber reports from West Prussia for example: 'Women's labour has disappeared completely in some areas; the wives of free day-labourers do their utmost to avoid it.' From East Prussia: 'The wives of free day-labourers work only very infrequently with their husbands ... Women's labour seems generally to be on the decline.' From Pomerania: 'The decline in women's labour is evident when compared with 1849' etc. (Weber, *Die Verhältnisse der Landarbeiter im ostelbischen Deutschland*, pp. 49, 185, 202, 377).

Developments in agriculture therefore by no means follow the same course as in industry; and this is easily explained when one considers the great importance which the private household still has in the countryside, and the different demands this makes on the housewife compared with the town. Only the severest distress, which both reduces the household to the extreme and necessitates an excess of overwork, will get the wife of the day-labourer or small peasant into wage-labour in the fields. It is indicative that English tenants give increased concern for children, for whom wage-labour is forbidden, as one of the reasons why women's labour has declined. The Education Act 'not only removed the labour of children from the tenant farmer, but also the labour of women; the women now stay at home to look after the children' (Kablukov, *Ländliche Arbeiterfrage*, p. 102).

Since wage-labour by married women on the land is a phenomenon which disappears as the position of the agricultural working class improves, there is no need for special protective legislation where overall social policy is sufficiently strong to effect such an improvement.

Similarly, the predominant form of wage-labour by young girls as house-servants requires no particular protective provisions separate from those affecting all house-servants, or the agricultural working class as a whole.

However, this statement does not apply to *migrant labour* by girls.

Migrant Labour

Migrant labour found its classical form in the now banned gang system in England. Marx described it in *Capital* in the following terms:

> The gang consists of from 10 to 40 or 50 persons, women, young persons of both sexes (13–18 years of age, although the boys are for the most part eliminated at the age of 13), and children of both sexes (6-13 years of age). At the head of the gang is the gang-master, always an ordinary agricultural labourer, and usually what is called a bad lot, a rake, unsteady, drunken but with a dash of enterprise and *savoir faire*. The gang-master goes from one farm to another, and thus employs his gang for from six to eight months in the year. The 'drawbacks' of this system are the over-working of the children and young persons, the

enormous marches that they make every day to and from farms and finally the demoralization of the gang. Girls of 13 and 14 are commonly made pregnant by their male companions of the same age. The open villages which supply the contingents for the gangs become Sodoms and Gomorrahs and have twice as high a rate of illegitimacy as the rest of the kingdom. (Marx, *Capital*, I, pp. 851–2)

Some types of German migratory labour are not much better. Let us listen to one witness who is above suspicion, that fond eulogist of the *Sachsengängerei* – or as fond as this institution could tolerate – Dr Kärger.

The *Sachsengänger* are workers from poor, economically backward districts, who move into the beet-sugar areas, in particular Saxony, to hoe and harvest, tasks for which the beet-farmers cannot find local willing and cheap workers. The *Sachsengänger* are recruited by agents who appear to bear an astonishing resemblance to the English gang masters. Recruitment takes place in the tavern, and is effected using every possible type of crooked trick.

If the recruiting agent is dealing with really stupid people, he makes a great show of the seal on the contract, giving the impression that the authorities have sanctioned the whole thing. Before the business gets going he tries to take on an aide who is skilled in a couple of languages (German and Polish): the aide moves around amongst the workers to make accepting the contract seem a plausible thing to do from their point of view, and acts as a bell-wether by being the first to sign the contract.

Unfortunately in some villages with Polish-speaking inhabitants, agents sometimes offer the people better conditions than the contract actually specifies. (Kärger, *Die Sachsengängerei*, p. 21)

The same agent who recruits the workers stays on as their supervisor and has ample opportunity to continue with his roguery. Having deceived them with the contract, he proceeds to exploit them through a hidden truck system:

Supervisors have been known to discriminate against workers in the distribution of jobs, by only giving them poorly paid and uncomfortable work, for not wanting to buy at 'his' merchants – that is, those he has taken under his wing in return for concessions. Even greater dangers face the *Sachsengänger* if the supervisor also controls the payment of wages.

He simply embezzles a portion of them, and in fact this is so widespread, 'that on some estates where this is supposed to have been abolished, the supervisors are impertinent enough to demand a small percentage of the overall wages of their workers by right'. As a consequence, this type of wage-payment has been abolished in many areas.

The workers under the supervision of these gentlemen are mostly girls, 'whose numbers regularly exceed those of the men severalfold' (p. 43), and mostly girls at a very tender age. Kärger counted 337 female and 150 male workers on 4 farms in Saxony. Of the young women 48.3 per cent were under 20, and 33.9 per cent between 20 and 25 – that is a total of 82.2 per cent under 25: 93.4 per cent were under 30. Unfortunately Herr Kärger forgot to note how many were under 16; perhaps he would not have found out even had he asked. The sugar manufacturers are unlikely to have betrayed all their trade secrets even to the likes of Herr Kärger.

Of the 150 men, 32 per cent were under 20, 19.3 per cent 20 to 25, and 73.3 per cent under 30.

These young, carefree, unworldly girls move around in groups together with the young men, under the leadership of the recruiting agent – who we have already identified as a strict moralist. It does not require a great deal of imagination to see that conditions bearing an awesome similarity to those of the English gang system are likely to develop.

Having arrived at the estates of our Christian and patriotic landowner, they are by no means out of danger. The work is hard, and the working hours inhumanly long.

> In the West – from what I have seen of such contracts – the work always begins at 5 in the morning, and ends at 7 in the evening, with a half-hour break for breakfast, one hour for lunch, and a half-hour break for Vespers. However, overtime is universally insisted upon. (Kärger, *Die Sachsengängerei*, p. 41)

That is, young girls are sweated for over 14 hours a day. Marx described how women work:

> The farmers have discovered that women only work steadily under the direction of men, but that women and children, when once set going, spend their vital forces impetuously – as Fourier already knew in his time – whereas the adult male worker is shrewd enough to economise on his strength as much as he can. (Marx, *Capital*, I, p. 851)

The methods used by these industrial slave-drivers to extract the maximum effort from their workers are well known from the 'patriarchal' regime. The murderous piecework system plays a major role, especially in tasks assigned to migrant labourers. But the East Elbians have invented even more inspired methods of forcing their workers into overwork. Weber gives us a hint of this in his book – which we have extensively quoted elsewhere.

We were repeatedly told that workers are more easily induced to overwork through the provision of 'refreshments' (schnapps) than through money. One inherently unpleasant aspect of overtime experienced in the Heiligenbeil district was that workers – if not as much as formerly – still require 'that damn schnapps' to get them to do it.

In other words, our Christian-Germanic nobles systematically get their workers drunk so as to stoke them up for work, just as in the seventeenth and eighteenth centuries mercenaries were plied with schnapps before battle to inflame them against the enemy, and quell their fear of the prospect of death. The Junkers evidently not only profit from Prussian schnapps as a commodity, but also as a foodstuff.

Migrant workers receive even less mercy than the permanent local workers. Let them get sick afterwards! There is no obligation to keep them through the winter and pay their medical costs.

But worst of all is the accommodation provided for migrant workers. Since it is not worthwhile building permanent homes for these workers, which would then lie empty for seven or eight months each year, the more primitive their accommodation the better. Although Herr Kärger has nothing but praise for the tenements built for the *Sachsengänger* on some farms, their main advantage is probably that the sexes sleep in separate areas – by no means an automatic institution. This was enforced by an order of the police.

Matters have not yet advanced quite as far in East Elbia.

In West Prussia accommodation is provided out of barracks, cattle stables and empty barns, into which workers crowd ten or more together. It is impossible to say whether the sexes are kept separated: a half, two-thirds or more are girls. This will be more likely on the more progressive estates than elsewhere. (Weber, *Die Verhältnisse der Landarbeiter im ostelbischen Deutschland*, p. 240)

How much one should share this expectation is revealed by the fact that a few pages earlier Weber himself complains that there are no opportunities for the separation of the sexes even in the dwellings of permanent *Instleute*. 'The family has to share their living room and bedroom with outsiders on gang-work (p. 183).

This economics of the rabbit warren is not a product of the 'state of the future', but of our present-day state where Christian-Germanic discipline and respectability still live on uncontaminated by Social Democratic poison, and where the noblest and best still reign untrammelled: it is our defenders of the family and marriage who, in their efforts to lower the production costs of schnapps and sugar, herd together their human stock into cattle sheds without distinction of age or sex.

That such scandalous conditions cry out for legislative remedy is now recognised even by bourgeois *Sozialpolitiker*.

The principal demand must be a ban on migrant labour by female minors. Dr Kärger will, of course, hear nothing of this – and he has his good reasons.

The proposal for a complete ban on migrant labour for girls below the age of majority results from the hope that it will reduce the dangers of moral depravity. My first observation is that I do not believe that the percentage of girls who abandon their virtue will be reduced by such a measure, as a girl who has been protected by her parents up to the age of 21 and is then cast out into life will be no more victorious in resisting the temptation of immorality than the younger girl. (Kärger, *Die Sachsengängerei*, p. 206)

The sentence may not be absolutely perfectly expressed, but our conclusion on reading it is that Dr Kärger would take Marx's report of girls of 13 and 14 getting pregnant under the gang-system very coolly indeed. He seems unconcerned as to whether this happens earlier or later.

But his main objection to such a ban on migrant labour is posed in terms of the interests of the fathers of migrant girl workers. What are these poor devils supposed to do with their young daughters if they cannot sell them off into contract slavery?

'To take a somewhat crass example, what should a small landowner from the Landsberg district, whom fate has presented with a gift of a daughter every year for six years, do with his blessings when the last of his daughters is 16?' We wouldn't dispute that this is a crass example: and if it is meant to offer conclusive proof, we can supply another, equally arbitrary, and no less conclusive example which is certainly no more crass. What happens if the farmer sends his six daughters to Saxony as migrant workers and each comes back with an illegitimate child? What's he going to do with his 'little blessings' then?

But Dr Kärger has another weighty reason: the exploitation of girls between 16 and 21 yields the greatest profit of all for beet farmers and sugar manufacturers, and prohibiting their employment 'should consequently be rejected from the standpoint of the interests of beet cultivation'. Our noble doctor is therefore fighting a genuine cultural battle on behalf of the right of beet cultivation to prostitute young girls. However, we Social Democratic vandals do not share his appreciation of such cultivation for sugar beet based on the barbarisation of people, and so we stand by our demand that migrant labour should be banned for girls below the age of majority.

Admittedly, this will not accomplish everything. Although a 21-year-old girl may be less easily corrupted than a 15 or 16-year-old since she has more experience and a more resolute character, the conditions under which present-day migrant labourers work are bad enough to corrupt even mature girls. Nevertheless, it would be going too far to ban migrant labour completely. Such a ban would deprive a large part of the working population of their freedom of movement, and rob them of a means of looking for higher wages than they can obtain at home. But migrant labour could take other forms than contract slavery and the gang system. These must be done away with. The most effective means of abolition would be the development of a public system of labour exchanges, which would supplant the trade in human beings now practised by the agents.

The need for strict regulations to enforce the provision of proper accommodation needs no further proof here. In addition a reduction in the inhumanly long working hours is also vital.

But not, of course, just for migrant labourers.

The Normal Working Day – Sunday Rest

This brings us to the issue of *the normal working day*, the main issue in the protection of workers.

Opponents of the proletarian movement are fond of saying that the normal working day – whose appropriateness and even necessity they no longer dispute for industry, although most are against reducing it – is incompatible with the conditions prevailing in agriculture, which lacks the regularity and uniformity of industry, is more dependent on external circumstances – wind, weather, rain and sunshine – and must therefore be more flexible and not squeezed into the straitjacket of a normal working day.

In fact, however, agriculture requires much less flexibility than industry. A farm's plan of work is fixed for the entire year, whereas an industrial enterprise may have to vary its operations depending on the state of business. Industrial entrepreneurs moaned more than anyone that the normal working day made it impossible for them to exploit the state of the market, and complete orders which had to be delivered very quickly. And they were much more vigorous than farmers in demanding flexibility in working hours, to satisfy the changing needs of the market – a much more capricious entity than wind and weather. But events took their proper course. Technical ability and organisational talent have surmounted all obstacles. The introduction of the normal working day has not killed off industry, simply industrial inefficiency.

There are examples of a normal working day in agriculture. However, we are unaware of any *legally* fixed normal working day. Attempts to implement such a regulation have been tried here and there, partly under pressure from angry farm workers, and partly, on more idealist grounds, by the agrarian ideologues themselves who were certainly well acquainted with the circumstances prevailing in agriculture. Dr R. Meyer notes in the Introduction to his essay on the 'History of the Normal Working Day' (in the *Zeitschrift für Sozial- und Wirtschaftgeschichte*, VI, 1):

> The legislative restriction of working time for men was first implemented in 1848 in Mecklenburg. (The revolt of the farm day labourers led to the establishment of a Commission of Arbitration over the disputed circumstances of day labourers (15 May 1848), which also regulated the working time on large estates) ... The Prussian conservatives Wagener and von Brauchitsch attempted to introduce a normal working day in 1869, but this foundered on the opposition of Herr Stumm ... In 1872 together with Herr Schumacher I got a resolution through the Conference of Rural Employers which demanded a statutory normal working day, and in 1874 or 1875 drafted a bill with Wagener which restricted the work of adults to 56.5 hours both in the town and on the land, which we communicated to Bismarck.

These efforts were not rewarded with success. However, since then economic developments now favour a normal working day on the land.

The techniques employed on large establishments have also introduced a greater regularity of work into agriculture than is customary on the small farm, and the growing pressure from farm workers is also pushing in this direction.

Protection of Rural Proletariat 379

The daily working time on the beet farms, contractually specified for the *Sachsengänger*, is nothing other than a normal working day. Weber also confirms that the tendency towards the fixing of a normal working day is growing. He reports from Lithuania, for example:

> The most effective way of reducing working time; beginning work at a *fixed* hour, not at sunrise, is quite recent in origin in many cases, and is only now being introduced into some farms in the southern districts. Starting times vary between 5 and 6 o'clock in the morning. In places a fixed time for finishing (between 7 and 8 in summer), which may not coincide with sunset, has also managed to get through. (Weber, *Die Verhältnisse der Landarbeiter im ostelbischen Deutschland*, pp. 48, 121, 84)

From the district of Königsberg: 'Farms on which work begins in summer at sunrise are usually of medium-sized holders: the large estates are more prepared to go over to fixed starting times – 5, 5.30 or 6 o'clock' (ibid., p. 121).

From Masuria: 'A fixed start to the day in summer is already established in quite a large number of instances, as are fixed finishing times too' (ibid., p. 84).

Weber also notes that farmworkers are becoming increasingly disinclined to work overtime. We can therefore already see the beginnings of a normal working day in agriculture in Germany, and although these first steps may still be small ones, this fact has less to do with the peculiarities of agriculture than the dependent situation of agricultural workers, whose power to insist on a reduction in working time and regular observance of it is still very slight. All the more reason why their comrades in industry should shoulder the task of bringing them the legislation which they cannot obtain by their own efforts.

What determines the limit to the agricultural working day is beyond the scope of this book; as in industry, what turns out to be the practically attainable limit will be quite variable – all the more so since it will be determined not simply by objective technical factors, but the very subjective factor of power. However, we see no reason why the eight hour day should not be the aim of the labour movement in capitalist society in both agriculture and industry.

One might object that agricultural labour is carried out under hygienically much more favourable conditions than industrial work: in the latter we have monotonous work in enclosed rooms, often filled with poisonous fumes, and in the former a variety of activities in the fresh air. Although this is quite a valid distinction in most cases, in turn the position of the wage-labourers in the town is also different to their counterparts on the land. As we have already repeated many times, the rural household is necessarily linked with an agricultural establishment. The day-labourers have not ended their working day once they get home after wage-labour – they still have to look after their small farm, clean the stables, get fodder for the cow, dig over the potato field and so on. Were wage-labour to occupy their entire time, from dawn to dusk, they would only have nights and Sundays for their own farm.

As in the case of the married female factory worker, the duration of wage-labour is by no means equivalent to the actual duration of work for the agricultural day-labourer. And any advancement in the position of the wage-labourers is associated with an increase in work on their own farms. This will not change overnight. The reduction in the agricultural worker's working day to eight hours therefore falls far short of giving preferential treatment to the agricultural worker over the town worker.

Although we might regard it as just as feasible to introduce a normal working day into agriculture as it is into industry, this does not mean both can be treated in exactly the same way. The length of the natural day has an entirely different impact on the length of the working day in agriculture to that prevailing in industry, where work is also carried out under artificial light. On the other hand, industry has a very different reserve army at its disposal from that available to agriculture. It may well prove necessary, therefore, to fix a different normal working day for each season, rather than a uniform working day for the whole year: whilst an eight hour day could be retained as the norm, a winter working day of six hours and a summer working day of ten hours could be worked. Overtime could be allowed for acts of God and urgent harvest work. At any event, we do not have to rack our brains too much over this question. Once the establishment of a normal working day for agriculture actually comes about, those with a direct interest will soon ensure that it has the necessary elasticity. Social Democracy's task will then not consist in raising anxious doubts about this elasticity, but in ensuring that it does not become a purely arbitrary matter, rendering illusory any limitations on working time.

Although we may concede that the normal working day in agriculture will not exactly resemble that practised in industry, we are not aware of any special characteristics of agriculture to justify confining the agricultural normal working day to the large farm, as the Zurich International Congress on Labour Protection recently decided. That small establishments are generally run in a more slovenly way than the large, and that the strict observance of regular working hours requires external compulsion applies just as much to industry as agriculture. And if Social Democracy demands the normal working day for handicrafts and the factory, then it should also demand the same rights for the wage labourer working for the large peasant as for those working for the estate owner. Its task is not to grant the small establishment a privileged position in relation to the large.

Although we may not be able to develop any enthusiasm for confining the normal working day to the large farm, this does not mean that we consider the normal working day can be applied to every type of agricultural labour. Distinctions have to be drawn – but not between the large and small farm.

Social Democracy demands the normal working day for every type of wage-labour, with *one* exception: work in the household. This is not because house-servants do not need their working hours reduced, but because the requirements of the household do not easily allow working hours to be restricted to certain times of the day. This applies both to the rural and the urban household. The rural household is intimately connected with the farm, or at least with certain aspects of it. The closer a branch of work on the land is connected with the household, the more difficult it will be to subordinate it to the normal working day. One therefore has to be very precise in specifying which types of labour will be covered by the normal working day. Field work will be more easily subsumable than work in the house or farmyard (especially the tending of animals), and the work of the day-labourer more easily than that of the domestic servant. The labours of the former are usually determined, regular and measureable – hoeing, mowing, threshing; that of the latter, variable, and not easily subject to control.

The institution of the normal working day will not therefore fully prevent the overwork of domestic servants. The normal working day is the form of the protection of labour which corresponds to the conditions of *modern* wage labour. To protect the domestic servant, this vestige of the Middle Ages, we have to resort to medieval methods. During that era, the natural day counted as the working day; there was no restriction on daily working time, but there was a restriction on annual working time through the numerous holidays which, corresponding to the thinking of that age, were occasioned by religious traditions. Religious holidays were legion (see p. 111). The struggle over the working day in the Middle Ages was the struggle over holidays – in the handicrafts, journeymen added 'drunken Monday' to the religious holidays. The suppression of the democratic classes by mercantilist-feudalist absolutism led to a reduction in the number of holidays, first in the Protestant and then in the Catholic countries. But the Sabbath remained.

Today even this is no longer so strictly observed, and least of all by that section of the population which still clings most to religion, the agricultural population. 'I can still remember the time', complains our 'country priest from Thuringia',

> when Sunday on the land was an evangelical sabbath: any business on the fields which could not be put off was performed very early in the day, at the latest before 6 o'clock. Only in years of really poor harvest would the priest announce on Sunday morning, at the behest of the mayor, that midday mass would not be held and field work would be allowed. I have also lived through decades in which although there was a Sunday Act on the lawbook, it was virtually repealed through the almost total forbearance of the authorities. Sunday work is increasing from year to year with progress in agriculture, with the increase in yields, with the ever more nervous haste and greed in buying and the steady decline in the old peasant trust in God, proper devotion to God and surrender to Him.

He had hoped that a new law on Sunday rest might bring an improvement, but soon everything was as before.

Sunday working has also increased in areas of large estates as well as amongst the peasantry. As with overtime, schnapps serves as the slave-driver here too (cf. Weber, op. cit., 1892, III, p. 289). Those pillars of piousness, who strive so hard to keep the population to religion, stoke it with booze in order to ignore its ordinances.

However, the decline in church attendance is no concern of ours: instead we should work towards preventing the meagre rest time which tradition still leaves the farmworker from being eroded yet further. Indispensable is the strict prohibition of all work on Sunday that is not absolutely necessary, and the securing of every second Sunday as a completely free day for the domestic servant, even if a normal working day is introduced into agriculture. At any event, the former is easier to win than the latter, and should therefore be demanded all the more vigorously.

As far as other provisions for the protection of workers are concerned, the problems encountered in agriculture will be much simpler than those seen in industry. The attachment of protective devices to machines, and the prohibition on using untrained, in particular, young workers, on them, is just as vital in agriculture as it is in industry. In contrast, night work does not yet play a role in the former – although this might change as electricity encroaches on to farming: and regulations regarding space, cleanliness, ventilation are certainly not necessary for field work.

The Housing Question

In contrast, housing policy poses the protection of labour much greater tasks in agriculture than in industry. We cannot rehearse the whole housing question here, however: and we certainly do not want to minimise the fact that housing misery in the towns creates conditions which are as bad as any on the land. Some sections of the industrial population live in even worse conditions than the agricultural – if this is possible; the living conditions exposed by Professor Singer in the industrial districts of Northern Bohemia are as dreadful as any of the 'rural shanties' revealed by Pastors Göhre, Quisdorp, Wittenberg and others. The garret which Göhre saw, in which four different couples slept on eight straw sacks on the ground, is no worse than the room in a workers' tenement visited by Singer in Trautenau: only 15.2 square metres in area, 'it contained a bed of the usual dimensions, which held one family consisting of five individuals (three adults and two children). A further nine persons of both sexes, young and old, lay sleeping densely packed together on the hard plaster floor – which lacked even a covering of straw' (Singer, *Untersuchungen über die sozialen Zustände in den Fabriksbezirken des nordöstlichen Böhmen*, p. 186).

Of course, the situation is not as bad as this everywhere: but wage labourers suffer from the virtually universal 'disproportion between the size of rooms and the number of their occupants', which Pastor Göhre observed in Chemnitz. Not only must married couples share their dwelling, and this usually means the bedroom, with half or fully-grown children, but also with lodgers of both sexes.

However, our concern here is not with how the poorer classes are housed in general, but with those dwellings which constitute part of the wage. The role of such dwellings is quite different on the land to that in the towns. In towns, living-in by wage-labourers in the employer's residence is a fast disappearing remnant of medieval handicraft customs; on the land, even the most modern large farm has to provide accommodation for some of its workers. Whilst the labour of the house-servant is no longer important in the handicrafts, and especially in large-scale industry, matters are quite different in agriculture. Agriculture is also distinguished by the number of contractually tied married workers with their own household, but living in the employer's house – the *Instleute*, and rent-fee farmers, who are contractually obliged to provide a number of days' labour in return for their accommodation.

However, of all areas of the welfare of workers – meaning, in the broadest sense, all those classes who perform so-called manual labour – workers themselves place least weight on housing. Any loss of nourishment will be immediately noticed by its effects on the body; remaining fit for work requires a proper diet, especially for those carrying out heavy work in the open air, such as farm workers. The pleasures of the palate, not simply eating but drinking and smoking too, are also familiar to the worker on grounds of tradition and physiology, are easily attainable, and hence greatly appreciated.

Dress provides the clearest expression of differences in social rank and social aspiration. As a consequence every aristocracy and hierarchy lays great store by rules of dress and insignia for the individual ranks and estates. The arrogance of rude soldiery is most clearly evidenced in the veneration which they demand for the so-called 'king's mantle'. Where there is no militarism, as in England, and where the soldier's uniform is an apparel of service, not of honour, an officer sporting himself in uniform when not on duty would be considered laughable.

The advance of democracy is accompanied by a tendency for differences in dress between the classes to disappear: as equals before the law, they demand the same respect in society. Proletarians do not want to bear the marks of their wage slavery outside work, do not want to distinguish themselves from the bourgeois in external appearance. Like the bourgeois, they want Sunday best too. The social rise of any stratum of the proletariat is probably more clearly revealed in improvements in their clothing than in their diet.

Housing is accorded the least importance. The physiological damage caused by poor housing is not felt as rapidly as that induced by an inadequate diet. Recognising the link between poor housing and physical deterioration requires observations and knowledge unattainable to those whose entire understanding is a product of our elementary schools, apart from that gleaned through personal experience. And what in fact is a dwelling for most workers today? Somewhere to sleep, basically. The worker arrives home late in the evening, dog-tired, and falls asleep. They leave early the next morning for the day's work. One room is quite sufficient.

Workers' frugality in the field of housing is even acknowledged by economists hostile to the working class. Although they might continue to rail against the workers' love of pleasure and finery, the champagne cellars of masons and the silk dresses of factory girls, we have not, as yet, come across any complaints about their luxury housing.

The gap between the proletarian standard of living and that of the middle classes is at its widest in the field of housing. But this also represents both the point at which workers offer least resistance to all the factors pressing down on them, and the point at which these factors are felt most acutely. The prices of factory-produced goods and many foodstuffs are falling, except where artificially kept up by tariffs and price rings. Set against money wages, many strata of the proletariat can be seen to be experiencing a rising standard of living. Matters are different with housing. Whilst ground-rents in agriculture are falling, they are rising rapidly in the towns: the price of housing is increasing fast and forcing workers either to spend a large proportion of their wages on rent or to cut back more and more as far as their standards are concerned. The position is not much better on the land, where wage-labourers obtain a house *in natura* as part of their wages. The more widespread the system of employers supplying housing, the greater will be the pressure to reduce production costs, then the more determined any resistance by workers will be to cuts in their rations or food allowances; and the higher the wages which have to be paid to them, the more employers will seek to worsen the housing provided to workers, or – where this is no longer possible – to oppose any improvement.

But if housing represents that element in the proletarian standard of living most resistant to improvement, and in which the tendency towards immiseration is felt most sharply, it also represents one of the most weighty forces holding the worker down. Inadequate housing does not only lead to physical deterioration, like an inadequate diet: it also leads to a degeneration in moral and mental capacities – in fact to the complete suppression of those most tender of feelings which develop out of the most intimate relationships. Anyone interested in understanding the shamelessness and brutalisation which prevails in slum districts would find it more instructive to examine where lumpenproletarians live, rather than investigate the shape of their skulls.

Migrant labourers and many other *working* proletarians also live in similar hovels to those of the poorest big city lumpenproletarians: married couples with children, young girls and lads, sick and healthy, all heaped together, huddled both for warmth and to make more space in their confined quarters. Worked like beasts of burden by day, housed worse than beasts of burden by night – what else could thrive there except animal brutality and lewdness? And the customary dwellings of factory workers, as described by Göhre above, or the dwellings of *Instleute*, who sleep together with gang-workers, are hardly suited to develop the more refined sensibilities.

However, there is one great distinction between town and country. Although the dire housing situation in the town is degrading and morally stultifying to the worker, the town also harbours forces which work against this, not only mitigating the effects of the housing problem but in places overcoming them completely. Work, in itself, in the town brings workers together, not simply to work but also for mutual stimulation, the discussion of public affairs, at least before and after work and during breaks. Labour on the land disperses the population over large areas and isolates them from each other. Town life outside work offers innumerable stimulations, associations, meetings, exhibitions, museums, theatres – even the pubs become an organ of public life, through which a part of the stream of urban culture flows. They are a place where workers can read newspapers and discuss what they have read. The individual develops independent thought; he or she becomes an individual and as such begins to feel the need for a home, a place in which to live, for friends, books, ideas. And if the stimulations of town life allow the better-off sections of the working class to surmount the degrading effects of the housing situation, these strata also develop a certain 'covetousness' towards housing and impel the worker to set even higher standards in this field.

The situation is different on the land. There are no stimulations to counter the degrading influences of poor housing. Work serves to isolate the population: associations and meetings are virtually impossible in view of the farmworker's economic dependency. No intellectual life exists to edify the worker. Public life rotates exclusively around the inn, which merely reflects the intellectual barrenness of the countryside. Any smidgeon of intellectual stimulation it might offer is generally drowned in booze, exacerbating rather than mitigating the depressing effects of the housing situation.

The specific effects of living in one's master's house, with one's employer, are also experienced far more acutely on the land. The public life of the town can offset these effects. A baker or master butcher who forbids his resident journeyman to bring Social Democratic newspapers into the house cannot prevent him from reading such papers in the public house, or stop his attending meetings in his free time. In contrast, the agricultural workers who live in the landowner's farmhouse are not only forced into complete submission in work but also outside it. Their intellectual life, political behaviour, personal relationships – everything is under observation; they enjoy no freedom of the press, no right of combination (even where this is guaranteed by legislation), and often not even the freedom to vote as they wish under universal suffrage. They are only distinguished from slaves by the fact that they occasionally change their master: in return for this freedom they can be thrown on the street once they become unfit for work.

Although no one would deny the importance of improving housing conditions in the towns, this is even more important on the land. Legislation to protect workers in agriculture would fall far short of accomplishing its most important task were it to exclude housing from its scope. Setting a minimum level of sanitary conditions for all living areas assigned to workers as part of the wage is required.

Such a provision, as extensive as the principles of hygiene dictate and applied without fear or favour, would have an enormously beneficial effect in the country. Not only would it bring about a significant improvement in the housing conditions of a large part of the agricultural labour force, but would also contribute to raising the overall standard of living of the rural population. Such a step would also prove a powerful means of clearing away those remnants of feudal employment relationships which still persist into the twentieth century: farmers would have to undertake a massive reduction in the number of workers living under their roofs and replace them with free day-labourers. The supplanting of domestic servants and *Instleute* by day-labourers, who would be free individuals outside work, would represent a great social advance.

Such an advance would admittedly be linked with some technical regression, since any landowner wishing to keep free day-labourers in their locality would have to ensure that they could establish their own household – that is, be able to farm a piece of land, be it their own or rented. The decline in the number of house-servants would lead to a multiplication of small farms at the expense of the large farm: however, the technical effects of such an increase would be slight, scarcely worthy of note when set against the social advance associated with the supplanting of the vestiges of feudal servitude by free wage-labour.

However, although the free day-labourers are socially on a higher level than the bondsman or *Instmann*, once they own their own home and a little land they lose the most important weapon of proletarian class struggle on the land, which is more effective even than the right of combination: *freedom of movement*. Their property chains them down.

There is only one obvious way of overcoming this obstacle: *the construction of worker housing for rent from public funds*. Such a demand is clearly dependent on a number of preconditions – primarily, the free self-administration of local parishes, rural districts and so forth, and universal suffrage for those representative bodies which influence their administration. The fulfilment of these conditions, together with the presence of an independent movement of agricultural workers with sufficient strength to be able to and to want to take up the struggle for representation on local councils, is necessary before Social Democracy could actually demand that parishes, or better, administrative districts on which the economic dominance of a small number of landowners is less apparent, should build houses to rent for farm workers. Such a step would in all likelihood bring agricultural labour to the greatest degree of independence attainable within capitalist society.

However, with the exception of England, we are not aware of any state in which raising this demand would lie in the interests of farm workers at present.

Rent on Land

A number of issues concerned with rent are closely related to the housing question.

As we saw in an earlier chapter, the price of agricultural land is only determined by ground-rent where it serves capitalist commodity-production. Where land is merely attached to the household, its price can far exceed capitalised ground-rent, and does so wherever circumstances favour the growth of population and the demand for land. And the price will be higher, the less the land is used for commodity-production and the more it is a mere appendage to the household – in general, this means the smaller the plot.

This is undoubtedly a major problem for the working population in the countryside, and constitutes one of the richest sources of the exploitation of the farm worker. The higher the price of a parcel of land needed to establish an independent household, the more they have to scrimp to save the purchase price and the more their standard of living is depressed. Under such circumstances the worker will be more inclined to try to borrow a part of the sum and so slip into debt-slavery and dependency. Where the land is leased, rather than bought, a high lease price will force the worker into greater dependency on wage labour: rents have to be met from money wages, not the product of the plot, which is not a commodity as far as the worker is concerned, or is so to only a minor extent. The higher the rent, the more eager and desperate the supply of labour power, and hence the lower any resistance to wage cutting. And the higher the rent, the more susceptible the worker becomes to rent arrears, which also become a source of debt slavery and dependence.

A successful struggle against this affliction would give a major boost to improving the situation and independence of the agricultural labourer.

This can be done where the tenant system operates: tenancy agreements simply have to be subject to the control of a court, which has the power to reduce unfairly high rents in excess of normal ground-rent down to the level of the latter; that is, to bring the rents of proletarian tenants into line with those of capitalist tenants. Such an institution was introduced in Ireland in 1881 by the supposedly Manchesterist ministry of Gladstone, and has been outstandingly successful.

The effects of a law of this kind, must, to some extent, have an effect opposite to that of the housing law outlined in the previous section. The latter forces large landowners to reduce the size of their holdings by chopping off small parcels for their workers; in contrast, the former renders such a separation less profitable than it would otherwise have been. One measure fosters the small farm, the other the large. However, these laws are not contradictory, but rather complementary: both work in the same direction, since each – if in different ways – are conducive to raising the standard of living and independence of the worker.

Matters are not quite as simple where workers actually buy their parcel. There is no practical legislative way to enforce a reduction in the excessive price of such parcels; and if such a measure were to exist it would be open to a number of objections. The landowners at whose expense the reduction in ground-rents is taking place, are often workers themselves. As beneficial as such a reduction might be to the worker buying land, it would rob those proletarians who have to sell their parcel as the former owner or co-inheritor of their few hard-earned, and saved, pennies. This provides yet another example of where the private ownership of land makes rational reform impossible.

14
The Protection of Agriculture

Social Democracy – Not the Representative of the Employers' Interests

The rent reform cited at the end of the previous chapter would not only be in the best interests of the agricultural labour force, but would also benefit agriculture. It would, and should, as already stated, only be to the advantage of the proletarian tenant; capitalist tenants would only gain once rents had been pushed down below the standard of normal ground-rents. But this would mean the end of the tenant system altogether, since landowners would find it more profitable to farm their land themselves. For the proletarian tenants the increase in income which would follow a reduction in rents could not only serve to raise their standard of living, but also allow the more rational organisation of the farm via the purchase of better tools, fertilisers and seeds.

The demand for reductions in excessive rents by means of special courts therefore represents a transition from measures to protect the *farm worker*, to measures encompassing the *interests* of *agriculture*.

Clearly, the latter is of less concern for Social Democracy than the former – the main reason being that Social Democracy is somewhat alone in its intervention on behalf of the rural proletarian. Matters are quite different when we look at agriculture. The interests of agriculture currently coincide with the interests of the agricultural entrepreneurs and the landowners, with the interests of profit on capital and ground-rent, in exactly the same way that the interests of industry concide with the interests of profit on capital in industry, and those of commerce with profits from trade. As important as these branches of the economy are for the overall life of our society – including that of the proletariat – they have other and more powerful patrons than the proletariat. Agriculture's distress is not caused by the inadequate representation of its interests or those of the landowners within the present-day state, or the neglect of governments and parliaments: it is due to causes which even a state friendly to agriculture will not be able to surmount as long as it remains rooted in the soil of present-day society and shrinks back from making any deep inroads into that society's basic organising principles.

Mere reasons of propaganda cannot possibly induce Social Democracy to take on the task of rivalling the agrarian charlatans in recommending miracle cures which promise immediate recovery for our ailing agriculture. By the same token it is also no part of its task to place even the true interests of agriculture – those in harmony with the interests of society as a whole – in the forefront of its efforts, just as it does not perceive its role as expending its energies in advancing the interests of industry and commerce. This is not because it places a low value on these interests, but rather because it is certain that they have ample opportunity to express themselves in the modern state, and that the state will do everything it can to foster them.

Social Democracy does not see itself in the role of agitator to industrialists and financiers; by the same token, it has no reason to seek to rouse farmers and landowners, both large and small, in the defence of their interests; its role is rather that of an observer, or possibly even a watchman, who looks to see that their special interests do not gain at the expense of the general interest, or their transient interests at the expense of long-term interests.

Social Democracy, whose duty it is to be active and positive in the interests of the proletariat, should adopt a basically negative, defensive, posture when it comes to protecting the interests of society at large under present-day circumstances. The positive elements must take a back seat as long as it lacks a real determining influence on political life.

This consideration alone is enough to ensure that Social Democracy will never be able to supplant the agrarian parties as far as the mass of independent farmers and landowners, who demand special concessions at the expense of society as a whole, are concerned – that is, those not dependent on supplementary employment. Despite all its theoretical goodwill towards the peasantry, Social Democracy, in practice, has never regarded it as necessary to mount a vigorous struggle for the agrarian measures pressed for most urgently by the peasantry.

Nevertheless, there are some areas within which Social Democracy can act positively in the interests of agricultural development.

Feudal Privileges – the Hunt

Social Democracy's prime efforts in this respect must be towards the removal of the *vestiges* of the feudal period, wherever they have been preserved or even revived. Social Democracy cannot be enlisted to support feudal privileges, the law of *entailment* and *Fideikommiss*.

However its opposition to the binding of property under *Fideikommiss* is not, as with bourgeois democracy's, aimed at encouraging its dismemberment into small peasant farms. For us, this would represent a serious technical step backwards.

In *East Prussia* the right of large landowners to exclude their holdings from rural parishes as *independent manorial districts (Gutsbezirke)*, and thus to offload their due share of the parish's burdens almost wholly on to the parish itself is much more pernicious than entailment. Landowners use the parish's roads and paths, their workers send their children to the parish schools, but they have no other obligation, or only the most minimal obligation, to bear any of the costs incurred in providing them. Instances, such as the following, can be found:

> Von Gouedies, a conservative Junker, has virtually dissolved the entire peasant parish in the village of Zuckersdorf, in the Rummelsberg district of Hinter Pomerania through the tactic of buying up land and incorporating it into his own property; *only two* independent peasants are left. These constitute the 'rural parish district', while the estate is an independent manorial district. The school currently needs rebuilding; but the costs fall exclusively on the 'parish', that is, the two peasants, whilst the estate owner gets off scot free as a 'lord of the manor'. The two peasants wanted to initiate proceedings against this, but they were advised not to: nothing would come of it. (*Die Epigonen der Raubritter*, p. 46)

The beneficence of the Prussian Junkers towards the peasantry is also illustrated in the *hunting rights* which they have created. This remnant of feudal privileges is not confined to Prussia, but extends throughout Germany and Austria.

The feudal privilege of the hunt had a double character. In the first place, it was a select sport, a 'feudal' sport, reserved for the nobility. Only land-owning nobles could indulge. The French revolution eliminated this, as with so many other privileges, and replaced the privilege of rank by that of land-ownership. Anyone might hunt on their own property. The 1848 revolution in Germany had the same effect. Nevertheless, here reaction swept away the equality of peasant and large landowner, although it was not able to restore the former feudal privilege. The large landowners (in Prussia of 75 hectares and upwards) could hunt freely on their own land; the small landowner could only do so on hedged land. The open plots of a number of small landowners (such as a commune or district) were joined into a hunting district, in which only hunting by employees or hunt tenants of the commune or district was permitted.

This restriction of hunting rights leaves us somewhat unmoved. Hunting is certainly not a means for economically or morally elevating the proletariat, or the mass of the population generally; irrespective of whether it is reserved for large landowners or can be enjoyed by all landowners, it will remain closed to the proletariat.

More important for us is the other privilege of the hunt handed down from feudal times: its legal precedence over agriculture. Agriculture, in particular peasant farming, has to serve hunting – not the other way around.

During feudalism's decline the peasants were obliged to feed the game for their gracious lord. They were forbidden to hedge their fields or scare off game animals (see p. 25). This naturally ceased in 1789, but game still occupies a privileged position in relation to the farmer's crops. Whereas the owner of pests is usually obliged to fence them in, this only applies at most to wild boar among the game animals. All other game is free, and the peasants may not shoot it even if it ruins their fields. Admittedly, the peasants are graciously permitted to fence in their fields and drive off game – but all that this means is that the cost of keeping game away from the peasants' crops has been shifted from the hunting lord to the peasants themselves.

The peasant has no influence whatsoever over the number and type of animals kept in the neighbouring woods belonging to a large landowner. And present hunting policy is diametrically opposed to the interests of agriculture.

Beasts of prey do not inflict much damage on the farmer. Even the tiger is regarded as an ally rather than an enemy by the East Indian farmer. Only a small number of particularly vicious tigers make unprovoked attacks on people, and the animals under their protection. And given the vast amounts of game in the typical jungle, the tiger does not need such a haul. By decimating the game which the farmer would otherwise be hard put to keep off the fields, the tiger earns the farmer's gratitude.

Europe does not have regal tigers, and is generally bereft even of wolves: the main predators are little foxes and martens. Like predatory birds, these inflict virtually no damage on the attentive farmers who take good care of their poultry at night. And they are invaluable in their assiduous and effective prevention of the excessive multiplication of mice and other rodents who devastate the farmer's crops. However, the hunter hates the small predator because it might also polish off a hare or deer, to the great displeasure of the sportsman, though not the farmer.

The farmer's interest dictates that the bulk of predatory game should be spared, at least within certain limits, whilst the number of specimens of herbivorous game animals be restricted. Current hunting policy demands the opposite, and has won out over the interests of the farmer.

Of course, there is now an obligation to pay compensation for damage caused by game. But look at how meagre it is. The hunting lord or tenant is relieved of any obligation to make good damage caused by certain animals (hares!). This is simply yet another illustration of the bare-faced impudence of the Prussian Junkers, who struck out any obligation to pay for damage by game from the 1850 Hunting Acts. After a number of Liberal motions to repeal this privilege had been rejected, the Centre Party introduced a game damage compensation law in 1891. This required the containment of all wild boars and compensation for damage caused by game trails originating from outside a district by the owner of the hunting district from which the game came, and compensation by hunting tenants for damage caused to land by *larger game*. Minor game animals and birds were left free to eat at large.

What was in any event a very modest law was twisted by the Junkers so that (1) any claim for damage from game trails and (2) the obligation to enclose game were both omitted; (3) in place of the obligation for hunting tenants to pay compensation, communes were made liable for repair – that is, the peasantry as a whole had to pay for damage caused by game; and (4) court proceedings were ruled out in instances involving damage by game. Disputes were to be settled by the local police, that is, the large landowner, or the district commission – large landowners again.

It takes the brazen effrontery of the Prussian Junkers, the Prussian government and the Prussian three-class voting system to offer this kind of compensation to the peasantry whose land has been damaged by game.

Although the position is a little better outside Prussia, farmers' needs are nowhere satisfactorily attended to in Germany or in Austria. It is well known that the Imperial Diet has explicitly recognised the hare's right to feed in the Civil Code. The pleasures of the hunt are more important than the people's nutrition. It is high time that this remnant of feudalism was got rid off.

But how to do it? Conferring a free right on each individual to hunt on their own land would offer little protection to farmers surrounded by large hunting tracts: they would have to neglect their field work and spend most of their time in a hide.

And although the peasantry on land surrounded by large hunting forests has been brought to the verge of ruin in some areas rich in game and forest, other peasant communes gain considerably by renting out land for hunting, especially in the vicinity of large towns where there is little game and woodland and where the hunter in search of sport is prepared to pay good money for the pleasure of shooting a hare or deer. Freedom to hunt for each individual landowner would remove a valuable source of income from some communes, without benefitting the peasantry, especially those on small parcels of land.

The best solution to the hunting question in contemporary society lies in the *restriction of the rights of private property, not their extension*. The privilege of large landowners to establish their own hunting districts must be eliminated along with that of the independent manorial district. Both should be incorporated into the parishes, or better the administrative districts. Hunting in the large landowner's woods must be brought under parish or district control, as presently happens with hunting on peasant land. Naturally, parish and district authorities will be the product of direct, universal and equal suffrage, and they should determine hunting policy throughout a hunting tract.

Nationalisation of all woodland would greatly simplify the whole hunting question – at least in democratic states. Hunting could then easily be accommodated to the requirements of agriculture in each individual district. No doubt we shall be able to get over any regrets as to the possible detriment to hunting as a sport.

Mixed Land Holdings – the *Gemenglage*

The scattering of strips belonging to different peasants, the *Gemenglage*, causes as much, and in some circumstances more, damage to agriculture than hunting, especially where the land is characterised by small peasant holdings: this is also a remnant of feudalism, of the medieval *Mark* constitution with its three-field system and enforced cropping pattern. Under this system, the arable land allotted to each individual farmer did not constitute a compact plot, but lay dispersed amongst the different furlongs. The elimination of feudal lordship and the introduction of full private property in land did not eliminate the fragmentation of the individual's property in land: in fact, it multiplied it, especially where the division of the individual parcels was a result of the equal inheritance of all a testator's children. Rational cultivation is impossible on such small and very small parcels. Huge amounts of time are lost moving from one strip to another, and much land is forfeited for paths, ridges and so on – in short, the *Gemenglage* is not only a powerful obstacle to any progress in peasant agriculture, but actually depresses it still further.

Some figures from the Sachsen-Meiningen area illustrate the extent to which the fragmentation of holdings has advanced.

The open-field of Leutersdorf, in the district of Meiningen, with 520.6 hectares of arable land, 37.6 hectares of pasture, 1.8 hectares of kitchen garden, 55.7 hectares of meadow and 191.2 hectares of woodland – all in all 835.9 hectares including paths, water, farmyards and buildings – is made up of 7,785 parcels owned by 76 households and 363 inhabitants. Herpf, with 598 inhabitants, has 1,808 hectares, of which 836 are woodland, and is divided into 10,973 parcels. Behrungen, with 695 inhabitants, in the Römhild district, has 13,910 parcels over an area of 1,378 hectares, of which 320 hectares are woodland. Wolframshausen, 423 inhabitants, in the same district has 9,596 parcels on 804 hectares, of which 145 hectares are woodland. (Heine, *Die bäuerliche Verhältnisse in Sachsen-Meiningen*, p. 10)

The best effects are achieved by rounding off (*consolidation*, joining, separation) the parcels belonging to each individual landholder into a compact pattern of ownership. A report from the Eisenach Oberland notes, for example:

Despite the substantial contribution to new communal works, 4-6 per cent, very much more is harvested after a successful consolidation than before, significant areas of previously unused land are made cultivable through improvements; hedges and ridges disappear, the *land's value often rises considerably within a short time of the achievement of a planned land pattern*, often by a third. A noticeable improvement in the economic circumstances of the separated fields soon makes itself felt. (Heine, op. cit., p. 31)

According to Meitzen, the consolidation of land in the open fields of Grossengottern and Altengottern (near Mühlhausen in Thuringia) totalling 12,934 *morgen* produced an additional yield of 59,339 Marks each year, 4.58 Marks per *morgen*. Total costs including irrigation ditches, new roads, bridges and so forth amounted to 139,902 Marks, that is, 10.50 Marks per *morgen* – unusually high because of the large amount of drainage work involved (Meitzen, *Der Boden und die landwirtschaftlichen Verhältnisse des preußischen Staates*, p. 438).

Despite such benefits, consolidation is proceeding very slowly. Cost is one reason. Not only is the procedure required a rather expensive one, but the act of consolidation also involves switching from the old three-field system with shifting pasturage to a higher, more intensive type of farming, requiring more capital. In the absence of the necessary cash, consolidation can become a cause of farmer indebtedness, and where the farmers are already deeply in debt could prove their ruin.

Moreover, consolidation cannot be practised by individuals on their own: it requires the assent of all those with a stake in the open field, since it relies on a mutual exchange of parcels. This is difficult enough to do in such a way that nobody loses, and even more difficult to do such that no one thinks they are losing. Bearing in mind the suspicious and conservative character of the peasant, it is clear that this issue presents us with yet another instance of private property in land placing an insuperable obstacle in the way of progress.

Enlightened absolutism resolved this problem by temporarily suspending private property in land. Much to its regret, liberalism also felt obliged to encroach on the sanctity of private property. Wherever a certain proportion of those with strips demanded consolidation, the others were obliged in law to participate and swap their property with someone else.

Despite this, the *Gemenglage* is by no means a thing of the past, and the improvement of agriculture requires that a good deal must still be done in this area.

Social Democracy has every reason to welcome such an advance from fragmented, irrational, and medieval cultivation to larger, more intensive and more modern farming: and where this can take place legally through further limitations on the rights of private property, it will not fail to support it with all the influence at its disposal.

But Social Democracy will have to be very cautious when it comes to the issue of a state subsidy for consolidation, something frequently demanded by the agrarians. The whole procedure implies an increase in ground-rents – as we saw, land-values can increase by up to a third. State subsidies have to be paid for by the taxpayers as a whole, including hard-pressed proletarians and petty bourgeois. Is it really their job to sacrifice part of their meagre income so that a number of landowners can rake in higher ground-rents? One could imagine circumstances in which such a subsidy would be appropriate, even from a proletarian standpoint. But there is no place for such largesse to landed property in the programme of a proletarian party.

Apart from limiting the rights of private property, Social Democracy also has a different task in this sphere: whereas consolidation – once the transitional stage has been overcome – ultimately brings undoubted benefits to the landowner, for the rural proletarian it implies a form of expropriation.

Ridges, stubble fields and so on offered the rural proletarian the opportunity to keep a goat or even a cow. Consolidation eliminates such public grazing places – 637 *morgen* of cultivable land was won from the open fields of Grossengottern and Altengottern when ridges and boundaries were removed – depriving rural proletarians of anywhere to keep the dairy cow so important to their households.

Dwarf-holders are also frequently damaged by consolidation, which mainly benefits middle and large peasants. But the smallholders have to pay just as much per unit area as the larger towards the cost of consolidation. And they are often cheated: their lack of influence in the village means they are assigned fields on the periphery, the most unfavourably located, involving the greatest losses in time in travelling to and fro.

Regrettable as all this is, Social Democracy cannot adopt a hostile stance towards consolidation. It is one of those instances where the interests of a particular stratum of the proletariat come into contradiction with those of economic development – something which Social Democracy must now allow itself to obstruct. As with the abolition of rough grazing for sheep, the collection of leaves for animal litter and the like, Social Democracy must try to ensure that the abolition of a right does not mean outright confiscation, and that it is compensated for through the guarantee of an allotment of land or some comparable gain, and that as few injustices as possible occur in the execution of the change. This can be partly achieved by giving the smallholder an equal say in the village and in the consolidation procedure, and partly by defraying the costs through a progressive land tax. Although we ought not to, and cannot, stand in the way of economic progress, we must strive to ensure that it takes place as painlessly as possible.

The Improvement of the Land

The same basic principles which guided us on the question of consolidation will also have to serve us when we turn to other tasks arising from the desire to improve agriculture.

Social Democracy already demands the nationalisation of forest and water. But as long as private property remains intact, we will welcome any appropriate limitations on its rights in the interests of the rational management of woodland and water.

The issue of water management is intimately connected with that of large-scale land improvement or so-called 'cultivation of the land' (*Landeskultur*). In fact, in essence, this is nothing more than those aspects of the management of water which serve agriculture: drainage and irrigation works, draining of marshes, recovery of land through dyke-building and the like.

Such works cannot be entrusted to individuals. During the earliest period of the capitalist mode of production, such tasks were assumed by the absolutist state, which increased landowners' ground-rents at its own expense, just as its subsidies raised the profits of industrial entrepreneurs. The liberal state introduced other principles into its policies for improvements. Meitzen writes on the Prussian experience:

> The main aim of the more recent concept of improvements (which emerged in the 1840s and 1850s) in contrast to the former system of public works, was the mobilisation of the activity of private individuals based on the profitability of such ventures, and the use of all appropriate means to strengthen and maintain private interest and self-help. There was no hesitation in compelling individuals to undertake required improvements if this was seen to be justified in avoiding a major problem. Other useful seeming works were encouraged by suggestion, the execution of preparatory work, technical advice and guarantees of assistance. Delays during the hazardous period of execution were eliminated as much as possible through aid and advances; the cooperative assistance of all those likely to benefit was sought in every possible way, and cooperatives were given every legal and actual encouragement to extend themselves to the fullest of their abilities. (Meitzen, op. cit., I, p. 463)

Social Democracy has introduced a different principle: it seeks the nationalisation of water, but not as practised in the absolutist state, where the state met all the costs and the landowners enjoyed all the benefits. The community must remain lord of the watercourses, and enjoy the returns from them, together with any increased yields which arise from its management of water.

Where this cannot be achieved, where private property is an insurmountable obstacle, there is no choice but to persevere with the liberal perspective: implementation by cooperatives of landowners at their own expense, not implementation by the state. State assistance will then consist not in the handing out of gifts to landowners but in restricting their property rights and overcoming the resistance of reluctant elements, whose collaboration is indispensable in carrying out improvements.

Exceptions would only be made where land ownership is not the beneficiary, or sole beneficiary, and where the public interest is also served, as with improvements in climate brought about by draining marshes, or the creation of a waterways by means of canals. Where this is the case, the state management of water can, and must, intervene directly. But landowners should also contribute in proportion to any subsequent increase in their ground rents; and expropriation should be demanded of any who fail to come forward with an appropriate amount. The draining of the Roman Campagna by the Italian government would benefit Rome and Italy as a whole. But it would be going too far were it to transform this desolate area into a blooming tract for the benefit of its rich owners, the Church of Rome and the noble families of Rome, at the expense of the impoverished Italian people.

Regard for the proletariat is not the only basis for objecting to expending public money on improvement works which are not urgently required for the public interest. The profitability of such works has also to be taken into account. Although talk of cultivating moorland or reclaiming land from the sea for agriculture sounds very positive, such works should evidently only be undertaken if they hold out the prospect of winning back a surplus over and above the cost of the works – except for works serving public hygiene and so forth.

The enlightened despotism of the last century, which developed capitalism's enterprising zeal but was inept at making capitalist calculations, occasionally paid very dearly for such attempts at extending the cultivable area bearing a ground-rent. Particular caution is advisable at a time when ground-rents are falling. A period in which capitalist accumulation is opening up immense tracts of fertile virgin soil outside Europe, in which within Europe fertile arable land is being turned back to pasturage, or even forest, is hardly the most expedient in which to expend large sums of money on transforming a few patches of infertile terrain into cultivable land. Roscher cites a work from as early as 1841 (*Aufzeichnungen eines nachgeborenen Prinzes*) which observes: 'Encountering the ruins of villages, dating from before the Thirty Years War, on marvellous soils in the middle of forests, makes one all the more uneasy at the prospect of the human and capital resources being put into the Danube marshes' (Roscher, *Nationalökonomie des Ackerbaus*, p. 122). Such improvements cannot alleviate the problems of agriculture, let alone those of the peasantry. What they lack is certainly not land.

However, a large number of potentially profitable improvements still remain unexecuted: they are obstructed not so much by a lack of money as by *private property in land*, the fragmentation of the land among a large number of owners. Money can always be borrowed if the proposed undertaking is a viable one: but most improvements can only be carried out over a large area, and not by individual landowners for themselves.

Carrying them out requires bringing landowners together. But this is difficult. Inertia, ignorance, and suspicion stand in the way: and the advantages which each obtains from large-scale improvements also vary.

Only limiting property rights, *state compulsion*, can establish the required uniformity. Once a certain proportion of those involved call for a project, and the project appears suitable, those opposed to it must be liable to give over their land to allow the works to be carried out and to bear a portion of the costs. Social Democracy will always support such methods for promoting the improvement of the land.

Control of Epidemics

Controlling the pests which threaten farm animals and crops, and hence the conditions for civilised human existence, is no less important than effecting improvements.

In Part I we already noted that the modern mode of production generates increasingly serious hazards to the health of animals and crops, and opens the door to animal and plant epidemics.

Recent measures to control the importation of animals and fruit are one consequence of this. However, serious as the real danger of ruin to entire districts and countries caused by the import of diseased specimens might be, restrictions on importation are often simply a disguised form of protectionism. Not only do they make it more difficult to import diseased livestock but block the import of livestock altogether. The demand should be not for a barrier to imports from abroad but to the movement of all diseased herds, whether foreign or domestic in origin. In fact, domestic herds are more dangerous since they are nearer and in more active interaction with the local countryside. Border inspections will be useless if they are not complemented by the vigorous control of epidemics within these same borders.

Once again private property emerges as the greatest impediment. The control of an epidemic, be it plant or animal, is pointless unless undertaken *simultaneously, vigorously* and *thoroughly* at all endangered locations. The failure of cattle owners to disinfect their stalls is enough to allow the banished pest to return. If all vineyard owners in a particular district decide to tackle phylloxera, but one declines, the vine pest will constantly return to afflict the others. Property rights have to be suspended in such a situation, at least temporarily: and state compulsion has to have precedence over individual economic freedom.

This is not only advisable in fighting the problem once it has arrived.

Prevention, as always, is the best policy. Not only should the pest's possible predators be protected and bred – those which attack the colorado beetle for example – but any necessary precautionary measures should also be undertaken in the actual techniques of cultivation or the arrangement of animal stalls. As with human dwellings, hygiene regulations can be decreed for stables and enforced through an inspectorate.

Compulsory inoculation with tuberculin, the isolation of sick from healthy animals, and the feeding of calves with sterilised milk have been proposed as a means of combatting bovine tuberculosis. In France, all imported cattle are subjected to inoculation. We make no judgement as to the effectiveness of the tuberculin inoculation, but if proven we would certainly applaud its compulsory application.

The existence of property rights will never cause Social Democracy to shy away from any compulsory measures necessary to combat pests in agriculture. Of course, it will also ensure that the most appropriate method of implementation is the one adopted.

Necessity, rather than desire, already forces the state to intervene in property rights to combat plant and animal pests. And although such measures are in the interests of agriculture itself, they still encounter stubborn opposition. Inertia and ignorance are not the only causes: peasants are also suspicious about the organs of the state, which usually confront them as an instrument of oppression and exploitation, as police officer or tax-collector. And peasants do not expect the bureaucracy, with its outmoded pedantry, to exhibit any understanding of the needs of agriculture.

The more state enforcement extends into the sphere of pest control, the more urgent the need for the enlightenment of the rural population – not just piecemeal but on a systematic basis. And this needs to be supported by the promulgation and implementation of compulsory measures by theoretically and practically trained specialists – not lawyers, police officers and former subalterns – in as close a degree of agreement as possible with the local organs of self-administration in parishes or administrative districts.

But who should bear the costs of these measures? The state? That would mean imposing part of the production costs of agriculture on the consumers – raising ground-rents at the consumer's expense. On the other hand, it would be unfair to impose the financial burden on farmers whose farms are suffering from a particular pest, since measures to control pests are in the interests of all farmers. Such a policy would also create a strong incentive for the individual to cover up any outbreak on their property.

The costs are often therefore imposed on all the farmers involved, and matters have progressed such that,

> for certain epidemic diseases – cattle-pest, pneumonic plague, anthrax – compensation will be paid for prompt notification should slaughtering become necessary, or losses be incurred. This represents an insurance against certain pests as far as the owner is concerned, and where compensation payments are borne by all livestock owners, one can speak of a *compulsory epidemic insurance*. The wish of the rural population for the inclusion of other pest diseases in compulsory pest insurance, in particular tuberculosis in cattle and red murrain in pigs, should be acceded to (Buchenberger, *Grundzüge der deutschen Agrarpolitik*, p. 188).

No objection can be raised against this type of state insurance.

But it does bring us to a further question – the significance of state insurance in agriculture.

State Insurance

Insurance is frequently claimed to play a different role in agriculture from that in industry; and although state insurance against every possible misfortune would be regarded as inconceivable for private industrial enterprises, this is held to be necessary for agriculture because of its exposure to the whims of nature, which have been tamed in industry.

However, uninterrupted production for the commodity-producer depends on social, as well as natural factors – and these are more capricious in industry than agriculture. Although agriculture might be more dependent on the moods of nature, it is less dependent on the moods of the market. The raw and auxiliary materials which industrialists have to buy can usually be produced by farmers for themselves: and even given foreign competition, the farmer's market is more secure and less victim to fashion than that of the industrialist. In fact, the markets can quickly turn nature's wrongs into their opposite as far as the farmer is concerned: a poor harvest can increase prices, more than making up for the lower yield.

Moreover, it is not possible to insure against the catastrophic misfortunes which afflict agriculture: insurance is only appropriate for those adversities which strike a few individuals out of a much larger number, so that a small sum paid by each individual is sufficient to provide adequate compensation for those hit. But drought or rainy summers, harsh winters and floods are afflictions which affect entire localities or even countries, causing such massive misery that insurance would be utterly powerless to help. Only the expenditure of all the resources at the disposal of society can assist, and even then they are not always available in the form required.

As long as Social Democracy does not have good reason to demand the nationalisation of the entire insurance system in both town and country, it could scarcely propose the simple wholesale nationalisation of agricultural insurance.

This is not to say that individual branches of insurance peculiar to agriculture do not merit some degree of intervention by the state: for example, livestock insurance and hail insurance.

Livestock insurance has a dual character: insurance against the threat of epidemics comes under the state as part of state measures against epidemics in general. In addition, there is insurance against livestock deaths not caused by disease.

This type of insurance is confined to small livestock-keeping farms. The death of an individual beast on a larger establishment will not seriously disrupt the farm's operation. The larger the herd, the more frequent the death of an individual head: such events are unavoidable elements in the establishment's costs. Like large shipowners, the owners of large herds of livestock are their own best insurers.

Small peasants are in a different position. The death of a cow could mean considerable damage to them, and frequently a fateful impediment to the whole of their farming operations. Their receipts are too meagre to allow the regular setting aside of a fund to depreciate the cost of their livestock, and individual accidents could remove their stock before they have lived out their useful lives.

Should this happen, the uninsured peasant has no other choice but to accept a loan from the livestock dealer, who then gets the opportunity, both as middleman and usurer, to exploit – and very effectively too – the peasant.

The obvious solution would seem to be for livestock-owning peasants in a village to band together and insure themselves against such accidents so that the costs of any individual accident are borne by all. This type of livestock insurance numbers among those endeavours which seek to confer the advantages of the large farm on the smaller through mutual cooperation. Useful and necessary as such efforts are, they represent only a meagre substitute for the large establishment.

By insuring itself, the large farm sacrifices neither the money for, nor loses interest in, the undertaking of preventive measures to avoid losses. Matters are quite different for the peasants. Lack of money, poor feeding and poor stabling already expose their stock to more risks from the outset. Paying the livestock premium certainly does nothing to improve their situation in this respect.

Peasants can make up for their lack of means to some extent through the greater care which they bestow on their livestock. However, insurance makes such care seem superfluous: it can often become a temptation to let an unfit animal perish in order to replace it with a better one at the expense of the insurance company.

As a consequence, despite the fact that attempts to organise peasant livestock insurance extend back to the cow guilds of the sixteenth century, and despite capital's eagerness to find new areas to bring under its sway, it has so far taken good care to steer clear of livestock insurance; and where it has become involved, the experience has mostly been a disagreeable one. Where peasants insure amongst themselves they can exercise some mutual control over their tending of livestock. This is completely impossible where livestock insurance is organised through capitalist enterprises. Capitalist livestock insurance is exposed to the permanent danger of fraud by the peasantry. And if the capitalists want to make money, they will attempt to defraud the peasants in turn. Small-scale cattle dealing does not suit big capital. As a result it generously concedes livestock insurance to the state and the communes – also a form of socialism.

Livestock insurance has not as yet extended beyond small local associations lending assistance, in one way or another, to the individual member in the event of a loss. These are associations of people who know each other very well; control is easy and simple, and damage to all through negligence or even deception by an individual is very difficult. However, these advantages have to be set against the disadvantage of the small number of those making up the circle of the insured: they can easily fail in the event of a local accumulation of livestock misfortunes, as a result of a shortage of feed perhaps, rendering illusory the whole idea of insurance.

The state should intervene here, either simply through linking the individual local associations with each other, allowing any short-lived but very heavy burden on one or more of these associations to be borne by the others and hence eased, or by decreeing a compulsory membership for individual livestock owners, thus extending the circle of those insured.

Where it can the proletariat prefers free democratic organisation to one imposed by the state bureaucracy. This also applies to insurance organisations: it does not require state assistance to extend its trade unions and benefit funds throughout the nation. However, if the peasantry feels the need for a national federation of local insurance associations, but declares its inability to accomplish this itself and calls on the assistance of an otherwise not especially friendly state bureaucracy, the proletariat should not seek to place obstacles in its path. If if can be of help, there is no reason to hold back.

The picture would, of course, change were such a call on the state to be a means whereby a number of farmers could extract subsidies at the expense of the taxpayer; for example, if the state, through endowing insurance funds, were to allow farmers to renew their livestock at the state's expense. A proletarian party cannot support such largesse.

Hail insurance differs from livestock insurance. The existence of such insurance cannot possibly lead to negligent or fraudulent farming practices. On the other hand, the threat of hail hangs over the large farm just as much as the small – a hailstorm can devastate both. Whilst livestock insurance, under certain circumstances, might become an obstacle to agricultural development and bolster the small irrational farm at the state's expense, this is quite impossible with hail insurance.

Hail insurance also differs from livestock insurance through the fact that whereas livestock insurance protects against hazards which affect the individual farmer's inventory, hail insurance covers hazards which totally cripple every farm in a locality, or even a whole district. Hail damage resembles flood damage in this respect, although it is usually confined to smaller districts. Insurance against it is therefore possible without imposing an excessive burden on the participants, as long they are sufficient in number. The impracticality of hail insurance organisation with a small area is revealed in the collapse of the hail insurance associations in Württemberg and Hesse, and the fact that small mutuality societies often have to raise extraordinarily large advances (for example, Ceres in Berlin in the years 1887–90: 175 per cent, 99 per cent, 133.3 per cent, and 100 per cent of the initial premium) (Buchenberger, *Grundzüge der deutschen Agrarpolitik*, p. 176).

However, where insurance is left to private enterprise the irregularity of hail in most districts is just as much an impediment to generalised insurance as hail's predilection for specific localities. A feeling of security easily builds up in areas in which no hail has fallen for a long time: this deters individuals from taking out insurance, particularly peasants who do not suffer from a surfeit of cash. And those areas which are especially endangered by hail are not welcomed by the private companies, or only on the payment of prohibitive premiums.

There is, therefore, an evident need for the state organisation of state insurance: this has already been introduced to some extent in Bavaria and Baden. The demand for compulsory state insurance can also be justified by the devastation which a hailstorm can cause and which can create such distress where no insurance is available that in many instances, as with flood damage, the state is obliged to intervene with assistance. The need for state help where insurance fails also justifies subsidisation by the state as it relieves it of the subsequent costs of emergency measures.

As little as we would otherwise clamour for an extension of the powers and social functions of the police state, state hail insurance seems to be a very useful measure.

One should not underestimate the possible effects of insurance, state or private. As useful as it is for the individual suffering damage, it represents a new tax for those who have to bear the costs, a tax which grows the more numerous the fields of insurance and the greater the extent of the damages insured against.

The possibilities of such damage are steadily increasing with the growth of modern cultivation – not only does it increasingly bring about epidemics to animals and damage to crops, together with flooding, but also, if the theory of the Chief Forester of Aargau, Herr Rinicker, is correct, more hail, which forms most readily in those areas where the high ground has been denuded of trees through the reduction in woodland. Insurance leaves the causes of the damage untouched: it fails, as we noted above, when we turn to the gravest problems which afflict farmers. It can, therefore, only be seen as a poor surrogate for measures designed to render farmers more independent of the moods of nature, and to subject these vicissitudes to their control.

Rational wood and water management, which reduce flood and hail damage; irrigation works, which combat aridity; drainage against waterlogging; rational breeding of strains of plants and animals which not only raises their yields but also their resistance; protection for insect-eating birds; hygienic stalls for animals; appropriate feeding and the like – these are all measures of far greater importance than insurance. But it has to be recognised that even some of these are in too much of a contradiction to the conditions of existence of the small peasant! Can one really be seriously demanding that small peasants ought to practise rational breeding and husbandry in clean, airy stables?

The Cooperatives – the Agricultural Training System

Livestock insurance at a local level is basically an attempt to obtain the advantages of the large-farm through cooperative organisation. We also touched on the *question of cooperatives* in our discussion of improvements. We conclude our observation on methods for promoting agriculture with a few words on the cooperative system. We can be brief as we have already dealt with the role of cooperatives in greater detail above.

One could well say that Social Democracy is sympathetic to the cooperative system in general, and to the agricultural cooperatives in particular. We do not overestimate them, however; we do not regard them as a means for saving peasant agriculture, since its benefits can be used equally well by the large as by the small farm. And where it strengthens the latter, it transforms its owner either into a capitalist exploiter, or one of the exploited. Moreover, we do not regard farmer cooperatives as a transitional stage to socialism, except in the sense that any limited liability company, and any large concern in general, represents such a transitional stage. However, cooperatives are – and in agriculture more than in industry – a powerful means for promoting economic development and the transition from the small to the large establishment, and are far preferable to the more typical capitalist means of effecting this development, the expropriation of small property. We cannot prevent the latter method of development in present-day society, but we do not have to support it. We can, however, support the cooperative system.

Nevertheless, our support should not go beyond removing possible legal obstacles to its development. State subsidies would represent nothing more than permission for individual groups of owners to improve their personal position via a grant from proletariat. And by encouraging dubious establishments and reckless financial conduct, such subsidies would not even be in the interests of cooperatives themselves. And this is leaving to one side the fact that control over a fund for subsidising cooperatives can become a means for buying political sympathy, a means of corruption like the Guelf funds.

A good portion of the cooperatives themselves reject state subsidies (see Dr H. Krüger's article on this subject in *Soziale Prazis*, VI, p. 338, VII, p. 203). One might term this Manchesterism, but state aid to promote the private interests of private individuals is no part of socialism. A social reform which conserves agricultural commodity-production by leaving the profits to the entrepreneur but the risks to the state – that is, the mass of the population – is no doubt a tempting ideal for agrarians, but such a policy cannot be executed on a large scale, nor is it in the interests of the proletariat.

There is one further method for promoting agriculture which does not hold back economic development – in fact, it markedly speeds it up: the extension of *specialist training*.

We already commented on the most important aspects of this issue in our discussion of the education system. No further arguments are needed to prove the readiness of Social Democracy to promote both agricultural and industrial training beyond the level of elementary and secondary schooling in any way possible, and its willingness to spend what is required on the introduction or improvement of agricultural secondary schools and colleges, agricultural laboratories and experimental stations, the establishment of model farms, the arrangement of exhibitions and the like.

This is sufficient to illustrate the essential elements in the development of agriculture within capitalist society and Social Democracy's intervention in this process. After what we have argued here we trust that no one will attempt to claim that our position represents 'Social Manchesterism'. However, the fact that our demands do not go beyond the limits of a bourgeois, democratic-social-reformist agrarian programme on many issues, and that we are exceeded in 'radicalism' by some of the programmes of the agrarians or land reformers is a crime to which we gladly confess our guilt. Our consolation is the hope that our agrarian policy preserves the unity of industrial and agricultural development, and that our standpoint is consistent with both: that we do not demand the opposite for agriculture to that which seems necessary in industry. Agrarians and land-reformers are not burdened with such worries: to them agriculture represents an independent whole. For the Social Democrat, however, agriculture is part of an organism, and can only develop in harmony with it.

Practicians may possibly find some of our demands inexpedient. In assessing whether this is so, what matters is whether they are useful for the promotion of agriculture, not whether they are useful in winning over peasants. We admit that some of our demands – not only those which relate to protective legislation, but also those which seek to limit property rights in land – may well have exactly the opposite effect.

However, should methods which are well-fitted for raising the standards of agriculture prove ill-fitted to winning the applause of the peasantry, this is not an indication of the unfitness of the methods but of the unfitness of present-day small peasant farming.

15
The Protection of the Rural Population

The Transformation of the Police State into a Cultural State

Although Social Democracy may not be able to compete with the agrarian parties when it comes to saving the peasantry, there is one area in which it has more to offer the rural population than even the most agrarian of the bourgeois parties.

But to make this clear, we must cast our net a little wider.

The entire movement of the modern mode of production tends to enrich the town at the expense of the countryside. We dealt with this above (p. 268) and merely intend to emphasise a few relevant aspects here. This enrichment follows necessarily from the accumulation of capital, which, together with the total surplus-value – including that produced by agricultural labour – becomes increasingly centralised in the towns. This tendency will not disappear until capitalist society itself disappears: the rural population therefore has a much greater interest in the coming of a socialist society than the urban population. The shift of industry into the open countryside and the industrialisation of agriculture do not alter this tendency in any way. Although such a shift might change the methods of exploitation for some sections of the rural population, the surplus-value squeezed out of them will continue to be centralised in the towns.

The subject of the disadvantage suffered by the country at the hands of the town is familiar to our agrarians. However, they are very mistaken if they believe that the way to make up for it is to disadvantage the urban population by raising the prices of food and raw materials. This will merely raise ground rents, and improve the position of the landowners. But these are not identical with the rural population, most of whom do not live from their ownership of land, but from their wage-labour. Even landowning farmers are in the main only apparently landowners; the real owner is the mortgage creditor in the town. And the large landowners also prefer to consume their ground-rent in the town. An increase in the price of food and ground-rents raises the price of estates, raises the mass of mortgage interest (as a result of sale and inheritance) and raises the amount which large landowners, or their children, have available to spend in the town. It also raises the exploitation not merely of the urban, but also of the majority of the rural population – and in the final analysis steps up the exploitation of the countryside by the town rather than reducing it.

Inasmuch as this tendency can be resisted within the present-day mode of production, Social Democracy does so through its efforts to improve the living and working conditions of the rural proletariat.

However, it is not the capitalist mode of production alone which exploits the country to the benefit of the town. The modern, centralised state also does so, even where it is completely under agrarian influence and seeks to do the exact opposite.

As with any state before it, the modern state is primarily an institution of domination. The bearers of modern state authority, parliaments and in particular princes, saw their main task as stripping the small more or less sovereign communities of the Middle Ages, out of whose conjunction the modern state arose, of their independence and means of authority. The urban and rural commune, the *Mark*, and the feudal territory, all lost their independence and the means of enforcement over which they had control. Justice, the police, the army, and tax administration all became tightly centralised.

In contrast, the modern state – again like any other previous state – is only an institution for the service of civilisation to a very limited degree. What it centralises are the *means of domination*. Cultural tasks are left to the communes and districts, or to private individuals: it shows no great interest in their centralisation. Elementary schools and to some extent even the higher school system remain a local concern. Universities are admittedly run by the state – it could not really burden the communes with them with the best will in the world; but in return they mainly serve the aims of domination, not culture – they are intended to drill usable state officials, not free-thinking scholars.

Welfare matters – in their broadest sense – are also a concern of the communes and, in part, private individuals: sanitation, the health system, care of the poor. The construction and maintenance of roads also remain partly a communal matter and partly a private one; the state only usually intervenes if it involves a military road – if it concerns war. State roads are aptly named *military roads*, and the railways have also only been nationalised in the militarised states – not in Switzerland, England or America. The *Kaiser* has observed that ours is the century of transport: but the spirit of our Prussian State Railways is not that of transport, but of militarism and profit-making.

The scientific and artistic institutions which the modern state maintains arose as an appendage to courtly pomp, as court theatres, court galleries, court museums, and east of the Rhine they still retain their courtly character today.

And those agencies of civilisation created or acquired by the state, alongside its means of domination, are also concentrated in the cities, in particular the seats of the princely courts. Both the rural and urban populations have to contribute to their upkeep, but only the latter really has access to their benefits.

The opposing tendency must begin to make itself felt within the state as soon as the proletariat gains any influence over its running. State authority is the most powerful lever for abolishing the capitalist system. The proletariat must, of necessity, strive to conquer it. But one should not imagine that the dictatorship of the proletariat means that one fine morning the city mob will overrun the ministries in a violent coup and use the state's means of enforcement to plunder the rich.

The proletariat cannot struggle for the possession of state power without at the same time raising itself and the state to a higher level. It cannot wield the state for its own purposes before it has succeeded in accomplishing this elevation. It is during this struggle that it first attains the necessary moral and intellectual qualities to enable it to become the ruling class – and abolish class rule. However, the proletariat's struggle for state power is not simply the struggle for the conquest of a means of power: by its nature it also necessarily entails striving for the transformation of absolute monarchy or oligarchy into democracy, together with reducing the state's activities of domination and stressing its cultural tasks – in fact the transformation of a police and militaristic state into a cultural state. This is of course self-evident and needs no further argument.

However, although this transformation will inevitably benefit the population as a whole, it will benefit the rural much more than the urban sector. The former have much more to gain.

A few examples will illustrate this.

Self-administration

Social Democracy demands the self-administration of the people at state, province and commune level. The last-named is much more important for the rural than for the urban population. The state official is an urban creature by nature, and has much greater understanding and sympathy for urban than for rural needs. The urban population also has quite different means available for influencing the bureaucracy than the rural, in particular a powerful press. This does not of course stop land-ownership being given preferential treatment by the government and bureaucracy at the expense of urban industry. But what type of land-ownership enjoys this agreeable position? It is large land-ownership, in fact that fraction of large land-ownership which is an urban class, which consumes its ground-rents in the town, and exercises its personal influence over the government and bureaucracy there. The interests of this land-ownership are also antagonistic to those of the mass of the rural population which it exploits: it is land-owning interests which mean that the rural population is disadvantaged in all local matters over which the state has any influence in any field in which the large landowner stands to gain – such as assessing local taxes, estimating damage by game and so on. As with the politics of the 'protection' of agriculture through tariffs and state largesse, the agrarian inclinations of state administration turn out to be means not for controlling the disadvantages suffered by the rural population, but of giving them added bite.

Self-administration of province, district and commune not only has to put a stop to the tutelage of and violations inflicted on the rural population by ignorant, overbearing and even downright corrupt officials, and check the excessive power of large land-ownership, at least where it rests on political factors: it must also bring economic benefits to the rural population by rendering a part of urban officialdom redundant, sending a portion off to the country where they will in the future consume their salaries – no longer as masters, but as servants of the people.

Militarism

For the rural population, restraining militarism is even more important than restraining the omnipotence of the centralised bureaucracy. Although militarism demands heavy sacrifices of the population as a whole, these fall hardest on the countryside. Industry, which generates an ever-increasing reserve army of unemployed, can more easily tolerate the reduction in labour caused by a standing army than agriculture, which suffers from a steady outflow of workers. Young people leave the country to become soldiers, all too easily lose their desire for a life on the land and are lost to agriculture forever. And those who do return are not always the best elements. The soldier is scrupulously protected from the effects of urban culture; the worst thing imaginable would be for him to absorb some of its spirit! Soldiers' taverns and brothels are the only places 'befitting' the defenders of the fatherland during their free time, the only ones which do not bring them revolutionary ideas. The only urban attainments they takes back to the countryside are their barrack-square manner and syphilis.

The taxes which the peasant pays for the upkeep of the army – both the obligatory variety and the voluntary ones he pays to keep his son in battle dress – also migrate to the town, where they are spent. Some urban industries, and some urban layers of the population live from militarism. The peasant derives only burdens and disadvantages.

Why then should the peasant turn out to be militarism's sturdiest pillar? No one would claim that peasants have a more developed national consciousness than the urban population, or that they have stronger ideals. Monarchist consciousness and enthusiasm for the 'king's mantle' do not suffice as explanations either.

The most likely explanation seems to us to be that the rural population is conscious of the fact that a hostile invasion would hit them hardest – much harder than the town dwellers, with the obvious exception of citadel towns. The horrors and devastations of war primarily afflict the open countryside. Hence peasants' anxiety that the Reich might be defenceless, and consequently their enthusiasm for the army, which keeps the enemy from their fields.

Winning the peasant for the struggle against militarism means proving that this does not imply leaving the fatherland defenceless.

However, the struggle against militarism has two aspects, often conflated but which ought to be kept strictly separate.

On the one hand, the desire for the establishment of a lasting peace. The war preparations of the big modern nations have now reached such insane dimensions that they make even the best patriots quake. Everyone is convinced that this cannot continue, that it will lead either to bankruptcy or to an annihilating war, the most insane of all wars – a war unleashed because the burden which was supposed to secure peace had become too great to bear.

Only one means seems capable of avoiding this – an entente between the great powers involving the disbandment of all standing armies and the voluntary subordination of the sovereign powers to the binding decisions of a World Court of Arbitration.

This is undoubtedly a very attractive idea, but utopian in a society in which conflicts of interest are so great that even economic struggles within a nation, such as strikes, cannot be resolved by arbitration. A lasting peace requires, at the least, that our great powers can arrive at a definitive resolution of all their points of difference, and make arrangements to prevent the emergence of new ones. We are, however, further from this than ever. National questions created by the development of the bourgeois state still remain unresolved; the division of Europe is not yet complete, and the most recent struggle for the division of the world has just begun. The antagonisms between nations produced by capitalist society are too deep to envisage that capitalist regimes could achieve a federation. The solution to this problem awaits the international solidarity of the proletariat, already a more powerful guarantee of peace than all the peace congresses of the bourgeoisie.

The demand for the replacement of the present standing army by a people's army, *a militia*, is quite different in character. It can be implemented in present-day society, even in the midst of the most acute international conflicts of interest. It does not seek to abolish the army, to diminish its external readiness, but simply to deprive it of its internal striking power. The army today is not only a means of external defence, but also serves to keep down the 'enemy within'; it is the most powerful of all the means of domination, the most powerful support of the ruling classes, inasmuch as their rule rests on political factors. It constitutes the *ultima ratio* which can be threatened against any attempt at peaceful emancipation by the exploited classes. The demand for a militia system is therefore an eminently civilising demand, a demand which must be important to anyone wishing social development to take the most peaceful path possible, with the minimum of violence and brutality.

The idea of a lasting European peace is mainly *economic* in aim. It wishes to relieve capitalist society of an increasingly unbearable burden. It impinges only on mutual relationships between governments; the relationship between government and people remains untouched. Laying down arms externally by no means implies internal disarmament. On the contrary: whilst the great powers constantly seek to outbid each other in terms of the size of their armies, making them increasingly into mass popular armies whose use against the population will become more and more problematic, the idea of disarmament does not rule out replacing current armies which are composed of soldiers from the people who will return to the people, by small armies of professional soldiers recruited from the lumpenproletariat, who – in return for good wages – will be quite willing to fire on their own mothers and fathers.

The demand, or better the desire, for disarmament is therefore that form for combatting militarism most likely to appeal to bourgeois circles, despite the limited prospects of actually realising it within bourgeois society. In contrast, such circles will work up very little enthusiasm for the replacement of the standing army by a people's army, although – or perhaps better expressed – precisely because, it is one of the prerequisites of those social conditions which will allow disarmament in the first place.

The idea of a people's army is primarily *political*, not *economic*, in purpose. It constitutes the indispensable precondition for a real democracy, in which the government is the servant, not the master of the people. In contrast, it is unlikely to imply a great deal of economic relief for the population. In this respect, the idea of a lasting peace is certainly superior.

The idea of a people's army by no means implies reducing the defence of the population: in fact it tends to strengthen it by drawing on all able-bodied citizens to be available for service. The costs involved are a matter for technical development: this cannot be predicted, but it will continue to celebrate its greatest and most fateful triumphs in the military sphere as long as the antagonisms between the capitalist nations continue.

The actual amount of direct economic benefit which the population as a whole would derive from a popular army will depend on numerous technical and political factors which are constantly changing and impossible to forecast at present. However, irrespective of the degree of benefit which we might estimate, one thing is certain: most of the direct benefits of a militia system will accrue to the rural population.

Regardless of the method of training in a people's army – and it can vary considerably depending on a large number of political, technical, economic and educational circumstances at different times and in different countries – such a system would inevitably lead to the virtual disappearance of the distinction between soldier and citizen. This is the essential hallmark of a popular army. Whilst the citizens remain defenders, even when no longer doing their training as soldiers – in Switzerland every able-bodied citizen keeps a gun at home – every endeavour is made to allow the soldiers to remain citizens. The period of segregation from the rest of the population – that is, training in the barracks – is kept to the indispensable minimum necessary for acquiring the skills of war, and as large a part of training as possible is carried out outside barracks. The systematic training of youth for military readiness plays a large role in any system of popular defence. But only a few months are devoted to training in barracks.

This means that the time taken out from the soldier's occupational life under a system of popular defence is at most an inconvenience, but not a serious burden on production. Although this point is important for all branches of production, it would be of particular relevance in agriculture with its shortage of labour. For agriculture the barracks symbolises the centralisation of the military in the town, and signifies one of the most pernicious forms of absenteeism – that of its best workers, who are not only transformed from workers into exploiters, albeit involuntarily, but also consume the results of this exploitation far removed from the countryside. Even someone who does not set great store by the direct economic benefits of a militia system would have to admit that it would remove one of the most oppressive forms of the exploitation of agriculture.

Nationalisation of Expenditures on Schools, Poor Relief and Roads

Social Democracy's desire to transform the state from an institution of domination into one of culture and civilisation does not only benefit the rural population in this negative way, through the struggle against the excessive power of the bureaucracy and militarism. The proletariat in struggle must also strive to make the state into a means for disseminating real culture and assume those cultural tasks which are too great for the individual or the commune, but whose fulfilment is indispensable for society as a whole.

We referred above (p. 344) to the fact that there are a number of cultural tasks which only towns can currently exercise, as long as such tasks are left to communal administration. These tasks are, however, just as vital for the countryside as they are for the town. Lacking in all other means of education and faced with an agriculture which is becoming an industry demanding far more scientific knowledge than most urban trades, the countryside needs good schools even more than the town. The same applies to provision for the poor. In the towns, where wealth accumulates, there are private individuals who can painlessly divest themselves of a little of their surplus in order to keep the dire poverty of others at a comfortable distance. In the open countryside private charity is virtually powerless in areas with a purely agricultural and small peasant population which does not live in plenty itself. And where large land-ownership does exist, able to intervene to mitigate poverty with its own plenty, the problem of absenteeism often means that the rich landowners never become aware of the poverty around their estates. The large landowners, who mostly live in the towns, would – were they charitable at heart – be more likely to donate to the urban than to the rural poor.

The Catholic monasteries and convents represent an exception to this: they generally own a considerable amount of land, and their inhabitants neither practise absenteeism, nor do they have sons or sons-in-law in the town – at least not legitimate ones – who might be relieving them of some of their ground-rents. The cloisters are highly suited to exercise charity in the country. But as much as one might want to acknowledge this, one has to admit that, considered as purely charitable institutions, their costs of administration are too high. Cheaper methods exist for producing the thin soup they serve up than the rich trappings enjoyed by the good fathers.

The situation is no better in the case of provision for the sick, and the system of public health generally on the land. Its intellectual desolation drives doctors into the towns: and while large numbers of young doctors fruitlessly scour the towns for a practice, the shortage of doctors on the land increases. Although it is always a bad thing for a proletarian to get sick, it is worse in the country than in the town. Workers in towns can often find a bed as 'subjects' for study in public clinics or obtain cheap medical advice: on the land they can search for a doctor for hours, and often have to content themselves with the drastic cures or 'sympathetic powers' of a shepherd or old wife. There are no hospitals, not even for the isolation of those with infectious diseases.

Roadways in the countryside are also neglected. The dispersal of the population, the long distances between settlements, and the low specific value of agricultural products, which can only be sensibly moved with first-class means of transport, mean that roads are of prime importance on the land. And whilst the population is increasingly herded together in the towns, it is becoming locally even more sparse in the countryside. At the same time, the towns have access to constantly expanding means for extending their communications; and the manufacture of cheap means of transport (omnibuses, trams, urban railways, packet trips etc.) is becoming such a lucrative business that capital is eager to get involved in it. In the countryside no one would consider using, and the poor communes are not able to use, their financial means to create the elements of transportation which are needed.

The antithesis between town and country therefore becomes even more glaring.

Social Democracy intervenes here by assigning to the state what the communes cannot afford. *The state should assume responsibility for the costs of education, provision for the poor, health care and transport.*

This does not of course mean that all these areas should be put under the administration of routinised bureaucrats. It should not mean any reduction in self-administration by communes, districts and provinces. In fact in most countries of continental Europe such self-administration will have to be extended. The commune is much less of an institution of domination than the state, and much less fitted for turning the school into a tool of government or for using poor relief or transport to corrupt electors in the government's own interests – or at least not where universal suffrage prevails.

Protection of Rural Population 419

There are also more progressive elements in a town council than in the state administration, which is much more subject to the influence of reactionary forces – backward rural areas, backward ruling classes, soldiers, priests and aristocrats – than the town. The nationalisation of rural schools could be beneficial under certain circumstances, but that of urban schools would definitely represent a step backwards.

Marx commented on the Gotha Programme of Social Democracy, which demanded 'universal and equal elementary education by the state':

> 'Elementary education by the state' is altogether objectionable. Defining by a general law the expenditures on the elementary schools, the qualifications of the teaching staff, the branches of instruction etc., and, as is done in the United States, supervising the fulfilment of these legal specifications by state inspectors, is a very different thing from appointing the state as the educator of the people! Government and Church should rather be equally excluded from any influence on the school. Particularly, indeed, in the Prusso-German Empire the state has need, on the contrary, of a very stern education by the people. (Marx, *Critique of the Gotha Programme*, p. 329)

There is no more reason to subject poor relief, care of the sick, transport and so on to a sclerotic state bureaucracy. In Russia, where the necessity of bringing the possibility of medical help to the rural population required the establishment of a system of public health care, the people only attained any importance in those provinces where the organs of self-administration, the *zemstva*, took the organisation into their hands. The indispensability of a precise knowledge of local needs and resources in providing poor relief, or establishing means of transport, needs no further argument.

Providing the state with new means of domination, without dire necessity, would be irreconcilable with the aim of transforming the state from an institution of domination into one of civilisation. Church poor relief was one of the foundations of its power: and every election bears witness to the effects of government control over the major national means of transport: constituencies loyal to the government have better prospects of seeing their wishes for railways, either main or branch lines, roads, bridges, etc., being fulfilled than areas loyal to the opposition, and this enables some followers of the government to get elected. Imagine the power the government would obtain if it controlled the entire system of local transport!

The role of state authority in this sphere should merely consist in collecting the resources raised by taxation and distributing them, according to agreed principles, for administration by individual provinces, districts and communes.

Free Administration of Justice

The demand for the free administration of justice and free legal assistance can be added to those demands raised by Social Democracy for replacing the state's functions of domination by those of civilisation which benefit the rural population more than the urban. This demand does not mean that all legal matters should be free of charge, that all legal proceedings should be contested at the state's expense – that is, at the expense of the proletariat – regardless of their nature. If two rich individuals inherit millions and argue over the spoils or if two companies tussle over a patent, Social Democracy could not countenance the demand that the proletariat should contribute to the costs of such litigation.

It would also be unreasonable to demand that anyone should have the right to seek legal redress at the state's expense simply at their own instigation, and for a wrong that perhaps only exists in their imagination. If the state pays the bill then the state must be allowed to decide which legal disputes are without foundation from the outset, and which not. However, this would lead to the institutions of the civil law taking on a fateful similarity to the current monopoly of prosecuting authority held by the state prosecutor. The state would acquire a new means of power. And the performance of our state prosecutors and judges is by no means such that we would want to see state officials take the place of independent advocates.

In our opinion the demand for the free administration of justice has to be understood as meaning that institutions should be created to enable those lacking in means to obtain justice, something frequently beyond them at present. These would include those arrangements already won or created by the proletariat here and there in order to facilitate proletarian access to justice. Such institutions would have to be generalised and their costs transferred from the individual corporations or communes which bear them at present to the state, but without any curtailment of the principle of self-administration. We are thinking here of the *Trade Courts* [*Gewerbegerichte* – predecessors of the Labour Courts], and the Labour Secretariats.

The most pressing needs for free justice may well be met firstly by the establishment of courts composed of trustees of the people, dealing with all small matters swiftly and free of charge and without excessive formality, under the guidance of stipendiary judges, and secondly through setting up information bureaux, in which specialist trustees provide free and impartial advice to those seeking justice as to their rights, the prospects for success in pursuing the case and the best way to redress the wrong.

The main advantage of such information bureaux is not that they provide individuals with the means for organising their own litigation, but that they will prevent many cases coming to court. This would prove a blessing, especially for the rural population.

The advocate lives from trials in the same way that the doctor lives from illness. And as the latter thrives on the maximum of illness rather than generalised good health, so the former hopes for as much discontent as possible. Although there may be many honourable members of these professions who would never let themselves be guided by such considerations, there are also quite a few who cannot resist them – more in the case of advocates than doctors. For doctors the issue is one of life and death, for the lawyer it is merely money, and whilst nature does not let itself be duped, this does not apply to the formalism of a somewhat limited judge faced with the wiles of the barrister. This is already a bad and unpropitious situation. Hardly surprising, therefore, that there are lawyers who, when confronted with a dispute which lends itself to settlement, albeit a modest one, will recommend a lucrative court case – lucrative for the lawyer that is, but ruinous for the client.

And more such cases exist on the land than anywhere else. This is not somehow the consequence of some mysterious 'addiction' to litigation on the part of the peasant, but rather of rural property relations. Most court cases turn on the subject of property. And nowhere is there more property than in the countryside, where even a large part of the proletariat owns land – frequently an absurdly small amount, but nevertheless a property sufficiently great to exercise a forceful sway over its owner's soul.

And if nowhere else has more property than the countryside, then the type of property peculiar to the countryside, landed property, is unique in its ability to create opportunities for property disputes. The land is simply something very special. In comparison, other things over which one can acquire property rights are transient, or – as with precious metals – where this is not the case, they can easily change their form and location. The land is rooted to one spot, and retains its essential form over hundreds of years. It represents the enduring conservative element in the economy, amidst the flood of the ephemeral.

This conservative character is also a characteristic of property rights in land; unlike property in other objects it preserves rights and obligations which are much more easily added to than shed over the course of the centuries. Property in a particular piece of land not only confers usage over a given area of land, but many other rights and obligations too. Things that would be quite inconceivable with any other type of property are nothing unusual as far as land is concerned: legal disputes continued from the seventeenth century, rights and obligations from the feudal period, stretching back into hoary antiquity, rights and obligations frequently not set down in writing and impossible, or at least difficult, to reconcile with modern notions of law. What a fertile source of litigation! And what a marvellous method for those with the necessary money and influence to acquire land by out-litigating the inconvenient current owner! The 'arm of the law' has certainly been of as much assistance in the expropriation of the peasantry by the aristocracy as the fists of its mercenaries. Open breaches of the law by large landowners are no longer to be feared. But the superior strength of their purses, which allows them to pursue a legal matter until the adversary succumbs exhausted, still persists. And it is doubtful whether this advantage enjoyed by private wealth can be abolished in a rational way under current social conditions.

Information bureaux staffed by people's lawyers could mitigate the worst effects, but scarcely do away with them totally. Their most beneficial role would be in preventing legal disputes between small landowners which are of little benefit in raising the level of peasant farming. The less money the peasants take to town to pay courts and lawyers, the more they have available for improving their living and farming standards.

All these measures will benefit the rural population much more than the urban, but they do not represent a privilege for country-dwellers and even less for landed property. In fact, they are eminently democratic and egalitarian in their effects. And neither do they signify protection for backward farming methods and the obstruction of economic progress: in fact, they represent a notable encouragement to the development of forces for new, higher social forms. And finally, they are not mere pious hopes, but lie on the path which social development must, of necessity, take.

The nationalisation of expenditures on schools and so forth is already a universal need, and all civilised states contribute to the costs of elementary schools: in France over 100 million francs annually (1893), double this in Great Britain (in 1893 over 160 million Marks), and in Prussia 53 million Marks (1896).

Very promising first steps have been taken towards the nationalisation of the care of the sick, at least in Russia, as we noted above. And as far as state responsibility for rural transport is concerned, increasing attention is now being given to the construction of local railways. But so far, this has been very scrappy: although pointing in the right direction it falls far short of meeting the demand.

The Costs of the Modern Cultural State

Governments are not lacking in goodwill; and no layer of the population is closer to their hearts than the rural population. What they lack is the means: *money*.

A general, and thorough, implementation of the programme sketched out here would undoubtedly require enormous sums of money.

Consider the nationalisation of school costs, for example. It is impossible of course to calculate exactly how much it would cost to bring about a general raising of the level of elementary education throughout the country up to the requirements of modern civilisation. But some idea can be obtained by looking at the costs of an elementary school in a large modern city and the costs of secondary schools. Simply raising Prussian rural schools to the level of the municipal schools of Berlin would cost the following:

Elementary school costs per pupil in Prussia (1896)

In the towns	35.50 Marks
In the countryside	29.67 Marks
In the Berlin area	67.24 Marks

Attaining the level prevailing in Berlin would double the costs of the elementary school system. In 1896 186 million Marks were spent on elementary schools of which 53 million came from the state. There were 5,237,000 pupils in elementary schools and 5,520,000 in all lower schools taken together. By Berlin standards, educating them would require 376 million Marks. And Berlin schools are by no means ideal. Average classes were as follows:

	No. of children per	
	Class	Teacher
In the countryside	56	70
In the towns	59	59
In the Berlin area	53	52

If one wished to arrive at 30 children per class, the resulting additional costs alone would increase the elementary school budget to around half a billion Marks.

But even this would not reach the minimum required of a rational elementary school system. It does not cover the free provision of materials, or food and uniforms for at least the poorer pupils; it does not cover equipping the schools with workshops and gardens, with industrial and agricultural teachers, with teachers and resources for organising and training the youth military service, or for providing general secondary education until 17 or 18 years of age. The latter would both bring about a significant increase in the number of those of obligatory school age and raise the costs of each individual pupil.

At present a secondary school student in Prussia costs 200 Marks, but a university student over 800 Marks. The costs of an ideal elementary school pupil could reasonably be put at 150 Marks. Even if the school leaving age were kept at 14, that is, with no increase to 17 years, this would bring the Prussian elementary school budget to around 800 million Marks: any extension of obligatory school age could easily round the figure up to a billion. Calculated for the Reich as a whole, this would add up to an elementary school budget of 1.5 billion marks. Even the military budget would pale in comparison.

We do not attempt to calculate the costs of the nationalisation of the other expenditures – poor relief, health care, transport, legal aid and so on. We lack the necessary background information. But they would certainly not be insignificant.

Set against these enormous demands, which would double or even triple the outgoings of our present-day state, the savings which such a reform programme would allow are minor in nature.

The supplanting of centralised bureaucratic rule by self-administration at state, province or municipality level will not mean the abolition of administration of public affairs by paid officials. Such matters are currently far too complex, diverse and extensive to be carried out as a secondary occupation, as a dilettante after-hours activity. They require trained specialists, paid officials, for whom such matters are their sole concern. The idea of government of the people by the people, meaning that public affairs should be attended to by representatives of the people, unpaid, in their free time instead of by paid officials is a utopia, and a reactionary, undemocratic utopia at that, irrespective of how democratic and revolutionary its representatives might feel themselves to be. Such a type of self-administration presupposes, in any communal system which has advanced beyond most primitive forms, an aristocracy – large peasants, feudal lords, rentiers of all types – who have the inclination and resources to dedicate themselves exclusively to public affairs since they live off the labour of others. Even the much-vaunted English self-administration was simply an aristocratic privilege. The more democratic modern large states become, the more they must – where they have self-administration – transform their officials from unpaid posts of honour into salaried positions. Compared with centralised bureaucratic rule, modern self-administration, modern democracy, does not mean a reduction in the number of officials, but rather their more even distribution throughout the country, their subordination to the will of the people and, linked with that, some change in the nature of their recruitment and promotion.

Whilst the advance of democracy does not lead to any great reduction in the number of salaried officials, it does lead to a progressive equalisation of their incomes. In monarchistic, aristocratic states, the highest offices are the privilege of the aristocracy and are correspondingly often extravagantly remunerated. In fact, the more such posts represent mere sinecures for greedy or hard-up, but lazy and ignorant, aristocrats, the higher the remuneration tends to be. The real work is attended to by workers from the bourgeois intelligentsia and proletariat, and is paid accordingly. The advance of democracy will lead to a reduction in the salaries of the highest officers, but an increase in the miserable salaries of the lower ranks, whose pay is often below that of proletarians working in private service; their compensation is a supposedly carefree old age, but also embraces the titillation of their vanity and arrogance, and often an unhealthy secondary occupation which arises from their office, namely corruption. A democratic state in which the official is not the master but rather the servant of the people, in which laws are not there only for the population, but rather, and primarily, for public officials, in which the uniform does not signify any particular right, but rather a particular obligation, will always find it difficult to find diligent officials if it does not pay them a salary corresponding to the class from which it recruits them. This alone will require a substantial increase in the salaries of lower officials the more the state becomes democratised – alongside other reasons too involved to go into here.

However, since the number of officials in poverty is large, and those overpaid is small, any advance towards equalising salaries will lead to a steady increase in expenditure on the salaries of public officials rather than a reduction. No savings can be made here.

The picture is more promising when we turn to the military sphere. General disarmament would release enormous sums, which although not sufficient to implement the reform programme outlined here, would permit a substantial raising of the general level of civilisation when compared with present standards. The seven to eight hundred million Marks which the German Reich annually spends for its army and fleet are no small matter. Such a sum could pay for an elementary school system which would command the admiration of the world, and place the Germany people at the head of the civilised nations. However, the prospects for general disarmament are, unfortunately, very poor. And no one would want to postpone serious reforms requiring large amounts of money until after successful disarmament – which may not be possible until we have a socialist system. The transition from a standing army to a people's army can, but will not necessarily, lead to a substantial absolute reduction in military expenditure. But such a reduction will never be sufficient to release enough funds to meet even a substantial fraction of the costs of a modern civilised state. And haven't we already observed that the lower strata of the population are already overburdened? Would we not want to use any savings from military reform to lighten their load?

Where should the money be found to transform the current state into a cultural state? Such a question poses bourgeois taxation policy a problem which it is utterly unable to solve. A glance at the principles of this taxation policy will show why.

Bourgeois and Proletarian Taxation Policy

Any taxation policy which aspires to be more than a mere plundering of the population must proceed from the question: what are the sources of social wealth from which taxes do and ought to flow? The question of how *individuals* should be induced to pay their taxes and how much they should pay is a secondary question which can only be satisfactorily tackled once we have answered the first.

If we consider the aggregate product produced by any given society from year to year, we can divide it into two portions. One portion serves to maintain and reproduce the labour-power engaged in production: it must accrue to the workers in production if society is to continue to exist. The excess over and above this constitutes the surplus-product from which the non-productive classes maintain themselves. In a capitalist society the surplus-product takes the form of surplus-value which accrues to the capitalist.

Looking at economic relationships in this simplified way clearly reveals that state taxes should and may only come from one source – the surplus-product, or surplus-value. This was very evident in the feudal period. The functions of the state were exercised by the king, the Church, the feudal lords; all drew their income, not from taxes in our sense of the term, but from their property in land, that is from the labour of the farmers. They drew on the surplus-product of these farmers, either wholly or partly, in the form of tribute in kind or as services, and in exchange they took on the functions currently exercised by the state – justice, police, national defence, relationships with the outside world.

Such tributes and services did not usually exceed the surplus-product; on the one hand, as Marx noted, because the unbounded greed of the money economy is not inherent to the natural economy, and additionally, because given the low level of weapons technology, the peasantry was not completely defenceless against the feudal lords; and finally, a peasant pressed too hard could flee, and given the shortage of labour-power, could always find work elsewhere, either with another landlord, or in the town.

It was in the towns that commodity production, the money economy, first arose. The product became a commodity with a specific value and price, and the surplus-product also took on the value-form. And that part of the surplus-product that had to serve to sustain the state became a part of the commodity-value realised in money. Money taxes replaced feudal tributes and services.

We have already described what this development led on to. The new state authority based on money taxes, which arose with bourgeois society, first had to crush the former masters of the commonweal, the Church and the feudal aristocracy. This struggle ended not with their destruction, however, but with a compromise which established their existence on a new foundation. From being masters of the state they became its servants; and in return the state protected their material interests. The new state taxes did not replace feudal services and tributes, but were added to them. With its new weapons technology, the flints and cannons of the professional army, and the boundless greed of the money economy, the centralised state was able to outdo the feudal lords in extracting money from the peasants, who could not hide themselves as easily from the state police as they could from the lord of a small feudal estate.

Feudal services and tributes were increased rather than decreased under the protection of the new state and this resulted in an enormous increase in money taxes. The princes scavenged money wherever they found it without the slightest regard to the continuation of production and the well-being of the population. And state protection of economically bankrupt feudal landed property led not to an increase, but to a fall in production.

Under these circumstances the surplus-product became increasingly incapable of satisfying the demands of the state: a part, in fact, a growing part, of the product needed to maintain and reproduce the working classes, had to be sacrificed to the greed of the state and its tax collectors, at least on the land. The prosperous peasantry of the fourteenth and fifteenth centuries became increasingly impoverished in the seventeenth and eighteenth; farming regressed and the peasantry slowly began to starve. Although this was partly attributable to feudal pressures which did not allow rational agriculture, and partly attributable to the demands of the rapidly growing money economy in relation to which the peasant natural economy was only slowly assuming the character of commodity-production, it was also in no small measure directly attributable to the insane extortion represented by taxes.

This was most starkly revealed in France, whose great revolution also represented the starkest reaction against such appalling conditions. The theoreticians of the aspiring French bourgeoisie were also the first to turn to thoughts of a rational taxation policy.

The Physiocrats were the first to state clearly and openly that taxation policy should be dependent on the economy: taxation policy had to serve the economy. The natural conclusion of this was the axiom: *tax should only be paid from the surplus-product*. However, the only labour that in their view created a surplus-product was agricultural labour. They therefore demanded the abolition of all other taxes and their replacement by a single tax (the *impôt unique*) on the agricultural surplus (*produit net*). However, such a tax, which would in essence have been a tax on large landowners, was not envisaged as being too onerous since the functions of the state were to be reduced to a minimum. The state associated with the feudal aristocracy had become a useless vampire, blocking economic activity in every direction: eliminating *this* state was the first precondition for economic prosperity. It was the Physiocrats who launched the expression *'laisser faire, laisser aller!'*

What the Physiocrats began was later continued by the radical free traders, who led the struggle of the bourgeoisie against the remnants of the feudal state in our own [nineteenth] century. Admittedly their theoretical basis was quite different, that of classical English political economy. But like the Physiocrats they also clung to the axiom of *laisser aller, laisser faire*, and demanded the reduction of state functions to a minimum. And like the Physiocrats they also aspired to a taxation policy in harmony with the requirements of production: in these respects it closely resembled the policy of their predecessors. Of course it never occurred to them to propose that taxes should be limited to a single tax on surplus-value. The question of surplus-value simply did not exist for them. However, they did reject indirect taxes, at least on necessary food, and demanded an income tax with exemption for low incomes; although such a tax does not fully coincide with the taxation of surplus-value, it does approach it very closely.

However, Manchesterism never achieved a complete breakthrough. The bourgeois state proved to be just as belligerent as the feudal. The French revolution, borne upon the ideas of the Physiocrats, unleashed a series of gruesome world wars which devastated Europe for over two decades and imposed terrible burdens on both the life and property of the people. The revolution of 1848 threatened to unleash a second era of wars – the same revolution which cleared the way for the rule of the radical free traders. Its defeat postponed these wars which were then later fought out by the executors of the revolution, the three autocrats, Louis Napoleon, Bismarck and Alexander II. The 20-year era of wars which began with a war in the East and ended with a war in the East was followed by the era of armed peace no less onerous to the population than war. As a result, all the civilised nations have experienced a steady increase in the burden of taxation and state indebtedness, interest on which requires additional taxes. At the same time, there has been an increase in the demands on the state as an agent of civilisation, despite governments' attempts to exercise strict 'economy' in this area. More schooling, transport and other provisions have imposed growing, and unavoidable, demands.

Instead of the peaceful state dreamt of by Manchesterism, the reality has proved to be a permanent armed camp; in place of *laisser faire* we see a constant expansion of the scope of state intervention in social life.

How should the growing demands of the state be met? From surplus-value, i.e. taxes on income, property or estates, or by taxing the necessities of the population – i.e. indirect taxes? This was the question. However, the bourgeoisie is the ruling class, and as such has always known how to shift the main burdens of the state off its own shoulders. There are states, such as France, which have no income tax at all, thanks to the autocracy of the bourgeoisie, which successfully overcame the aristocracy a hundred years ago and which has always appreciated the value of the petty bourgeoisie and peasants as a bulwark against the proletariat. This explains why food is so highly taxed in France; the bulk of the state's revenues come from grain duties, indirect taxes, including taxes on salt, sugar and drinks, and a tobacco monopoly. According to the 1897 budget revenues were as follows:

	Francs (million)
Duties	410
Indirect taxes	559
Tobacco, match and gunpowder monopoly	421
Total	1,430

Total state revenues came to 3,386 million francs. Stock-exchange duties yielded 8,700,000, property income tax 65,800,000. The other taxes (stamp duty, etc.) are far from serving as a substitute for income tax.

Of all the modern states, the bourgeoisie enjoys least hegemony in England, a country where ironically the capitalist mode of production developed earliest and in its purest form, but where, as a direct consequence, the bourgeoisie encountered a strong proletariat, unconstrained by a petty bourgeoisie and peasantry at a time when it was still faced with a strong aristocracy.

As a result we find virtually no indirect taxes on *necessaries*. But surplus-value is also spared as much as possible. English taxation policy rests on a compromise; it introduced an income tax (incomes below £160 are exempted), but not a progressive one (in fact there is a slight regression for incomes between £160–500 according to the 1894 Act), and hence large incomes are not more highly taxed than moderate incomes. Estate duties work in the same way as income tax. In addition there are high indirect taxes and revenue tariffs on mass luxury articles such as spirits and tobacco. In 1896 these indirect taxes yielded £48,714,000, while income tax and stamp duty, the lion's share of which is made up of estate duty, yielded £34,830,000. Total receipts were more than £100 million.

The other civilised states tread a path midway between that of England and France. On the Continent, with the exception of Switzerland, surplus-value is much less burdened with tax than the people's necessaries. And in general, indirect taxes are tending to rise, not only absolutely but also relatively. This is highly irrational, since, as with salt tax for example, it not only affects poor, larger families relatively more than more affluent families, but also absolutely. They are also irrational because their collection swallows up a large part of the revenue. But they are more comfortable: the people feel their effects less than direct taxes and – and this is what is crucial – the mass of the population does not resist them as the bourgeoisie resists direct taxes, which were a considerable burden on their incomes. And the bourgeoisie is still the class whose interests are decisive. The declining classes, handicraft workers and peasants, also encourage the spread of indirect taxes via their tariff policies. Export industry is almost exclusively big industry. Handicrafts and peasant farming merely supply the domestic market. They want to secure this market. They therefore favour protective tariffs which, far from protecting them, simply become new indirect taxes which they themselves largely have to bear.

The bourgeois parties, both Manchesterist and Protectionist, have not advanced beyond the two types of taxation policy sketched out above – not even bourgeois democracy, which is not a capitalist party, and not an anticapitalist party, but rather a party for the reconciliation of class interests, the party of those interests which capitalists and proletarians, petty bourgeois and peasants, all have in common. It lacks resoluteness towards the capitalists. It dare not burden them with the whole of the tax burden. At the same time it wants to bring relief to the lower classes. Its entire taxation policy therefore culminates in the aspiration: *as low a level of taxation as possible* – an ideal irreconcilable with the growing tasks of the modern state. Irrespective of goodwill and good intentions, it is impossible to transform the state into a cultural state on the basis of bourgeois democracy.

The tax policy of proletarian democracy – Social Democracy – is quite different in character. Its rallying cry is not the *reduction* of taxes, but their *transfer* to the shoulders of those able to bear them. It takes up the old Physiocratic demand, that taxes should only be paid out of surplus-value. Admittedly, surplus-value in the developed capitalist mode of production is not as easy to pin down as the Physiocrat's *produit net*, which, in the mainly self-sufficient natural economy of the peasant, appeared as the material surplus of products produced above and beyond their needs and delivered to the feudal lord. Surplus-value only comes into view after a number of apportionments and transformations which obscure its actual magnitude – and therefore render taxing it fully virtually impossible. The taxation of individual sources or portions of surplus-value can easily lead to anomalies, including the passing on of tax liabilities. Thus urban landowners use their monopoly position to shift the taxation of their ground-rents on to their tenants.

We do not propose to delve any deeper into the question of what is the most rational form for taxing surplus-value – this goes beyond our brief. It is sufficient to refer to the programme of German Social Democracy: it demands that those state expenditures which are to be covered by taxation should be met by a progressively rising income and wealth tax and an inheritance tax rising with the size of the estate and the closeness of the family relationship. This combination seems to be the most certain to bite into surplus-value.

Bourgeois democracy also demands this type of taxation, and to some extent has obtained it; but it lacks the resolution to squeeze large sums out of capital. Only Social Democracy can muster the required ruthlessness. And only Social Democracy can demand social reforms which require significant state expenditure, and simultaneously aim to replace all other taxes by income, wealth and inheritance taxes.

Given the growing demands on its finances even bourgeois democracy is sometimes compelled to make exceptional demands on surplus-value in order to meet the state's requirements: but in doing so it does not choose the form of *taxation*, but rather *public borrowing*. Although this is sometimes for economic purposes, such as the construction of railways or canals, it is usually intended for utterly unproductive spending – the acquisition of cannons and battleships, paying for wars and the like.

It is a curious fact that in monarchist states, everything in the state is Imperial or Royal – with the exception of the debts. The soldier's uniform is the king's mantle, but the king would protest mightily if it was proposed to name the debts raised to pay for this royal uniform the 'royal debts'. These are graciously donated to the nation. In this respect even Russian absolutism turns out to be highly republican.

Such loans can be compared to the voluntary contributions which the ruling classes, aristocracy and clergy were called upon to make in feudal times whenever the fatherland was in danger. There is, however, one difference: the feudal lords did not demand interest on what they laid at the altar of the fatherland – whereas for the capitalists, interest is the main consideration. Perhaps one could equate the privileges in perpetuity which rich lords, bishops, monasteries and towns obtained in return for their contributions with the never-ending interest payments payable on our current national debt.

After military spending, interest payments on public debt are the largest item of expenditure in all modern states. In England, out of a total budget of 2,000 million Marks, the fleet and army take $c.800$ million and interest on the national debt 500 million. In France the army and the fleet take $c.700$ million, and interest payments 1,000 million!

In the German Reich, interest on state debt is only 74 million Marks, compared with spending on the army and the fleet of 700 million. But the German Reich is still young; it obtained billions of Marks from France in the war which gave birth to it and since then has not had to fight another. In the same period in which the German Reich succeeded in raising its overall indebtedness to 2,261 million Marks – after beginning with reparations of 4,000 million Marks – the English national debt fell from 15,600 million Marks to 12,400 million – without grain, meat, petrol or similar tariffs! And for a real comparison, one would also have to add in the debt of all the member states of the Confederation. The Prussian state debt alone is 6,500 million Marks, and interest 229 million (1898); the debts of Bavaria, Saxony, Württemberg add up to 2,500 million. Taking all German state debts together we arrive at figures comparable with England, with the difference that in Germany the direction of movement is rapidly upwards, and with the English, down.

Alongside military spending, the elimination of interest payments from a modern state's budget would release the most resources, either for lightening the load on the population, or carrying out major social reforms. General disarmament and a general cessation of interest payments on government stock would release well over a billion Marks annually for such purposes in large modern state. And a lot could be accomplished with such an amount!

State bankruptcy is nothing unusual; nevertheless, we would not want to assert that a regime such as the one assumed here, under proletarian influence but not yet able to overcome the capitalist mode of production, would cancel interest payments unless under great pressure to do so. Selecting only a few capitalists and confiscating their property would represent a gross violation of the principle of equality before the law: the fact that quite a substantial proportion of state bonds are held by the smallest capitalists would make this even less justifiable. Confiscating the small savings of small people cannot be claimed to be in conformity with the intentions of a democratic government.

What is certain is that such a regime would have to make a definitive break with the raising of new loans, and attempt to pay back existing loans as quickly as possible. Fresh loans would be tantamount to renewing the subordination of state authority to the yoke of capital. Public borrowing is one means by which the bourgeois state can use the surplus-value appropriated by capital for state purposes. The only means recognised by proletarian democracy for achieving such purposes is taxation.

However, although proletarian democracy might choose to show little consideration for capital, it cannot tax away surplus-value just as it wishes. Raising taxes so as to confiscate surplus-value is totally inconceivable: the state under discussion here is not a socialist commonwealth, in which such considerations would have no meaning since a society which is mistress of its means of production does not need taxes to gain access to its surplus-product. Rather, we are talking about a state in which, although the proletariat has sufficient political power to influence taxation policy, the capitalist mode of production still prevails. And as long as this is the case, as long as society for one or other reason is not able completely to take over the functions of the capitalist, surplus-value will continue to play an important economic role. Like the feudal lords or Roman aristocrats before them, the capitalists cannot consume the entire surplus-product provided by their workers. They must 'forgo', must 'save'. Only a part of surplus-value is consumed, the rest is accumulated – that is, turned into fresh capital. And alongside the advances of the natural sciences, this accumulation of capital constitutes the major force for economic progress in our century. If economic progress has advanced faster in this century than in any other previous century, if it has created enormous productive forces dwarfing all previous wonders of the world, if – for the first time in world history – it has created the possibility of a socialist society on the basis of a higher civilisation, then – together with the natural sciences – this is due to the accumulation of capital. And as long as the productive forces are not the property of society, and are not regulated by society, rendering the accumulation of capital impossible would mean obstructing progress and stunting the preconditions for socialism.

Fortunately for progress, capital's urge to accumulate is so strong that it can be treated fairly roughly without great upset. Labour legislation and workers' organisations have so far turned out to foster rather than obstruct economic progress, and have not inflicted the slightest harm on the accumulation of capital. It has now reached such a scale that it is beginning to pose a dilemma for the capitalists. The mass of surplus-value accruing to them year in, year out, is so enormous that, despite their incredible luxury, they still manage to set aside as much money as can easily be induced to breed yet more surplus-value. A number of national bankrupticies – Argentina, Portugal, Greece etc. – and bankruptcies of giant concerns, principally the Panama affair, have occurred over the last years without causing excessive disruption to economic life, without encroaching on the capacity of capital to invest yet more hundreds of millions in completely unproductive state loans, and still promote the development of new industries and means of transport with even greater energy than before.

Surplus-value can be tapped considerably more than at present, without fear of jeopardising economic development.

It would be utterly futile to attempt to calculate, even approximately, how far one could in fact go.

But irrespective of how high one estimates the sums which can be raised for the state in this way, the possibility must also be accepted that they might prove insufficient to cover all those costs required to allow a cultural state to raise the entire population to the level of modern civilisation. A second method of obtaining surplus-value will have to be added: the state – or the commune, for which the following also applies *mutatis mutandis* – must set about producing surplus-value for itself.

Economic and political development is pushing in this direction anyway. There are a number of natural private monopolies – mines, the major means of transport, lighting plants and so on – the exploitation of which, in the absence of competition, not only leads to the exploitation of their workers, but also to the exploitation of the consumers. In addition, the concentration of capital also creates artificial private monopolies via cartels, and so forth, which have a similar effect. The entire population, not merely the proletariat, are up in arms against these monopolies. But legislative control over them never goes further than mere half measures: there is only one way to put a stop to the exploitation of the community which they practise – their acquisition and operation by the community. As long as the big capitalists have the state in their pockets – as is the case today – this is neither an easy nor a desirable thing, however. The proletariat cannot demand that a hostile state power be granted a further domain. And the capitalists are powerful enough to frustrate any nationalisation inconvenient to them, and impose conditions on any nationalisation which does succeed such that they gain from it. The nationalisation of the Austrian and Prussian railways was certainly not carried out at the expense of the shareholders.

These objections lose their relevance in a state in which the proletariat is able to endow the state with the required ruthlessness towards capital, and where the mass of the population has enough control over the state to have no cause to fear a multiplication of its spheres of power. The nationalisation of private monopolies can speed ahead – and other things being equal, this will take place all the more rapidly, the greater the needs of the state and the more limited its capacity to tax surplus-value. And such a nationalisation would also be effected under conditions which, although not a confiscation, will guarantee a plentiful income to the state, part of which it can use to improve the position of its own workers, part in the interests of the consumers, and part to promote its civilising work on a truly grand scale.

The operation of such state monopolies would still not be socialist: under the prevailing conditions it would in fact serve commodity-production, not immediate production for society's needs. But it would nonetheless differ fundamentally from the administration of monopolies under the bourgeois state. Under a proletarian taxation policy, monopolies would be a means of conveying surplus-value to the state; under bourgeois taxation policy, they are a powerful means of indirect taxation, raising the price of necessaries to the state's advantage.

The criterion for placing a branch of production under proletarian state monopoly is the level of its form of production: most suitable are establishments which are organised bureaucratically, and which have passed from being individual property into the anonymous ownership of a joint stock company or a syndicate, and are already outside the sphere of competition.

In contrast, the criterion for placing a branch under bourgeois state monopoly is the importance of its products as either necessities or luxuries for *the mass of consumers* (tobacco, spirits, salt). The level of the development of production is of no concern – such monopolies embrace backward branches of production carried out in mainly small establishments (tobacco). The monopoly has to exclude competition *artificially* and obtains its income by exploiting consumers, and often its workers more than would have been the case under free competition between private concerns.

Just as state monopoly should not be confused with socialism, so proletarian state monopoly should not be confused with bourgeois state monopoly.

The nationalisation and municipalisation of private monopolies under the state and communes; the replacement of indirect taxes by progressive income, wealth and inheritance taxes; the end of state borrowing – these constitute the heart of proletarian taxation policy. No proof is needed to see that such a policy would not only provide enormous relief to the proletariat, but to the working population in general. In fact, it could prove to be more important for small handicraft workers, retailers, and small peasants than for the wage-proletariat. Whilst many strata of the latter are moving upwards, the former are facing ruin. For the rising strata of the proletariat, current bourgeois taxation policy represents an impediment to their rise; but for the declining classes it means an acceleration of their ruin. The tax burden falls heavier on small peasants and the petty bourgeoisie than on wage-labourers, and the former have a much greater interest in a proletarian tax policy than the proletariat itself.

The taxation policy outlined here would not only provide relief to the working population, but also enable the state to pursue an energetic welfare and culture policy, quite unlike that facilitated by the bourgeois tax system, wherever capitalist production was highly developed and the mass of surplus-value large.

Taxing the people's needs has to be kept within limits if the ruin of the mass of the people and hence the community as a whole is to be avoided. And taxing surplus-value under a bourgeois taxation policy will never be adequate.

Only a proletarian taxation policy can really squeeze it, can tax away all those sums which the capitalist class currently invests in foreign and domestic loans to governments, and more, without impairing the development of industry, or even the bourgeoisie's purchasing power. And producing surplus-value by nationalising the major monopolies places the most important productive forces of the nation in the service of the community and allows the state to use the countless, presently unutilised workers for the work of civilisation. This will increase the material resources of the state and local authorities enormously. The growing concentration of capital is bringing more and more areas towards state exploitation: opening up new sources of income for the state, without burdening the population by multiplying its enterprises, therefore has limits.

Whether the proletariat will ever really come to expound its own taxation policy is doubtful. This would require a situation which our discussion has simply presumed: considerable political power on the part of the proletariat together with the uninterrupted continuation of the capitalist mode of production. Both are virtually mutually exclusive, or at any event could only coexist for a short time.

Nevertheless, we consider it necessary to examine what kind of taxation policy the proletariat would pursue were it to come to political power today. The significance of a social objective consists less in whether it will be achieved than in whether it provides a faithful pointer of the direction in which a social movement is travelling. The significance of the *objective* lies in the significance of the *movement* and the accuracy with which it shows the *direction* required. One can only have a clear perception of a movement if one has recognised its goal.

Should social circumstances be such that a specific taxation policy of the type indicated here is superfluous when the proletariat comes to political power, then at least such a policy provides a goal for proletarian democracy *today*; and the extent to which the proletariat acquires political influence will be indicated, amongst other things, by the degree to which its taxation policy is realised. The stronger Social Democracy becomes, the lower the levels of indirect taxation, and the greater the importance of income, wealth and inheritance taxes: the national debt and interest payments will be reduced, and the large capitalist monopolies will be nationalised and municipalised both sooner and more cheaply.

The Neutralisation of the Peasantry

If we collect together the demands which have emerged from our studies, we find the following:

I. **Measures which Benefit the Rural Proletariat**
   a) Abolition of the Servants Ordinance; combination on the land; establishment of the right of free movement.
   b) The prohibition of wage labour by children under 14; the prohibition of agricultural work between 7 pm and 7 am for all children and young persons without exception; the prohibition of migrant labour by young persons up to 18; compulsory education for elementary and secondary schools.
   c) Protection of migrant workers; the prohibition of migrant labour by women and girls under 21; prohibition of the gang system, and replacement of recruiting agents by public labour offices.
   d) The introduction of a normal working day averaging eight hours for fieldwork, with permission for overtime during harvests and urgent work necessitated by natural circumstances; establishment of Sunday rest for house-servants.
   e) Establishment of minimum necessary standards for rural worker housing in the interests of health and morality; vigorous enforcement of housing standards on the land;
   f) Reduction of excessive rents through special courts.

II. **Measures for the Protection of Agriculture**
   a) Abolition of the *Fideikommiss*.
   b) Abolition of manorial districts and their integration into the rural communes.
   c) Abolition of hunting districts belonging to large land-ownership, and their incorporation into the rural communes.
   d) Limitation on the rights of private property in land in order to promote:
      1. Consolidation, the abolition of scattered strip holdings.
      2. 'Cultivation of the land' – improvements.

3. Prevention of epidemics.
e) Nationalisation of hail insurance, and possibly stock insurance – but the latter without any contribution from the state.
f) Legislative facilitation of cooperative mergers.
g) State promotion of the agricultural training system.
h) Nationalisation of forests and water.

III. Measures in the Interests of the Agricultural Population

Efforts to overcome the exploitation of the countryside by the town and the abolition of the cultural antagonism between town and country through:
a) Implementation of maximum self-administration at parish and province level.
b) Replacement of the standing army by a popular militia.
c) Nationalisation of expenditures on schools, poor relief and roads.
d) Nationalisation of the health system.
e) Free administration of justice.
f) Replacement of the existing taxation system by progressive income, property and inheritance taxes, and the equitable nationalisation or municipalisation of profitable private monoploies and cartels.

These could be characterised as the demands of a Social Democratic agrarian programme should one wish. But, in our view, this would not be an appropriate characterisation. The points listed under I are already, in essence, contained in Social Democracy's current demands for labour protection; the same applies to the points under III which comprise our immediate political demands. And of the points under II, the only demand of crucial importance, the nationalisation of forests and water, is similarly not purely agrarian in character, not merely in the interests of agriculture, but also of industry, general hygiene and so forth. The remaining demands, despite their importance, are relatively speaking too minor to be able to constitute the basis for a major party programme. These 'small measures' have also already been implemented in many progressive countries: Social Democracy's only distinction from other parties in their regard is its degree of ruthlessness towards the rights of private property wherever they conflict with the general interest of rational cultivation. And this itself must demonstrate that, essential as these 'small measures' are in the interests of the development of agriculture, they are inadequate when set against the great burdens which private property in land and capitalist commodity-production is increasingly imposing on agriculture.

As we have already noted, our intention has not been to present an exhaustive programme. We would regard agrarian action programmes for specific issues and localities as entirely appropriate: but these cannot be worked out by theoreticians alone – practitioners must help too.

Our sole concern was to use a number of concrete examples to indicate the general direction which Social Democratic agrarian policy ought to follow, assuming the correctness of the developmental path of agriculture which we sketched out. It is then an easy matter to decide how to proceed in individual instances.

Hopefully we have succeeded in showing that the belief that nothing can be done to save the peasant economy, and that such a policy contradicts the basic principles of Social Democracy, does not necessitate nihilism on these questions of social policy. Social Democracy can adopt the same position as it does with the handicrafts and domestic industry, a position which allows a rich and fertile activity not only in the interests of the rural proletariat but in the interests of agriculture and the rural population in general too.

Of course doubts might be raised as to whether the presentation of this agrarian policy will succeed in binding the peasantry to Social Democracy. At heart Social Democracy will always be a proletarian and an urban party, a party of economic progress. And it will always have to struggle with the deeply rooted prejudices found in a conservative peasantry, ill-disposed to the urban system and rooted in the patriarchal family, with its complete subjection of maids and servants, wife and children. It will never be able to offer the peasant as much as the agrarian parties, who are not only closer to them in character but who can also promise much more since they do not believe in the necessity and inevitability of economic progress: they see nothing wrong in inverting the previous situation, and letting the rural population feed off the urban, and agriculture off industry and commerce.

Social Democracy is unlikely to win over peasants who cling to their old farming practices. But it may be possible to put such peasants into a neutral position. And even this would be a significant gain. Economic development will of course continue to sweep over them, and Social Democracy will also have to deal with the peasants should they stand in its way. But they still nevertheless frequently constitute a force whose power should not be underestimated; if it is at all possible to remove its obstructive effects, it would be foolish to ignore the opportunity.

But what makes the peasant into the enemy of Social Democracy is not the latter's practical politics. Of course the peasants cannot work up any enthusiasm for it – after all it refuses to sacrifice the consumer to their interests, it opposes attempts to increase ground-rents through artificial increases in food prices, it rejects entails, the Servants Ordinance, and limitations on free movement. But Social Democracy also struggles against the high tax burden imposed on the peasant, against the excesses of the bureaucrats and large landowners – and the peasant is quite happy about that. What outrages peasants is the idea of the expropriation of land-ownership which the victory of Social Democracy supposedly implies. In their eyes this means being chased out of house, home and farm, chased off their property, which will then be shared out amongst the have-nots. A study of Social Democratic agrarian policy would be incomplete if it did not clarify this issue. Our concluding chapter is therefore dedicated to this task.

16

The Social Revolution and the Expropriation of Landowners

Socialism and the Small Enterprise

At the end of Part I we made reference to the fact that the transition from capitalist to socialist agriculture can be accomplished without expropriating peasant landowners. What was said there should suffice to dissipate any fears which the peasantry might have in this respect.

However, we still have a number of other arguments on this issue.

Not only do small peasants have nothing to fear from a victory of the proletariat: neither do the owners of small enterprises in general, including the handicrafts. Just the opposite in fact.

As we have shown, they will be the prime beneficiaries of the transformation of the state from an institution of domination into one of civilisation, and of the shifting of the burdens of public spending onto surplus-value or surplus-product.

However, their response to the early stages of a socialist society will vary according to whether their establishments are parasitic or not. Small establishments can be termed parasitic if they have long since become technically obsolete and economically superfluous, and if their owners only cling on to them either because a purely proletarian existence seems even more uncertain and miserable than their present life, or they are denied any opportunity for existence within the wage proletariat. Consider the number of small enterprises, especially of the retail sort, which are established by wage labourers who have been disciplined or become unemployed for one reason or another, and who raise a loan in order to establish an independent dwarf-enterprise as a means of avoiding sinking down completely into the lumpenproletariat.

For statisticians the unemployed are only those lacking any occupation at all. At the last count this was only a few hundred thousand. But were the moment ever to arrive when the state offered to guarantee all the unemployed a decent living, the increase in those requiring work and money from the state would be astounding. And the number of dwarf-enterprises would diminish considerably.

The better the position of workers in the large enterprise, the shorter their working hours, the higher their wages, and the more secure their income, the more willing the owners of parasitic small enterprises will be to abandon the reactionary experiments through which they seek to prolong their wretched existences at the expense of the community in general. And the sooner they will decide to abandon their outmoded and superfluous enterprises and become workers in modern factories. This would be bound to increase significantly the volume of productive forces available to the nation, at the same time eliminating a prolific source of poverty and distress.

However, there are also essential as well as parasitic small enterprises in those spheres not yet conquered by the machine, which do not serve mass production. There is of course scope for disagreement as to which enterprises belong in these categories, and the technical conditions also change from day to day. The machine has now penetrated into the arts and crafts, once regarded as a safe bastion for the small enterprise, as much as it has into baking or shoe-making. Nevertheless, some of the handicraft industries would in all probability survive into the early stages of socialist society, and the increase in popular welfare could even enable some branches of the handicrafts to experience a renaissance inasmuch as the demand for cheap mass articles will fall and that for more expensive and more individualised craft products will rise. At the same time, proletarian taxation policy (if one could still speak of taxes) will ease the burdens currently imposed on handicraft workers. Their general education will improve and the opportunities for greater technical and artistic education will multiply. One could even say that socialist society is not only *not* based on the complete demise of the handicrafts, but it could lead to a fresh blossoming of some of its branches. However, the social character of these newly flourishing handicrafts will be quite different to the present. It will simply constitute one exception to the general type of production.

The vast bulk of the means of production and the economically crucial part will be social property; production will be social. The small handicraft workers, even if they remain independent in their own workshops, will be completely dependent on society: and society will be the sole provider of their raw materials and tools, and usually the sole purchaser of their products. They will have to adapt themselves to the organism of social production, accommodate themselves to it and, despite their isolation in their own workshops, they will become social workers.

The development of the peasantry will also proceed in the same direction. The innumerable owners of parasitic dwarf-holdings will be glad to shed the semblance of their independence and their property if the large-scale socialist enterprise offers them palpable advantages.

But non-parasitic small peasant holdings, those which still fulfil important functions in economic life, will also become limbs of social production, like the handicraft enterprises, even if they remain fixed in their apparent isolation. The nationalisation of mortgages and the agricultural industries, on which farmers depend, will mean that society will have more power over them than over handicraft establishments.

However, the peasantry need not fear that it will suffer under this dependency. To be dependent on the state is certainly more agreeable than being exploited by a few sugar barons. But the state will give to, rather than take from, the peasantry. Peasants and agricultural workers would be especially valued workers in the transition from capitalist to socialist society.

The enormous extension of industry for the world market and the simultaneous flooding of the world market with foreign grain – two phenomena which are intimately connected – drive the rural population and specifically its most able elements into the towns. Once the domestic market regains its primacy in the domestic economy, one of its main expressions will be a growth in the importance of agriculture. The greater purchasing power of the masses will call for more food; and a reduction in exports will reduce the supply from abroad. An all-round rational policy for agriculture with the aim of the highest possible yields will become indispensable.

Agriculture will require the best means of production and the best labour-power. This latter aspect is not so simple, however. All agricultural workers are fit for some type of industrial labour, but few industrial workers could currently work in agriculture. Although suitable training should enable youth to carry out agricultural work as well as industrial intellectual work, this prospect will not be of much help during the initial problems of socialism.

The agricultural worker and the small peasant, who are the most poorly provided for in the present-day society, will inevitably become highly-prized, and will achieve a very favourable social position. How could anyone think that a socialist government will drive peasants from their fields? This would be insanity, beyond even what our most unscrupulous and stupidest opponents have declared us capable of.

A socialist regime would have to attempt to structure agriculture as advantageously as possible simply in order to feed the population. The displacement of commodity-production by the production of use-values also offers the possibility of transforming the peasants' money payments – the mortgage interests and other tributes still demanded of them – into payments in kind; this would represent an enormous relief for them. A proletarian regime would also have every interest in making sure that the peasants could work as productively as possible, equipping them with the best technical aids. Far from expropriating the country-dweller, Social Democracy will place the best means of production, completely inaccessible during the capitalist era, at their disposal.

Of course the most technically advanced means of production can only be used on a large-scale establishment, and a socialist regime would have to work to extend these as fast as possible. Expropriation will not be necessary to induce peasants to consolidate their fields and go over to cooperative, or communal large-scale farming. Should the cooperative large-scale enterprise prove to be advantageous for the cooperative worker, then the example of nationalised large-scale enterprises will suffice to move the peasants to follow suit. The major obstacles presently standing in the way of the development of cooperative agriculture – the lack of examples, the risk, the shortage of capital – will no longer exist and the enormous obstacle represented by unconstrained private property in land will have been reduced to the minimum by the nationalisation of mortgages, the growing dependency of the peasant on the nationalised agricultural industries, and the right of the state to administer and intervene on matters of improvements, and human and animal hygiene.

In view of all this, in view of the interest which a socialist regime will have in the uninterrupted continuation of agricultural production, in view of the high social importance which the peasant population will attain, it is inconceivable that forcible expropriation would be chosen as the means for educating the peasantry into the advantages of more advanced farming.

And should some branches of agriculture or regions exist in which the small establishment remains more advantageous than the large, there will be not the slightest reason to force them to conform to the model set by the large farm. These will be neither branches of industry, nor districts of any great significance for national production since the large enterprise has already established itself as superior in most of the crucial branches of agriculture. The shift of the economic centre of gravity from the world market to the domestic market will inevitably bring these branches, especially grain production, into even greater prominence.

Individual small establishments in agriculture are just as compatible with socialist society as those in the handicrafts; and what is true for the latter also applies to the former. It does not matter a great deal whether the land they cultivate is private or state-owned. What is important is not the name, not the juridical categories, but the economic results.

This is of course merely a *hypothesis* not a *prophecy*. It does not say what *will* happen but what *could* happen. What will in fact happen is no more known to our opponents than it is to us; like ourselves they can only base themselves on those factors about which adequate knowledge currently exists. But if we project the path which these factors are presently tracing into the future, then we shall, in fact, arrive at the development indicated here.

The wishes and intentions expressed by Social Democracy in its official demonstrations and in the writings of its most prominent representatives nowhere contradict the conclusions presented here. Nowhere do we find the demand for the expropriation of the peasantry.

Just before the 1848 March revolution, the Central Committee of the Communist League, of which Marx and Engels were members, formulated the 'Demands of the Communist Party in Germany'. The three points which related to agriculture were as follows:

> 7) Princely and other feudal estates, together with mines, pits, and so forth, shall become the property of the state. The estates shall be cultivated on a large scale and with the most up-to-date scientific devices in the interests of the whole of society.
> 8) Mortgages on peasant lands shall be declared the property of the state. Interest on such mortgages shall be paid by the peasants to the state.
> 9) In localities where the tenant system is developed, the land-rent or the quit-rent shall be paid to the state as a tax. (Communist League, 1848, pp. 3–8)

Not a word about encroaching on the property rights of the peasants. The only thing to be nationalised are the mortgages on the peasant lands, not the land itself.

Once the wounds of the defeat of 1848 were healed and the workers' movement regained its momentum and began to stir itself, the land issue reappeared on the agenda. It was dealt with at a number of congresses of the International. The most well known and most important were the discussions at the Basle Congress in 1869 which decided: (1) The Congress declares that society has the right to abolish private property in land and transform it into communal property; (2) Congress declares that it is necessary in the interests of society to accomplish this transformation.

Congress did not state *how* this transformation was to be accomplished. It declared: 'Whilst Congress acknowledges the principle of communal property and land it recommends that all sections should investigate practical means for its implementation.'

Liebknecht made a number of speeches on these resolutions in Saxony in March 1870, the most extensive of which were later reworked into a brochure published in 1873 under the title *Zur Grund und Bodenfrage* (republished in a second edition in 1876). He writes:

> In France, and in particular in Germany, this question is by no means as straightforward as in England. Agricultural workers are naturally either already in favour of a rational restructuring of land and property relations or can be won over easily. For the most part, it is only the *small peasants* who, despite already being proletarians or rapidly heading towards the proletariat, still cling to their 'property', even though in the most instances this is only nominal, purely imaginary property. An order for expropriation would undoubtedly stir most peasants into serious resistance, perhaps even open rebellion.
>
> The state was therefore to avoid anything which might actually or apparently damage the interests of the peasantry. Enlightenment as to the advantages of socialism had to be accompanied by practical measures to relieve the heavily burdened peasant population. This would principally involve the nationalising of mortgage debts, reducing the rate of interest, and linking additional loans to a commitment on the part of the peasant to undertake rational cultivation. With state support, the individual farms would gradually pass over to cooperative large-scale farming (see pp. 176-9).

Liebknecht characterised the expropriation of the rural population by a revolutionary government as patent folly.

The rapid growth of industry and the proletarian movement in the industrial centres has pushed the rural question into the background in the years since 1870. It has been put back on the agenda – not only for the bourgeois parties, but also for the proletarian parties – by the onset of agricultural distress. Engels has set the tone for the current discussion. What he stated in 1848 he repeated in 1894, asking: 'What, then, is our attitude towards the small peasantry? How shall we deal with it on the day of our accession to power?' And he answers:

> To begin with, the French programme is absolutely correct in stating: 'that we foresee the inevitable doom of the small peasant, but that it is not our mission to hasten it by any interference on our part.' Secondly, it is just as evident that when we are in possession of state

power we shall not *even think of forcibly expropriating the small peasants* (regardless of whether with or without compensation) as we shall have to do in the case of the big landowners. Our task relative to the small peasant consists in the first place in effecting a transition of his private enterprise and private possession into cooperative ones, not forcibly, but by dint of example and the proffer of social assistance for this purpose. And then, of course, we shall have ample means of showing to the small peasant prospective advantages that must be obvious to him even today.

Even as far as bigger peasants were concerned Engels thought:

Most likely we shall be able to abstain here as well from resorting to forcible expropriation, and as for the rest to count on future economic developments, making also these harder pates amenable to reason. (Engels, 'The Peasant Question in France and Germany', pp. 634–5, 638)

These comments accord fully with our own sentiments. Not only do they show that expropriation of the peasantry is not in the interests of socialism: they also show that socialists have no intention of doing this.

The peasantry has nothing to fear from Social Democracy; in fact they have everything to gain from it. The fact that they cannot fulfil all their wishes in present-day society is not due to any lack of goodwill towards them, but because many of these wishes must remain pious hopes, beyond fulfilment by *any* party. Social Democracy cannot compete with the agrarian parties when it comes to *promises*. But Social Democracy is actually doing what needs to be done for the rural population in present-day society: and it alone can do it in full measure because it has less respect for capital than any of the bourgeois parties.

Peasants can expect much more from the transition to a socialist society than from any social reforms carried out within the confines of present-day society. Expropriation is the capitalist method for moving from a lower to a higher form of production. In present-day society a peasant is constantly faced with the dilemma either of resisting progress, which means general decline, or being swept away by the expropriating force of capital. Only socialism offers the possibility of participating in social progress without falling victim to expropriation. Socialism will not only *not* mean expropriation, but also offers the most certain protection from the threat of expropriation presently constantly hanging over the peasant.

The Future of the Independent Household

And although we expect the large enterprise to prove superior to the smaller in most branches of agriculture, although the cooperative or communal form will supplant the smaller once the proletariat, having won power, sweeps away all the obstacles to its advance, and although arable land will be consolidated, this does not mean the abandonment of the independent *household*. Despite the fact that the unique link between farm and household will be severed, there is no reason for the peasant's home to become communal property. Modern socialism rests on common property in the means of production, not in the means of consumption. Private property is still possible in the latter. And of all the means for enjoying human life and bringing some happiness into it, one of the most important, if not the most important, is possession of a home. Communal property in land is by no means irreconcilable with this.

We would be venturing into very treacherous territory were we to discuss the housing system of the future here. Whether the individual of the future prefers living in a palatial *Phalanstère* à la Fourier, or in separate cottages à la Bellamy, whether one individual prefers the one, and another the other, both can develop alongside each other: what is certain is that *if* they feel that it is important for every family to own their own home, the fundamentals on which a socialist society is based would not prevent this.

Technical development is of course already leading to a reduction in the work required in the individual household and to an extension of paid employment by women. The reason why the former is taking place so slowly is a consequence of the cheapness of female labour-power. Women's labour in the household is not paid with money and, therefore, apparently costs nothing; and the woman is the most willing and unremitting beast of burden. The proletarian can therefore cling to the technically backward individual household. For the affluent classes, the maintenance of an independent household means comfort, having their own slaves, maidservants, always on hand for the exclusive service of their own dear selves.

The stronger the proletariat becomes, the more difficult servants will be to find: their demands will increase, and the affluent will find it increasingly difficult to maintain their households. Those conscientious housewives who most assiduously defend the sanctity of their own hearth – as long as they have a servant to clean it – will be amongst the most energetic in demanding measures to reduce the work of the private household or allocate it to particular trades once they have been forced to do the work themselves; to cook, to wash, to raise children, and – horror of horrors – to polish boots.

Another push in this direction must inevitably come from the victory, or even the mere strengthening, of the proletariat among working women. The reasons why they are currently forced to carry out the most unproductive tasks, inadequately, at home, rather than have them taken care of by well-equipped establishments outside the home are poverty and necessity. The increasing affluence of worker families will not express itself in the burdening of yet another domestic slave but rather in the unburdening of the housewife. The reduction in housework, currently proceeding much more slowly than technical progress could allow, will then speed up. This will mean the disappearance of the economic foundation of the family. But not the family itself. For in the meantime, another, higher basis for the family has emerged – *individuality*.

People are by nature social beings, 'gregarious creatures', and it takes some time before they begin to perceive and experience their individuality as something distinct from society. As long as individuals caught up in the struggle for existence could only survive through their bond with society, and as long as social development proceeded so slowly that tradition, that is the sum of inherited views of the community as a whole, completely dominated the intellectual life of the individual, no form existed within which the individual could develop. The foundation for the free development of the individual, at least for the aristocracy, had to await the growth of the productivity of labour and the division of society into classes, which released some members of society from the need to spend all their time in the struggle for existence, physical labour and war; they acquired the time to develop a specific intellectual life, and because of their wealth and slaves, were able to live independently of society, and even in contradiction to it: and this was true in particular whenever major catastrophes suddenly placed society on a new basis and interrupted the dead hand of tradition. Consider, for example, Greece after the Persian wars, Italy after the Crusades, and Western Europe after the great discoveries and the Reformation. The individual *personality* was born; individual art appeared alongside impersonal folk art, individual philosophy alongside impersonal religion.

It was, however, the capitalist mode of production which first succeeded in stripping this herd character from wider and wider spheres of the population, transforming the individual, the 'superman' from an aristocratic phenomenon into a more democratic one. This feat was accomplished by dissolving all the traditional organisations which had previously held the mass of the population together in the struggle for existence, and by declaring permanent economic revolution – toppling tradition from its leading role and forcing everyone to develop their own perspective based on their own observations: and finally, through the fact that the modern mode of production has created an unprecedented number of 'workers by brain', not least due to the mass of surplus-products produced by this mode of production – at the same time giving them a much less secure and satisfactory status than before.

Individualism – the desire for the free development of the personality – will inevitably become stronger and more generalised in a socialist than in capitalist society, the more widespread welfare, education and leisure become within it.

The possibility of the individual's free activity will admittedly be reduced in quite a number of ways under socialism in one very important sphere, that of economic life: on the other hand, the present meagre opportunities for individual activity outside economic life will be greatly expanded through the reduction in working time.

This will increase the importance of the family and the home. Nowhere else offers the same opportunity for the individual personality to live itself out so fully, without the obstruction of the hostile or at least confining will of others: a place which it can adorn and shape as it wishes, constrained only by material, not personal considerations, in which it can live freely with its loves, friends, books, ideas and dreams, its scientific and artistic creations.

The growth of individualism also means the growth of individual sexual love, which finds satisfaction only in the joining and living together of one individual with another particular individual of the opposite sex. Such marriage, based on individual sexual love, also requires that individuals should have their own home.

The more the economic element disappears from marriage and the individual element enters into the foreground, the greater the change in the relationship between parents, especially fathers, and their children. As an economic institution marriage has the task, on the one hand, of creating the necessary economic foundation for the household through the dowry or labour-power of the housewife and the earnings of the husband; and on the other hand, of supplying heirs for the patriarchal property, which includes the father's occupation. Individualistic marriage not only replaces the economic motive for matrimony by personal attraction between the partners, but the relationship between the parents and children also becomes an individual one. Children are cherished by their parents, not as heirs, but as individuals, not forced to become successors within a caste irrespective of their aptitudes and abilities, but allowed to develop as free individuals.

The germs of individual marriage and the family are already very strong; but they are constantly frustrated by the fact that poverty and distress on the one hand, and wealth on the other, still allow economic considerations to take precedence over personal ones. A socialist society free of these extremes, in which the importance of the individual household grows even smaller, will inevitably allow the individual character of marriage and the family to come to the fore. This personal character already constitutes the common standard for judging the moral worth of a family and marriage. A *decent* marriage is held to be one in which the personalities, not the economic circumstances of the partners, are of importance; the morally worthwhile bonds within the family are the personal bonds between its members, not material links. According to the modern viewpoint the son who sees his father merely as a future source of an inheritance or the father who forces his son into an occupation or marriage in order to expand or conserve the family wealth are not considered to be acting morally. The disappearance of the private household does not mean the abolition of marriage and the family. The home does not have to disappear along with the stove. Modern civilisation can offer familial bonds other than the cooking stove and the sink. The disappearance of the individual household simply means the transformation of the family from an economic into a purely ethical unit: it signifies the realisation of a moral demand already brought to maturity by the development of individualism made possible by the modern productive forces.

Socialism will not therefore suppress the demand of fully developed individuals for their own home; rather it will generalise it, at the same time creating the means through which its satisfaction can also be generalised.

Peasants should not fear for their homes. A socialist regime will not pass by without leaving a trace, but the changes which it will bring – the hygienic and the aesthetic – will not be to the detriment of the peasant home.

The decline of the peasantry is possibly revealed nowhere more clearly than in their houses. We have already referred to the hovels inhabited by agricultural workers: but peasant dwellings are often no better than miserable and filthy stalls. Yet the peasant does have a feeling for cleanliness and for beauty – a fact apparent wherever they live in a state of well-being. The peasant houses of the past, such as those of the Swiss or Russian peasants, are the delight of architects;

now peasant art lives on only in urban villas. The originals are falling into dilapidation and there are no successors on peasant farms. However, with well-being and leisure, the peasant can be an artist once more. And these benefits will be restored to the peasant by the victorious proletariat. It will not simply emancipate the wage slaves of industry. The countryside too, whose wonderful natural beauties now stand in such stark and tragic contrast to the ignorance, poverty and squalor of its inhabitants, will be transformed into a blooming garden, lived in by a free, happy and proud people.

Bibliography

Agahd, K., 'Die Erwerbstätigkeit schulpflichtiger Kinder im Deutschen Reich' in *Brauns Archiv für soziale Gesetzgebung und Statistik*, Vol. XII (1888), Berlin.
Appun, C.F., in Peschel, O., *Völkerkunde*, Leipzig, 1897.
Auhagen, O., *Die ländliche Arbeiterverhältnisse in der Rheinprovinz und im oldenburgischen Fürstentum Bielefeld*, 1892 (see Verein für Socialpolitik).
Backhaus, A., 'Die Arbeitsteilung in der Landwirtschaft' in *Conrads Jahrbücher* (1894).
Bernstein, E., 'Der Sozialismus und die gewerbliche Arbeit der Jugend', *Die Neue Zeit*, XVI, pp. 37ff.
Braf, A., *Studien über nordböhmische Arbeiterverhältnisse*, Prague, 1881.
Bray, C., *The Philosophy of Necessity*, 2 vols, London, 1841.
Brentano, L., *Theoretische Einleitung in die Agrarpolitik*, Part 1, Stuttgart, 1897.
Buchenberger, A., *Grundzüge der deutschen Agrarpolitik*, Berlin, 1897.
Buchner, M., *Kamerun*, Leipzig, 1887.
Buckle, H.T., *History of Civilisation in England*, Vol. I, London, 1899 (Thinker's Library ed. 1930).
Communist League, 'Demands of the Communist Party in Germany' (1848) in K. Marx and F. Engels, *Collected Works*, Vol. 7, pp. 3–8, London, 1977.
Conrad, J., 'Getreidepreise', in *Handwörterbuch der Staatswissenschaften*, Jena, 1890.
Drill, R., 'Die Agrarfrage in Österreich', *Die Zeit*, Nos. 100–2 (1896), Vienna.
Engels, F., (1886) Foreword to 'Die schlesischen Milliarden' by Wilhelm Wolff in *Marx-Engels Werke*, Vol. 21, p. 247, Berlin, 1962.
Engels, F., (1894) 'The Peasant Question in France and Germany' in Marx and Engels, *Selected Works in One Volume*, London, 1970.
Fick, L., 'Die bäuerliche Erbfolge in rechtsrheinischen Bayern', *Münchener Volkswirtschaftliche Studien*, 8 (1895).
Filzer, J., *Anschauungen über die Entwicklung der menschlichen*

Gesellschaft, Kitzbühel, 1895.

Gerlach, A., 'Fleischkonsum und Fleischpreis' in M. Sering (ed.), *Handwörterbuch der Staatswissenschaften*, Jena, 1890.

Goltz, T. von der, *Handbuch der gesamten Landwirtschaft*, 1890.

Goltz, T. von der, 'Ackerbau' in M. Sering, *Handwörterbuch der Staatswissenschaften*, Vol. 1, Jena, 1890.

Goltz, T. von der, *Die ländliche Arbeiterklasse und der preußische Staat*, Jena, 1893.

Hamm, W., *Die Naturkräfte in ihrer Anwendung in der Landwirtschaft*, Munich, 1876.

Heine, A., *Die bäuerlichen Verhältnisse im Herzogenthum Sachsen-Meinigen* in *Schriften des Vereins für Socialpolitik*, Leipzig, 1883.

Juraschek, F., *Übersichten der Weltwirtschaft*, Berlin, 1896.

Kablukov, [?], *Ländliche Arbeiterfrage*, Stuttgart, 1887.

Kärger, K., *Die Sachsengängerei*, Berlin, 1890.

Kärger, K., *Die Verhältnisse der Landarbeiter in Nordwestdeutschland*, Leipzig, 1892 (see *Verein für Socialpolitik*, 1892).

Kirchhof, F., *Handbuch der landwirtschaftlichen Betriebslehre*, Dessau, 1852.

König, F., *Die Lage der englischen Landwirtschaft*, Jena, 1896.

Köttgen, C., 'Ist die Elektrotechnik nach dem heutigen Stand ihrer Entwicklung schon befähight, mit begründeter Aussicht im dem Dienst der Landwirtschaft zur Erhöhung des wirtschaftlichen Reinertrages zu treten?' in *Thiels Landwirtschaftliche Jahrbücher*, XXVI, Vols. 4–5, 1897.

Krafft, G., *Lehrbuch der Landwirtschaft auf wissenschaftlicher und praktischer Grundlage*, Berlin, 1875–8.

Laveleye, E. de, *Essai sur l' économie rurale de la Belgique*, Brussels, 1863.

Liebig, J. von, *Familiar Letters of Chemistry*, London, 1859.

Liebig, J. von, *Die Chemie in ihrer Anwendung auf die Agricultur und Physiologie* (7th edn in 2 vols with an Introduction: no English translation of this edn), Brunswick, 1862.

Liebknecht, W., *Zur Grund- und Bodenfrage*, Leipzig, 1874.

Lippert, J., *Kulturgeschichte der Menschheit in ihrem organischen Ausbau*, Stuttgart, 1886.

Marx, K., (1850) 'Discussion of "Le Socialisme et l'impôt"' in K. Marx and F. Engels, *Collected Works*, Vol. 10, p. 326, London, 1978.

Marx, K., (1867) *Capital*, Vol. I, Harmondsworth, 1976.

Marx, K., (1875) 'Critique of the Gotha Programme', in Marx and Engels, *Selected Works in One Volume*, London, 1970.

Marx, K., (1884) *Capital*, Vol. II, Harmondsworth, 1978.

Marx, K., (1894), *Capital*, Vol. III, Harmondsworth, 1981.

Maurer, G. von, *Geschichte der Dorfverfassung*, Erlangen, 1866.

Meitzen, A., *Der Boden und die landwirtschaftlichen Verhältnisse des preußischen Staates nach dem Gebietsumfange vor 1866*, Berlin, 1868.

Menger, A., 'Das bürgerliche Recht und die besitzlosen Volksklassen' in *Brauns Archiv für soziale Gesetzgebung und Statistik*, Berlin, 1888.

Meyer, R., *Die ländliche Arbeiterfrage in Deutschland. Sozialismus, Auswanderung. Mittel gegen beide*, Berlin, 1873.

Meyer, R., *Ursachen der amerikanischen Konkurrenz*, Berlin, 1883.

Meyer, R., *Der Kapitalismus 'fin de siècle'*, Vienna, 1894.

Miaskowski, A. von, *Die schweizerische Allmend*, Leipzig, 1879.

Miaskowski, A. von, *Das Erbrecht und die Grundeigenthumsverteilung im Deutschen Reich*, Leipzig, 1882.

Mill, J.S., *Principles of Political Economy*, London, 1852.

Nordhoff, C., *The Communistic Societies of the United States*, London, 1875.

Nordenskjöld, A., *Die Umseglung Asiens und Europas auf der Vega*, Leipzig, 1881.

Perels, E., *Die Anwendung der Dampfkraft in der Landwirtschaft*, Halle, 1872.

Quesnay, François (1760), 'Maximes générales du gouvernement économique d'un royaume agricole', in *Collection des Economistes*, Paris, 1841.

Roscher, W., *Nationalökonomie des Ackerbaus*, Stuttgart, 1873.

Royal Commission on Agriculture, *Report of Mr. Henry Pew on the Country of Norfolk* (C-7915), London, 1895.

Royal Commission on Agriculture, *Final Report of Her Majesty's Commissioner appointed to inquire into the subject of agricultural depression* (C-8540), London, 1897.

Sax, E., *Die Hausindustrie in Thüringen*, 3 vols, Jena 1882, 1884, 1888.

Schönberg, G., *Handbuch der politischen Ökonomie*, Tübingen, 1896.

Sering, M., *Die landwirtschaftliche Konkurrenz Nordamerikas im Gegenwart und Zukunft*, Leipzig, 1887.

Sering, M., *Die innere Kolonisation im östlichen Deutschland* in *Schriften des Vereins für Socialpolitik*, Vol. 56, Leipzig, 1893.

Singer, J., *Untersuchungen über die sozialen Zustände in den Fabrikbezirken des nordöstlichen Böhmen*, Leipzig, 1885.

Sismondi, J.S de, *Études sur l' économie politique*, Brussels, 1837–8.

Smith, A., (1776) *The Wealth of Nations*, Books I–III, Harmondsworth, 1981.

Sombart, Werner, *Sozialismus und soziale Bewegung*, Jena, 1896.

Stöckel, C.M., *Errichtung, Organisation, Betrieb der Molkereigenossen-*

schaften, Bremen, 1880.

Thaer, A.D., *Einleitung zur Kentniss der englischen Landwirtschaft*, 3 vols, Hanover, 1798.

Verein für Socialpolitik, *Bäuerliche Zustände in Deutschland* in *Schriften des Vereins für Socialpolitik*, Vols. 22–4, Leipzig, 1883.

Verein für Socialpolitik, *Die Verhältnisse der Landarbeiter in Deutschland*, Leipzig, 1892. Comprises: Volume I, Kärger, *Die Verhältnisse der Landarbeiter in Nordwestdeutschland* (*Schriften des Vereins für Socialpolitik*, Vol. 53); Volume II, Auhagen, *Die ländliche Arbeiterverhältnisse in der Rheinprovinz und im oldenburgischen Fürstentum Bielefeld* (*Schriften des Vereins für Socialpolitik*, Vol. 54); Volume III, Weber, *Die Verhältnisse der Landarbeiter im ostelbischen Deutschland* (*Schriften des Vereins für Socialpolitik*, Vol. 55).

Verein für Socialpolitik, *Verhandlungen der am 20. und 21. März in Berlin abgehaltenen Generalversammlung des Vereins für Socialpolitik über ländliche Arbeiterfrage und über die Bodenbesitzverteilung und die Sicherung des Kleingrundbesitzes*, Leipzig, 1893.

Webb, S. and Webb, B., *History of Trade Unionism*, London, 1898.

Weber, M., *Die Verhältnisse der Landarbeiter im ostelbischen Deutschland*, Leipzig, 1892.

Index of Authors

Agahd, D.:
  child-labour, 353–4, 356
Appun, C.F., 28
Auhagen, H.:
  large and small farms, 115
  day-labourers, 181
  migrant workers, 193, 234
Backhaus, A., 41
Braf, A.:
  rural industry, 186
Bray, C.:
  the Ralahine cooperative, 126–9
Brentano, L.:
  on value, 62–3
  on land, 85
Buchenberger, A., 114
Buchner, M., 28
Buckle, H.T., 27–8
Comte, A., 27
Conrad, J.:
  Prussian latifundia, 154–5
Drill, R., 120, 144
Engels, F., 2, 34, 325
  on dialectics, 3
  February revolution, 332–3
  the peasantry, 447–8
Fick, L.:
  illegitimacy, 163
Filzer, J.:
  sexuality of rural workers, 219
Gerlach, A., 102
  meat consumption, 36
Goltz, T. von der:
  mechanisation, 45–6, 229
  supply of labour-power, 166

Instleute, 324
  child-labour, 356, 359
Hamm, W.:
  the microscope, 55
Heine, A.:
  parcellisation of peasant land, 396
Juraschek, F.:
  phylloxera in France, 216
Kablukov:
  women's labour in England, 372
Kärger, K.:
  mechanical reaper, 47
  child-labour, 110, 357, 358
  Heuerling, 162, 226
  rural labourers' holdings, 180
  rural industry, 188, 269
  Sachsengänger, 196, 373, 374, 376
  rural labour shortage, 227
  the 'rural labour question', 351–2
Köttgen, C.:
  electrical power, 50, 98
Krafft, G., 98, 200, 267
  Austrian latifundia, 157–9
Lafargue, P.:
  mortgage costs in France, 106
Liebig, J. von, 27
  soil fertility, 53–4
  agricultural institutes, 57
  grain milling, 285
Liebknecht, W.:
  socialisation of land, 447
Lippert, J., 370
Marx, K., 2, 3, 4, 9, 12, 66–7, 72, 101,

225, 116, 307, 325, 427
  organic composition of capital, 77
  absolute ground-rent, 79
  interest, 84
  economies of scale in commerce, 104
  concentration and fragmentation of holdings, 164
  forestry, 376
  the gang system, 372, 374
  education, 419
Maurer, G. von, 22
Meitzen, A., 107, 171, 291, 396
  agrarian improvements, 399
Menger, A.:
  Servants Ordinance, 346
Meyer, R., 135
  land-ownership, 153
  overseas food competition, 247, 251
  child-labour, 358
  the working day, 378
Miaskowski, A. von, 165
  dismemberment and agglomeration of holdings, 175
  common pasturage, 341
Mill, J.S.
  the peasantry, 110, 134
Nordenskjöld, A., 28
Nordhoff, C.:
  agricultural cooperatives in the USA, 129–30
Owen, R., 126
Perels, E., 45
  agricultural mechanisation, 46
  steam-power, 48
Quesnay, F.:
  advantages of large farms, 133
Ricardo, D., 66

Rodbertus, J.K., 7, 8, 79, 85
Roscher, W., 39, 111, 400
  small farms, 324
Sax, E.:
  domestic industry, 188
Schönberg, G.:
  domestic industry, 182–3
Sering, M.:
  medium-sized farm, 108–9
  cooperatives, 124, 279
  large farms, 152
  new peasant plots, 166
  size of holdings, 176
  women's labour, 371
Settegast, H.:
  transport costs of agricultural produce, 35
Singer, J.:
  housing conditions, 383
Sismondi, J.S., 15, 16
  on the peasantry, 13–14, 134
Smith, A., 133
  value, 65–6
Sombart, W., 10–11, 135
Spencer, H., 27
Stöckel, C.M.:
  dairying cooperatives, 269–70
Thaer, A.D.:
  agricultural academies, 39, 56–7
Thünen, J.H. von, 148
Webb, S. and B.:
  agricultural trade unionism, 347
Weber, M.:
  on the Instmann, 162, 376
  miners in Silesia, 189
  child-labour, 356
  women's labour, 371–2
  migrant labour, 375, 376
  working time, 379